Behavior Management

A PRACTICAL APPROACH FOR EDUCATORS

D1207556

Behavior Management

A PRACTICAL APPROACH FOR EDUCATORS

FOURTH EDITION

James E. Walker
Vice President for Academic Affairs
University of Northern Colorado
Greeley, Colorado

Thomas M. Shea
Professor, Department of Special Education
Southern Illinois University
Edwardsville, Illinois

Merrill Publishing Company
A Bell & Howell Information Company
Columbus   Toronto   London   Melbourne

Cover Art: Jennifer Burke, a senior at Marburn School, created the tie-dyed art; her instructor is Sue Robertson. © Jennifer Burke.

Published by Merrill Publishing Company
A Bell & Howell Information Company
Columbus, Ohio 43216

This book was set in Korinna.

Administrative Editor: Vicki Knight
Production Coordinator: Mary Harlan
Art Coordinator: Lorraine Woost
Cover Designer: Cathy Watterson

Photo Credits: All photos copyrighted by individuals or companies listed. Mark Freado, p. 33. Merrill/photographs by Kevin Fitzsimons, pp. 129, 157; by Jean Greenwald, pp. 1, 54, 93, 222; by Lloyd Lemmerman, pp. 187, 269.

Copyright © 1988, 1986 by Merrill Publishing Company. All rights reserved. No part of this book may be reproduced in any form, electronic or mechanical, including photocopy, recording, or any information storage and retrieval system, without permission in writing from the publisher. "Merrill Publishing Company" and "Merrill" are registered trademarks of Merrill Publishing Company.

Previous editions copyrighted 1984, 1980, 1976 by C. V. Mosby Company.

Library of Congress Catalog Card Number: 87-62597
International Standard Book Number: 0-675-20829-7
Printed in the United States of America
2 3 4 5 6 7 8 9 — 92 91 90 89 88

To
Gwenn, Jamell, and Jabrina
and
Dolores, Kevin, and Keith

Preface

This fourth edition of *Behavior Management: A Practical Approach for Educators* has been extensively revised to improve its readability and usability. Revisions are based on developments in the field of behavior management reported in the literature since the original manuscript was prepared and on feedback from many professionals and students.

During the last two decades the proliferation of behavior management philosophies, techniques, and instructional methodologies has increased the complexity of the educator's responsibilities and functions. New information is being published almost daily on the various perspectives of human behavior, including the psychodynamic, biophysical, environmental, and behavioral points of view. Of these perspectives the behavioral point of view appears to have had the most significant impact on classroom and school management procedures and practices. However, because of their overall importance in the broad field of behavior management, the theories and techniques associated with the psychodynamic, biophysical, and environmental perspectives are also reviewed in detail in this edition.

Revisions in the text are, in large part, a result of direct and indirect feedback from students and faculty who have studied the third edition. We have been informed of the text's strengths and weaknesses by many undergraduate and graduate students of education, by teachers participating in in-service programs, and by our professional colleagues. We have attemped in this revision to retain the text's strengths and minimize its weaknesses.

The text is written to provide a practical guide to experienced teachers, teachers-in-training, parents, and paraprofessionals for applying behavior management techniques both in general and special educational settings and in the home. It is designed to aid teachers working in self-contained classes and resource centers, teachers engaged in itinerant and consultative service, and elementary and secondary regular classroom teachers having responsibility for normal and exceptional children. It may be used as a basic text for preservice and in-service courses and as a self-study guide. It is designed for use by parents of normal and exceptional children.

Behavior management is introduced in Chapter 1. This chapter includes presentations on guidelines for behavior management and on the application of behavior management techniques to individualized education programs (IEPs), mandated for all handicapped children by Public Law 94-142. Chapter 1 concludes with an overview of the psychodynamic, biophysical, environmental, and behavior modification perspectives of human behavior and educational practice.

The basic principles of behavior modification are presented in Chapter 2. The exposition of each principle is supplemented by practical examples from classroom teaching experiences.

In Chapter 3 the reader is given step-by-step instructions for modifying behavior in the classroom. Each step is discussed and exemplified. Chapter 3 includes an extensive list of reinforcers for use in the classroom and school setting.

Several specific methods of increasing appropriate behavior and decreasing inappropriate behavior are reviewed in Chapters 4 and 5.

Chapters 6 and 7 provide an overview of behavior management techniques associated with the psychodynamic, biophysical, and environmental theoretical perspectives presented in Chapter 1. In the final chapter the ethics of behavior management are discussed.

Chapter 8 is an overview of behavior management procedures and practices for implementation by educators wishing to involve parents in coordinated home-school management programs. The chapter includes a parent-teacher interview technique for assessment purposes. This material is also applicable to the training of paraprofessionals.

Quizzes and skill-building projects are presented at the end of each chapter. Answers to the quiz questions are presented in the *Instructor's Manual.* A copy of each worksheet and form presented earlier is provided at the end of the text.

The text is written in nontechnical language for maximum readability by a broad audience of professionals, paraprofessionals, college students, and parents. This style was chosen in order to avoid the unnecessary technical jargon that causes so much of the professional literature to lose its significance and impact. Although based on the results of current research, the text does not provide an extensive review of the literature. Such a review would limit the text's practical application. The reader will, however, find, in the reference sections, lists of journals and texts to serve as a beginning point in a review of the literature.

The primary goal of this work is the *ethical, effective,* and *efficient* management of the behavior and learning problems of children and youth as they learn to explore, manipulate, and ultimately control their world for their personal satisfaction and benefit and for the benefit of society.

Acknowledgments

We thank the reviewers—Dr. Andrew Brulle of Eastern Illinois University, Dr. Tom Kampwirth of California State University–Long Beach, Dr. Robert N. Freeman of Georgia Southern College, and Dr. Frances T. Harrington of Radford University—for their time and their constructive suggestions which strengthened the fourth edition. We would like to acknowledge the assistance and support of our many colleagues, friends, and long-suffering students who have been exposed to and have responded to the materials in this text. We have profited greatly by their comments.

Harvey Gaines and Jean Wildhaber served as our right arm throughout the writing process by typing, correcting, and retyping the various drafts of the manuscript.

Contents

CHAPTER FIVE

CHAPTER SIX

CHAPTER SEVEN

CHAPTER ONE

An Introduction to Behavior Management

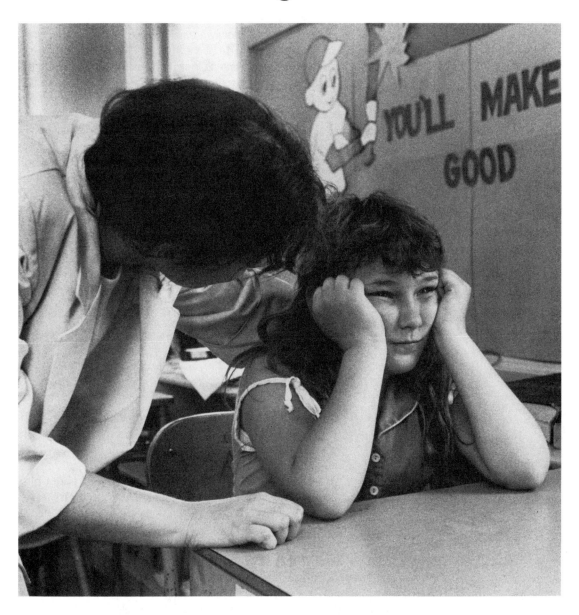

Ms. Justine watches as Tami, wiping her eyes with a tissue from the decorative dispenser on the corner of the teacher's desk, slowly leaves the fourth-grade classroom. It has been a long, trying day for both of them.

As the little Swiss clock on the desk chimes 4 o'clock, Ms. Justine leans back in her chair to ponder her dilemma. Right now, she hates teaching. She hates reprimanding and scolding children, especially Tami, who tries so very, very hard to sit still and pay attention during her lessons. It seems as if this little drama has happened with Tami and some of the other children a dozen or more times since the school year began last month.

The children are too active to settle down to their lessons. Ms. Justine yells and hollers, scolds and reprimands, but it doesn't appear to help. They never change. Perhaps they never will.

Something must be done. The children have to learn their lessons. Tami in particular needs help. She is 2 years behind in reading and a full year behind in spelling; she has practically no measurable skills in subtraction and division. Tami must learn these skills before the end of the school year or confront another failure in the fifth grade.

Ms. Justine knows her present methods of behavior management are not only ineffective but also are taking too much out of her personally. She is exhausted when she gets home after school. Her stomach is always upset. She is grouchy and short-tempered with her husband and children.

Perhaps there are more effective methods Ms. Justine could apply in an effort to help Tami and the others attend to their lessons.

Larry sits in the gym bleachers, anxiously waiting for Mr. Veritas to finish organizing the volleyball game. The whole class, except Larry, is choosing sides and preparing to begin the game.

Larry wishes he could be part of the activity, but he can't. He's afraid to let the others know that he's a poor player. He doesn't know exactly why he's a poor player, but every time a group game is organized, he must refuse to participate. He says, "No, I won't," "I can't," "I don't feel good," or "That's a dumb game."

Larry knows Mr. Veritas is unhappy with him but also very concerned about him. But Larry just can't play those games. He thinks it's really too bad that Mr. Veritas doesn't like him, because Mr. Veritas is a nice guy and would be an interesting friend.

Mr. Veritas quickly organizes the teams, and the volleyball game begins. He believes that he must hurry and talk to Larry.

"Poor kid," Mr. Veritas thinks, "he's really OK, but he just won't play team games. Perhaps he refuses because of his weight problem. No, others in the class are as rotund as Larry, and they play team sports. Perhaps Larry is afraid he's not a good enough player. I'll talk to him again and see what I can do to help."

2

Perhaps there are effective methods for helping Larry increase his participation in team activities.

Ms. Komfort hums a little tune to herself as she cruises along Interstate 55 out of Memphis. What a marvelous day! What a great year it has been at John F. Kennedy Elementary School with her 25 first graders!

For the first time in her teaching career Ms. Komfort has interested, responsive, and enthusiastic children in her class. If the last 4 months of the school year are as good as the first 5 months, she will remain in teaching forever.

"Sure hope it continues," she thinks.

Perhaps there are techniques to help Ms. Komfort maintain her children's enthusiasm for learning throughout the year.

Teachers wish to teach; it is what they are trained to do, their function, and the purpose for which they are employed and assigned to a school, a classroom, and a group of children for approximately 180 days each school year. Frequently teachers are frustrated in efforts to attain their goals because of the behavioral and remedial problems of the individual children in their classrooms.

As a result of the theoretical, experimental, and pragmatic efforts of many scholars and practitioners during the twentieth century, teachers have been made increasingly aware of a number of variables that must be considered if effective and efficient classroom transactions are to be established between teachers and children. Teachers have become keenly aware of the following:

1. Every child is a unique individual, *similar* to all other children in many respects, yet *different* from all other children.
2. No single set of therapeutic or remedial procedures is effective under *all conditions* with *all children.* We must remain open-minded and give thoughtful consideration to many theoretical and methodological points of view if we are to effectively aid children.
3. No matter how well designed and executed classroom-centered intervention processes may be, their effectiveness will be limited unless they relate to the individual child's needs and desires (Caplan, 1963; Morse, 1985, 1964).

Educators have also become aware that in reality the child's cognitive, affective, and psychomotor learning domains are inextricably interwoven. We understand that the child acts and reacts as a whole being. We recognize that a remedial intervention in the cognitive domain may influence the child's affective behavior, that intervention in the psychomotor domain will in all probability affect the child's cognitive and affective learning, and so on.

EXAMPLES ■ Todd, a 6-year-old first grader, was diagnosed by a neurologist as "a hyperactive child with suspected minimal brain damage." According to his teacher, Todd was disruptive in the classroom, constantly running about, hitting children, tearing paper, and so on.

Todd's neurologist prescribed medication to slow the boy down in school. The medication has been effective in modifying Todd's behavior. He has begun to learn his ABC's and numbers; he has learned to use scissors for cutting-and-pasting activities; his behavior has improved in the classroom, especially during group activities. Todd has been heard to say, "See how good I am," and "I'm a big boy now."

It is evident that changes in Todd's hyperactive psychomotor behavior have influenced his cognitive skills (learning his ABC's and numbers) and his affective behavior (in group activities). In addition, his self-concept appears to have improved. ■

■ Scott, an 11-year-old fifth grader with a visual-perceptual handicap, had experienced difficulty in throwing and catching a ball and in running bases.

Scott is now enrolled in a program that includes physical therapy, visual-perceptual training, and adaptive physical education. As a result of these interventions he has developed skills in throwing, catching, and running.

Scott's teacher has noted that as Scott is increasing his competency in the psychomotor area, he is also improving cognitively (in such activities as reading and writing) and socially (his group behavior and peer relationships have improved).

Again, it is evident that changes in one learning domain influence the individual's competency in the other areas of learning. ■

■ Maryellen, a 13-year-old ninth grader, was diagnosed by a school psychologist as a "slow learner."

Maryellen had experienced difficulty in academic subjects throughout her school years. Although she could learn and did learn the basic skills, she required more time and instruction than her classmates. As a consequence of her academic difficulties, Maryellen usually received Ds and Es on report cards. Over the years she developed an "I don't care" attitude toward school work and school. This attitude caused her to be frequently reprimanded and punished by her teachers.

On entering high school, Maryellen was placed in a remedial program. In this special program academic work was designed to be responsive to Maryellen's rate and level of learning. Evaluations were based on individual performance.

Presently Maryellen's teacher reports she is a happy, highly motivated slow learner.

It is evident that changes in Maryellen's academic program influenced her affective behavior. ■

This text is written primarily from the point of view of learning theory and behavior modification. However, behavior modification is but one of the conceptual frameworks available to the practitioner for use in efforts to change behavior. *Behavior modification is not a panacea that can effectively solve all problems of all children.*

Other conceptual frameworks (biophysical, psychodynamic, and environmental) have made and continue to make significant contributions to our knowledge of the behavior of children. The reader is encouraged *not* to cast aside these other points of view—not to become an exclusivist.

Behavior management interventions based on social learning and behavior modification theory are presented in detail in Chapters 2 to 5. Interventions based on psychodynamic theory are presented in Chapter 6; those derived from environmental and biophysical theory are presented in Chapter 7.

The remainder of this first chapter is devoted to an overview of the conceptual frameworks or theories of the causes of human behavior. An effort is made to operationally define behavior management and demonstrate the relationship between the conceptual frameworks and the intervention derived from them. The chapter includes a discussion of United States Public Law 94-142 and the mandated individualized education program (IEP).

Definition of Behavior Management

The majority of school staff meeting and discussion time is often devoted to considerations of behavior management. The same few, but important, questions are asked repeatedly:

- ☐ How can this child's behavior be changed?
- ☐ How can this classroom's group behavior be changed?
- ☐ Should I punish this behavior?
- ☐ Should I discuss this behavior with the individual?
- ☐ Should I ignore this behavior?
- ☐ Will this intervention work?
- ☐ Is it ethical to use this intervention technique?
- ☐ Will it harm or hurt the child?

Hour after hour of teacher and parent time is devoted to discussions of these and similar questions and concerns about the management of children's behavior in the classroom, school, and home.

In this text *behavior management interventions* are defined as all those actions (and conscious inactions) teachers and parents engage in to enhance the probability that children, individually and in groups, will develop effective behaviors that are personally fulfilling, productive, and socially acceptable (Shea & Bauer, 1987).

Behavior management is a complex problem that cannot be approached from a simplistic point of view. It is a teacher function that must be studied, planned, and objectively used and evaluated, with equal emphasis given to all relevant variables: the individual or group whose behavior is being studied, the behavior under consideration, the setting in which the behavior occurs, the individual applying the intervention, and the purpose of the intervention. A specific technique that is an effective intervention for one specific behavior of one specific child in a particular setting may be ineffective under another set of circumstances when applied by a different individual to change a different behavior. More specifically, behavior management must be individualized.

Self-discipline is the goal of all behavior management. It is the process of attaining control over one's personal behavior in a variety of circumstances in association with many individuals and groups. Self-discipline is discussed in greater detail in the next section.

Behavior Management Guidelines

The following are guidelines to be considered in the application of any behavior management intervention (Kauffman, Pullen & Akers, 1986; Shea & Bauer, 1987; Tisdale, 1985). They are presented here primarily to stimulate thought and discussion.

Model and Leader

Outside of the family, the teacher is in all probability the most important element in the child's environment. No other variable in the school appears to have a greater potential impact on a student than the interpersonal relationship developed between teacher and child.

Educational programs can be (and have been) operated successfully under extremely adverse conditions (without adequate facilities, materials, equipment, funds, personnel, transportation, and so on). However, no program has ever been successfully operated without teachers who can and do relate positively and productively with children.

Authentic teachers must be authentic people—real people. It is difficult to select for employment an authentic teacher by the traditional means of application and personal interview. However, there are several personal traits that successful teachers appear to have in common:

☐ *Self-insight:* The teachers know how they wish to work with children. They have some understanding of why they engage in the activities that make up their lifestyle.

☐ *Self-acceptance, self-appraisal and realistic self-confidence:* The teachers accept themselves as they are but seek to improve themselves. They are realistically confident in themselves and their capability to be effective but are not so overconfident of their abilities as to be considered naive; they do not have an "I can do anything" attitude. They can make honest and forthright statements concerning their strengths and weaknesses without excuses.

☐ *Love and acceptance of children:* The teachers love and are able to demonstrate their love for children. They understand that love and compliance are not identical. Sometimes love is demonstrated through discipline. They accept children as worthwhile human beings even though they must at times reject a child's behavior. They are capable of accepting, without reservation, individuals who are different from themselves—whether these individuals are short or tall, male or female, black, white, brown, red, or yellow, rotund or slim, deformed or normal, intelligent or retarded, or conforming, deviant, or radical.

☐ *An understanding of the behavior of children:* The teachers not only understand human behavior at a cognitive level but are also able to empathize with children who manifest deviancy. They continually seek insight and understanding into such a child's behavior.

☐ *Curiosity and willingness to learn:* The teachers have a bit of the child in their adult person. Like children, they are curious about their environment and enthusiastically explore it. They enjoy learning.

☐ *Patience with self and others:* The teachers realize that they are imperfect and that they make mistakes. They also recognize this quality in others. They realize that learning is a slow, complex, process for many individuals. However, they continually strive to attain learning goals for themselves and their students.

☐ *Flexibility:* The teachers are flexible. They know when to change a lesson, intervention, or activity for the benefit of the students and when to change in order to attain a broader objective.

☐ *Humor:* The teachers have a well-developed sense of humor. (Mistakes, accidents, and humorous happenings occur in the classroom daily. Teachers who cannot laugh will certainly cry.) The teachers are capable of laughing at themselves and with their students. They never laugh at their students.

Teachers become models for the children they instruct. For better or worse, children will probably model at least some of their behavior after a teacher. It is of questionable value for children to have teachers who are highly skilled and knowledgeable in specific subject areas and activities but who lack the capacity to understand and accept themselves and their students.

In addition to the personal traits just presented, effective teachers need specific knowledge and skills to successfully work with children. Following are work characteristics of such individuals:

1. They establish routines in the daily lives of those in the classroom group.
2. They establish and enforce behavioral limits. They accomplish this difficult task without personal emotional involvement.
3. They do not permit emotionally charged situations to get out of control. They intrude themselves into conflicts and cause them to end in fairness to all involved.
4. They are consistent. All children are confused by teachers who condone a specific deviant behavior one day but do not condone the same deviation the next day.
5. They personally investigate an incident before acting rather than taking action on the basis of second- or third-person information and rumors. They confer with all children and adults involved in the incident before acting.
6. They ignore certain behaviors. Many unacceptable behaviors manifested by children are normal, age-appropriate behaviors. Others are simply not of sufficient potential impact to require a response by the teacher. Effective teachers are selective in responding to and ignoring behaviors.
7. They communicate verbally and nonverbally with their students. They talk *with*

students, not *to* them. They learn that many of the concepts they considered to be universal knowledge are mysteries to many students. They are tuned-in to the language and action of youth.

8. They learn to avoid personal confrontations with students when it is therapeutically appropriate. However, they confront an individual or group when necessary for the benefit of that person or group.

9. They learn to change activities and lessons for therapeutic purposes. Some teachers are so personally committed to "their thing" (lesson or subject) that they fail to recognize student disinterest, dislike, and resistance.

10. They work both independently and as team members by communicating with colleagues and supervisors. They hold themselves accountable for their actions or lack of action. They know they cannot succeed in isolation.

11. They make a direct appeal to students when the students' actions are confusing and discomforting to them personally. Frequently a direct appeal to a child's basic humanness and common sense will solve behavior problems as quickly and as effectively as sophisticated behavior management interventions.

12. They provide each child under their supervision with security. Effective teachers communicate to students that they will be provided needed security from physical and psychological harm while under teacher supervision.

The new teacher seldom arrives in the classroom with these specific behavior management skills in addition to instructional competence in all the needed subject matter areas: reading, writing, mathematics, language, and so on. These skills are developed through experience and with the assistance of colleagues and supervisors.

Self-Discipline

Self-discipline is the desired result of all behavior management interventions presented in this text. Self-discipline, or the process of attaining self-control over one's personal behavior in a variety of circumstances in association with a variety of individuals and groups, is not an instantaneous process. Self-control is developed by nearly all human beings over a long period of time (years) and includes a number of developmental phases. During the process of attaining self-control, children naturally progress and regress as they and their environment change. A child may appear perfectly self-controlled one day and not the following day. Progress—maturing and growing —is often measured in slowly increasing lengths of time between occurrences of unacceptable behavior exhibited by the child.

The word *discipline* is derived from *disciple,* or follower of a master's teaching. This concept contains the idea of something learned from a teacher whose example the learner personally desires to model. The best discipline is derived from the respect and understanding of one human being for another. Discipline should be cooperative and voluntary, not simply imposed from above by an authority figure (Chetkow, 1964).

In education harsh, punitive, and negative disciplinary techniques are avoided. The majority of children, especially those with behavior problems, have a poor or distorted self-image as a result of repeated failure and negative discipline. Many of these children have psychologically isolated themselves from the effects of negative discipline. Benign and positive interventions leading ultimately to self-discipline are suggested to teachers of both regular and special classes.

Time

All children at one time or another during their school years exhibit some behavior problems. This simple fact is all too frequently forgotten by teachers.

It is not unusual to have a teacher become extremely frustrated with a child because the child's deviant behavior does not respond to intervention immediately. This same frustration among teachers is also exhibited relative to academic skill training. Perhaps we are too impatient and too easily frustrated as a result of living most of our adult lives in a society conditioned to instant change, instant solutions to problems, and little or no frustration. The teacher must be patient and adjust to slow, time-consuming progress. Miracles and instant "cures" are few in number and difficult to observe when they do occur.

Children learn certain habitual ways of acting and reacting in their environment. These coping skills are developed over a span of years. Although unacceptable to others, they have been and continue to be more or less successful for the child. The child cannot (and should not be forced to) relinquish these copying mechanisms or survival behaviors immediately and begin using "new" (and from our point of view more acceptable, more productive) ways of coping.

To change deviant behavior requires time and energy. Teachers must be patient and focus on the child's progress rather than on the desired end product.

Objectives and Goals

Although teachers develop long-term goals for the children with whom they work, such goals are generally not a daily concern. Long-term goals are divided into a series of properly sequenced immediate objectives. The immediate objectives provide structure for the group's (teacher and students) daily, weekly, and/or monthly program of lessons and activities. The long-term goals provide the needed direction for the overall program for the individual child.

An important objective for each child enrolled in school is to have a pleasant and positive experience. The program must be enjoyable and rewarding for the child, or it will not meet the normal childhood needs of seeking out and exploring the new, the different, the unknown, and the exciting.

Although the teacher has many academic remedial objectives for a particular child, these remedial tasks cannot be so demanding of the child's time and energy that school becomes drudgery. School must be a positive experience, offering the child a variety of opportunities to learn new skills and to participate in new activities of a nonacademic as well as of an academic nature.

Empathy, Not Sympathy

Behavior problem children do not need their teacher's sympathy. Ill-founded sympathy distorts the problems the teacher is attempting to help the child overcome. It places the teacher in an emotional condition that prohibits objective analysis of the child's behavior. A teacher who becomes deeply emotionally involved in a child's problem frequently functions in a biased, nonhelpful way. Such a teacher reacts to the child and others concerned with the child's welfare on a subjective rather than an objective level.

Although relationships based on sympathy are to be avoided in the educational setting, those based on empathy are necessary and should be encouraged. The teacher must be able to understand how the child feels and must be able to perceive the child's world from the child's point of view. This capacity is frequently referred to as "taking the position of the other" or "being in the other person's shoes."

The capacity to empathize permits the teacher to provide the child or group with direction, guidance, and support when such assistance is needed.

Expectations

Many years ago we might have been told by our grandparents or parents, "As the twig is bent, so grows the tree." Some teachers ignore this simple truth. However, during the last decade, researchers have confirmed what our grandparents took for granted: Our expectations for children have a significant effect on their performance (Beez, 1972; Rosenthal & Jacobsen, 1966; Rubin & Balow, 1971, among others).

This self-fulfilling prophecy means that, to a significant extent, if we believe a child is and will continue to be an incompetent, the probability is increased that the child will function as an incompetent. If we believe and communicate to a child that he or she will not learn to read, behave, compute, socialize, speak, and so on, the probability is significantly increased that the child will not accomplish these tasks. Conversely, if we believe and communicate to a child that he or she will learn to behave, read, play, socialize, and speak, the probability is increased that the child will respond to our expectations and learn these tasks.

As educators, we must maintain high but realistic expectations for students. Classrooms should be environments developed around a "can do" attitude. Children must be told repeatedly throughout each day: "You can do it." "You know and I know you can do it." "You did it!" "Great!" "Super!" "Beautiful!"

Obviously such a "can do" attitude is meaningless and perhaps harmful unless the program is designed to ensure that the child receives the needed support and skill training required to complete a task and fulfill our expectations.

Freedom and Independence

As a general policy students should be encouraged to grow and learn as much as possible without teacher assistance. Within realistic limits, anything that children can do for themselves, they should do. The instructor's function is to facilitate, not to dominate, the child's activity program. The teacher is available to instruct, demonstrate, assist, counsel, and offer encouragement. All young people need freedom to explore, investigate, and implement new behaviors without adult interference if they are to grow. Often they will succeed in their efforts; occasionally they will fail and require assistance.

Although constant failure is not recommended, occasional failure is a part of every person's life. The teacher cannot and should not shelter children from all failure; at times they should be allowed to confront the logical consequences—success and failure—of their actions. (Dreikurs & Grey, 1968). It is the teacher's function to help the child learn to cope appropriately with both success and failure.

Complete freedom for many children becomes counterproductive. A child attends school to learn productive skills and behaviors. The teacher is responsible for planning the curriculum for or, preferably, in cooperation with the child. To do otherwise would be irresponsible and a disservice to the child. Behavior management and curriculum are partners; one is of little value without the other.

Democracy without structure, discipline, program, or predictability becomes anarchy. Children are learners; they are not adults skilled in the principles and practices of democracy. They must be encouraged to learn and apply democratic principles in the classroom and school under teacher supervision if they are to live by these principles as adults.

Models of Human Behavior

What makes us behave as we do toward self, others, and the environment? How can we change our behavior and the behavior of others from inappropriate to appropriate? From unacceptable to acceptable? From destructive to constructive? From "bad" to "good"?

These questions embody our purpose—our goal. They are the age-old queries that have gnawed at our intellect and emotions since the beginning of time.

What makes us behave as we do? How can behavior be changed?

Four of the responses theoreticians have made and continue to make to these questions are the psychodynamic, biophysical, environmental, and behavior modification explanations of human behavior. In this section these theoretical models are related to the behavior of children.

Ideas, Actions, and Outcomes

"What we believe about the behavior of students affects how we respond and act toward them" (Wood, 1978). In an intervention, ideas, actions, and outcomes are tied together and greatly affect each other. Ideas, in and of themselves, are inert unless active energy is added to their influence. Active energy, by itself, is meaningless and chaotic unless it is directed. In an intervention the conceptual framework directs and channels the action by providing an analysis of the nature of the problem that dictates the intervention and by suggesting the outcome toward which the intervention is directed.

"One form of intervention, carried out within two different conceptual frameworks, can have radically different meanings and lead to radically different experiences and outcomes for the participants" (Rhodes & Tracy, 1972b, pp. 23 and 24).

Educators' perceptions of children, if Rhodes is correct, are in large part determiners of the behavior management interventions selected and imposed. For example, the teacher who perceives the child as primarily determined by the environment approaches the problems of behavior management from a radically different point of view from the teacher who perceives a child as controlled primarily by intrapsychic or biophysical factors.

Historical Perspective*

According to Hewett and Forness (1984), there are four historical determiners of our behavior toward ourselves and others:

1. The need and desire to *survive* in a harsh and hostile environment
2. *Superstition,* or the need to respond in some manner to the unknown
3. *Science,* or the need to investigate, analyze, and explain the unknown
4. *Service,* or the need to assist, guide, protect, and make whole fellow human beings of lesser fortune

Humans have moved among these determiners throughout recorded history, first emphasizing one explanation then another. Movement among these forces is determined by natural forces, irrational and rational beliefs, social and economic conditions, religion, law, and knowledge. We have striven for a rational explanation of behavior but we have frequently regressed to irrational explanations during trying times. However, during each historical period we have developed some explanation of our behavior, frequently a combination of two or more of the historical determiners.

As we approached the twentieth century, our explanations of human behavior focused more on science and service and less on survival and superstition. However, with all of our contemporary knowledge of human beings and our environment, the elements of survival and superstition still exist in our explanations of human behavior.

Each of the models of human behavior presented in the following section is an explanation of behavior; each has led to the development of an educational strategy or methodology for application with children having behavior problems.*

---

*The reader is especially referred to Hewett and Forness (1984), and Rhodes and Tracy (1972a, 1972b) for excellent overviews and discussions of our attitude toward and treatment of the handicapped during the various historical periods.

*The material on the psychodynamic, biophysical, environmental, and behavior modification models of behavior is adapted from Shea, T.M., and Bauer, A.M. (1987). *Teaching children and youth with behavior disorders.* (2nd ed.). Englewood Cliffs, N.J.: Prentice-Hall.

Psychodynamic Model

As used in this text, the psychodynamic model refers to a group of theoretical constructs that have evolved during the past several decades from the original theoretical formulations of Freud (1949). These formulations have in common a belief in the existence of a dynamic intrapsychic life. Proponents of this model vary in their views on the following: the impact of the environment on the individual's intrapsychic life, the basic instinctive forces energizing psychic life, and the functions of the components of the personality (Roberts, 1975).

The effects of nonintrapsychic variables, such as the environment and heredity, have been discussed by Adler and Jung (Munroe, 1955), Berne (1964a, 1964b), Erikson (1963, 1974), and many others.

Psychodynamic theorists see the causes of human behavior as being within the individual. Behavior is determined by a dynamic intrapsychic life. The relationship between the individual and behavior problems from the psychodynamic perspective is depicted in Figure 1.1.

Freud perceived the personality as being composed of three interrelating components: the id, the superego, and the ego.

The id is the lusty infant who wants immediate gratification. Physical pleasure is what the id is after, and it will use the libido (sexual energy) to get what it wants. The id's typical remark in the personality dialogue is "Gimmie. I want it. Now!" Because of its animalistic antisocial nature, the rest of the personality and society have kept the id mostly unconscious. It still influences us, but unconsciously....

The super-ego is the conscience. Should and shame are the staples of its vocabulary, and its favorite line is, "You should be ashamed of yourself!" While the id is predominantly unconscious, the super-ego is partly conscious and partly unconscious. The unconscious part contains the "remonstrations and rules we were taught. "Don't do that. Don't play with ... Nasty! Nice people don't ..." The super-ego is judgmental.

Between the id and the super-ego lives the hero and executive of the Freudian personality structure, the ego. Not only is he caught between the id and the super-ego and

FIGURE 1.1
Etiology of behavior from the psychodynamic perspective.

forced to moderate their conflicting pressures, he also is the one who is mostly aware of outside, social reality. Thus, his line to the others is, "Now, let's be realistic about this. . . ." The ego generally straddles the conscious and the unconscious. In a healthy personality he is the manager and can call the shots without being overpowered by the id or the super-ego. Each of the three parts has a genius all of its own. The ego's armamentarium includes his "ego defenses." Sublimation, for example, is the redirection of socially unacceptable impulses into acceptable channels: Don't play in the toilet, dear. Why don't you go out and play in the sandbox? A large part of our work as teachers is to provide socially acceptable outlets for otherwise destructive desires.*

From the psychodynamic perspective, personality development occurs as the child moves through a series of psychosexual steps which must be completed in order for the individual to avoid later problems (Erikson, 1963). The first stage is the *oral* stage, in which the individual's first contact with the environment occurs, relationships are initiated, and a basic attitude of trust or mistrust is developed. The *anal* stage follows, centering on elimination and conformity to demands for control. At the end of this stage, the individual either accomplishes autonomy or experiences shame and doubt. The third stage is *phallic,* in which the child becomes increasingly interested in the feelings of pleasure associated with the genitals. At this time the individual must develop his or her personality and self-identification. The next stage of psychosexual development, *latency,* usually occurs during the elementary school years. During this period the individual channels energy into learning. Finally, during adolescence, the *genital* stage occurs, in which the individual's previous identities are consolidated.

Efforts to apply psychodynamic theories to educational processes have led teachers to develop the psychodynamic-interpersonal educational, or psychoeducational, strategy. This strategy is

> . . . concerned with the psychic origin and meaning of maladaptive behavior, as well as the child's interpersonal relationships with others, particularly the teacher. This orientation, shared by most psychotherapists, is consistent with the high priority given by them to understanding psychological causal factors and the development of a positive, trusting relationship between adult and child in formal education training. (Hewett, 1968, p. 9)

Significant contributions to this educational strategy have been made by Berkowitz and Rothman (1960), Bower (1961), Glasser (1965), Morse (1965, 1985), Redl and Wineman (1951, 1952), Nichols (1984), and others. Although diversification exists among these theorists and practitioners, the primary objectives and methodologies to be applied in the educational setting remain relatively constant.

> A primary goal is to understand why the child is behaving as he is in school. This goal may be achieved by some through interpretation of behavior in a psychodynamic context, using psychoanalytic concepts. Others may view the child more in relationship to his

---

*From Roberts, T.B. (1975). *Four psychologies applied to education: Freudian-behavioral-humanistic-transpersonal.* Cambridge, MA: Schenkman Publishing Co.

total environment and be concerned with understanding why he lacks adaptive capacities for dealing with the stresses and demands associated with learning and adjustment in school. For the teacher, a major goal is the communication of acceptance to the child and the establishment of a secure and meaningful relationship. Formal educational goals are of secondary importance. (Hewett, 1968, pp. 17 and 18)

In the classroom emphasis is placed on (1) developing a mentally healthy atmosphere, (2) accepting the child and the pathological conditions without reservation, and (3) encouraging and assisting the child in learning, beginning at a level and under circumstances in which the child can perform successfully. Assuming the role of educational therapist, the teacher accepts the child, tolerating and interpreting the child's behavior.

Psychodynamic theories no longer dominate educational programs, as was the situation in the 1950s and 1960s. However, this theoretical perspective remains a dominant force in contemporary society in the United States in such forms as popular literature, child care books, movies, novels, television shows, and casual conversations.

In Chapter 6 several intervention strategies associated with the psychodynamic model are reviewed in detail.

Biophysical Model

The biophysical theory of the etiology of learning and behavior problems of children places emphasis on organic origins of human behavior. The proponents of this conceptual model postulate a relationship between physical defects, malfunctions, and illnesses and the individual's behavior. This relationship is depicted in Figure 1.2.

Schroeder and Schroeder (1982) discussed the two primary subgroups of biophysical theories: (1) biophysical deficit theories and (2) developmental theories. The deficit subgroup includes theories related to genetics, temperament, neuropsychopharmacalogy, nutrition, and neurologic dysfunction. Developmental theories include

FIGURE 1.2
Etiology of behavior from the biophysical perspective.

neurological organization, perceptual motor learning, physiological readiness, sensory integration, and development. Many of the interventions evolving from these subgroups of biophysical theory are discussed in Chapter 7.

Although not the dominant theory of causation in the education of children, the biophysical model does have proponents among professionals and parents concerned with severely emotionally disturbed, autistic, learning-disabled, perceptually handicapped, and developmentally disabled children.

The practitioner who is influenced by the biophysical model is concerned primarily with changing or compensating for the individual's malfunctioning organic mechanisms or processes that are causing the inappropriate behavior.

Some proponents of this theoretical perspective believe the individual's external environment to be a relatively unimportant factor in behavior (Rimland, 1969). Others accept the importance of the external environment and believe that it is the factor that triggers an inherent organic predisposition within the individual organism (Rosenthal, 1963).

As a result of extensive biophysical research with children having severe behavior disorders (autistic, schizophrenic children), Rimland concluded:

> Why do psychiatrists and psychologists believe there are people whose mental disorder is functional rather than organic? Why do they reject the plausible premise that the "functional" cases differ from the organic cases only in that our knowledge is at present too limited to identify the "organic" defect in the "functional" cases? (p. 703)

Rimland's prediction is that as our knowledge and understanding of human behavior and the physical organism develop, we will find that psychosocial factors have a minor influence in the etiology of severe behavior disorders.

Biophysical handicaps can be classified into four groups (National Foundation-March of Dimes, 1975):

1. *Structural defects:* One or more parts of the body are defective in size or shape (spina bifida, clubfoot, cleft lip).
2. *Functional defects:* One or more parts of the body are malfunctioning (blindness, deafness).
3. *Inborn errors of metabolism:* The body is unable to convert certain chemicals to other chemicals needed for normal body functioning (phenylketonuria [PKU], Tay-Sachs disease).
4. *Blood diseases:* The blood is unable to conduct its normal functions (sickle-cell anemia, hemophilia).

These organic defects may be a consequence of either heredity or environment (trauma). Environmental effects may occur before, during, or after birth.

Several curative and preventive medical interventions have been developed to mitigate or modify the effects of biophysical defects. Among these interventions are prenatal and postnatal health care, proper nutrition and diet, megavitamin and similar therapies, general and specific physical examinations, symptom control medications, and genetic counseling. These interventions are presented in detail in Chapter 7.

Among the proponents of biophysical theories as they apply to the education of children and youth are Cruickshank and others (1961), Fernald (1943), Frostig and others (1961), Getman (1962), and Kephart (1960).

An excellent summary of this theoretical perspective as it applies in the educational setting is provided by Hewett (1968):

> The primary goal of the sensory-neurological strategy is to discover the child's sensory and neurologically based deficit, often through extensive observation and diagnostic testing. Once these deficits are uncovered, the child is viewed as a learner who must be trained to accurately perceive and comprehend stimuli and to demonstrate motor efficiency before he is given complex learning tasks. (p. 24)

In the educational setting the teacher who is influenced by the biophysical model will emphasize order and routine in the classroom and daily schedule, frequent repetition of learning tasks, the sequential presentation and learning of tasks, and a reduction or elimination of extraneous environmental stimuli.

Environmental Model

The impact of the environment on human behavior is a dominant theme in contemporary society. Many decisions made by governments, corporate groups, and individuals are made with a conscious awareness of the relationship between people and the environment. Environmental impact studies are standard, accepted components of all proposals to construct highways, airports, dams, lakes, industrial complexes, highrise buildings, and so on. Both professionals and lay persons are increasingly concerned with any environmental changes that may affect human behavior, such as those concerning recreation areas, water pollution, waste disposal, strip mining, or nuclear power. Many are concerned with the effects of environmental changes on employment, human services, neighborhood composition, and so on.

Sociology traditionally is the study of the development, structure, interaction, and behavior of organized groups of humans. Sociology is composed of a number of subgroups focusing on specific areas of this social science, such as social psychology, small-group study, or educational sociology.

In an educational setting sociology focuses on the formal and informal composition of and interactions among groups. It is concerned with groups both within an organization and outside it that affect the organization. Applied to the education of children, sociology is the study of social forces that in some manner affect individuals and groups.

Ecology is the study of the interrelationships between an organism and its environment. As it applies to education, ecology is the study of the reciprocal relationship between the child or group and others (individuals, groups, and objects) in the environment.

Sociology and ecology as etiological models of human behavior are depicted in Figure 1.3.

The environmental theorists maintain that isolating a child's behavior from the environment in which it occurs denies the phenomenal nature of that behavior (Rhodes & Paul, 1978). Environmental theorists assume instead that "the child is an inseparable part of a small social system, an ecological unit, made up of the child, his family, his school, his neighborhood, and community" (Hobbs, 1966, p. 1108). Reactions of others in the child's ecosystem influence the way the child acts (Algozzine, 1980). The environmental perspective emphasizes the individual's behavior problem as a product of a "particular collective in a particular environment or place at a particular time in history" (Rhodes & Paul, 1978).

An environmental theory of importance to educators is the *deviance perspective.*

> The deviance perspective focuses on mental illness as the breaking of social rules. In particular, mental illness is related to implicit rules governing ordinary social interaction. From a deviance perspective, two important questions arise. (1) What are the social forces promoting conformity or rule-breaking? (2) What relationships exist between those enforcing the rules and those breaking the rules? (Des Jarlais, 1972, p. 263)

In an effort to respond to these two central questions, theorists have generated several models to account for deviant behavior. Reviewed by Des Jarlais (1972), these frameworks include:

☐ *Anomie:* The theory of anomie as a cause of mental illness was first proposed by Durkheim (1951). Anomie is defined as a lack of social rules or inhibitors within the structure of a society that effectively limit or regulate individual and group behaviors. This phenomenon occurs in rapidly developing or changing societies, such as contemporary society, in which socially sanctioned norms have not

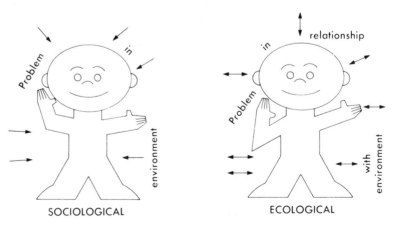

SOCIOLOGICAL   ECOLOGICAL

FIGURE 1.3
Etiology of behavior from the sociological and ecological perspectives.

evolved or been institutionalized rapidly enough to monitor the efforts of individuals and groups to attain their needs and desires.

☐ *Social disorganization:* The theory of social disorganization was developed from the findings of a series of urban studies. Among the researchers associated with this school of thought were Hawley (1950) and Park and Burgess (1925). This perspective attempts to measure and characterize the differences between communities considered organized or "natural" and communities considered disorganized. Characteristics of the organized community, in opposition to those of the disorganized community, include low crime and delinquency rates, stable family units, a low rate of mental illness and so on. The sources of such characteristics of the community (both organized and disorganized) are assumed to be related to such variables as the availability of employment, education, religious services, recreational facilities, and the like. The disorganized community lacks appropriate services.

☐ *Labeling theory:* The labeling of children who deviate from the norms and rules of the school and community has long been a concern of educators. Many fear the effects of the label and its implications for the child's behavior and educators' expectations of the child (Algozzine, Mercer, and Countermine, 1977)

The theory of labeling emphasizes that one does not become a deviant by breaking rules. One must be labeled a deviant before the social expectations defining the particular form of deviance are activated. Once an individual is officially labeled a deviant, this person assumes the role expectations of that particular form of deviance in order to conform to the expectations of society.

This theoretical perspective is closely related to Parsons's (1951) concept of the sick role. He proposed four societal expectations that encourage individuals labeled "sick" to assume this role:

1. Sick persons are relieved of their normal role obligations.
2. Because they are sick, they are not morally responsible for their condition.
3. Sick persons must express their desire to return to normal functioning.
4. Sick persons must seek technically competent help from appropriate caretakers (psychiatrists, psychologists, social workers, teachers).

Reviewed by Wagner (1972), a variety of interventions have evolved out of environmental theories. Many of these interventions are reviewed in detail in Chapter 7.

The application of the environmental model in educational programs for children is characterized by (1) an awareness of the impact of the environment on the group and/or individual and the monitoring and manipulation of the environment for the benefit of the individual and/ or group, and (2) an awareness of the dynamic reciprocal interrelationship that exists between the group and/or individual and the environment and the monitoring and manipulation of this relationship for the benefit of the individual and/or group.

In summary, the environmental framework is based on several assumptions about behavior, the environment, and the interactions between an individual and environment (Swap, Prieto, & Harth, 1982). These assumptions are:

1. The child is not disturbed. Disturbance is a consequence of either the environment's effect on the child or the interactions between the child and the environment.
2. Environmental interventions, to be effective, must in some manner alter the ecological system in which the child functions. The implementation of environmental interventions is based on an assessment of the child, the specific environment in which the child is functioning, and the interactions between these two elements. Although the interventions may focus on one or more of these factors, it impacts on all of them.
3. Environmental interventions are eclectic. It will be apparent in the discussion in Chapter 7 that environmental interventions are chosen from many theoretical perspectives. Interventions are selected and applied as needed within the environmental framework.
4. Interventions in an ecological system may have unanticipated consequences. Because of the complexity of the child, the environment, and the relationship between the two elements, it is difficult to predict with certitude the specific effects an intervention may have on the relationship's many variables. Thus, frequent and careful evaluation of the impact of interventions is essential.
5. Each interaction between child and setting is unique. This assumption recognizes the uniqueness of each child, the environment in which he or she is functioning, and the reciprocal relationship between child and environment.

Behavioral Model

Behavioral psychology is the predominant educational psychology taught in colleges and universities in the United States today (Kavale & Hirshoren, 1980).

The statement "What you do is influenced by what follows what you do" (Sarason et al., 1972, p. 10) is an excellent summary of the essence of the behavioral theory, specifically in reference to behavior modification. Behavior modification is the primary focus of Chapters 2 to 5 of this text. A brief overview of this model is presented here to facilitate the reader's efforts to compare and contrast it with the three previously presented models of human behavior.

The behavior modifier is concerned primarily with what behavior an individual exhibits that is inappropriate or unacceptable and what intervention can be designed and imposed to change this observable behavior.

For the behavior modification practitioner *behavior* is defined as all human acts that are observable and measurable, excluding biochemical and physiological processes (Roberts, 1975).

The behavioral theorists and practitioners see the causes of human behavior as existing outside the individual in the immediate environment. Thus the individual's behavior is primarily determined by external forces. The relationship between the individual and his or her behavior as perceived by the behaviorist is depicted in Figure 1.4.

FIGURE 1.4
Etiology of behavior from the behavior modification perspective.

Those adhering to the behavior modification model assume that all human behavior (adaptive and maladaptive) is the consequence of the lawful application of the principles of reinforcement.

According to Roberts, the principles of reinforcement are:

1. Reinforcement always follows the exhibition of the behavior. According to "Grandma's law," you eat your vegetables first, then you may have dessert.
2. The behavior should be reinforced as soon as possible after it occurs. Teachers who do not return papers or who delay their return a long time are guilty of professional misconduct in the perception of the behaviorist.
3. The reinforcement must be appropriate for the individual or group being reinforced. A reinforcer is only effective if the individual or group being reinforced perceives the reinforcer as rewarding or punishing.
4. Many small rewards, presented frequently, are more effective than a few big ones. The principles of reinforcement are presented in depth in Chapter 2.

These rules are an indication of the behavior modifier's belief that human behavior is controlled by the individual's impinging environmental stimuli. The individual's behavior is changed by manipulation of environmental stimuli.

Behavioral theory, including behavior modification techniques and their applications to individual and group behavior problems, has its roots in the writings and research of Bandura (1969), Eysenck (1960), Hull (1943), Skinner (1953, 1971), Thorndike (1932), and Wolpe (1961), among others. Although there have been and continue to be debates among theorists relative to various constructs and interventions within this theoretical model, practitioners have successfully applied its principles to a variety of human problems. Among the problem behaviors that have been modified as a consequence of the application of behavior modification interventions are the symptoms of psychoses, autism, neuroses, marital conflicts, specific learning problems, motivational handicaps, and speech problems. Researchers and practitioners have successfully modified tantrums, verbal and physical aggression, interpersonal interaction patterns, eating habits, mutism, and so on.

Various behavior modification interventions in the school have been successfully implemented with exceptional children by Haring and Phillips (1962), Hewett and Taylor (1980), Orme and Purnell (1970), and others.

The goal of behavior modification interventions in the classroom with behavior-disordered children (and, indeed, with all individuals) is best summarized by Hewett (1968).

> The basic goal for the behavior modifier is the identification of maladaptive behaviors which interfere with learning and assisting the child in developing more adaptive behavior. Every child is considered a candidate for learning something regardless of his degree of psychopathology and other problems. This "something" may only represent a starting point (e.g., chair sitting) and be but a small part of the eventual "something" the teacher hopes to accomplish (e.g., reading), but care will be taken to insure its mastery before more complex goals are introduced. The child's behavior is viewed in the broadest possible context without rigid adherence to a priority ranking of behavioral goals on the basis of inferences regarding emotional conflicts or brain dysfunctions.

There are a variety of behavior modification interventions that may be applied in the effort to change behavior. These interventions are presented in detail with practical examples in Chapters 4 and 5.

The procedures for applying behavior modification in the educational setting require the teacher to (1) observe and clarify the behavior to be changed, (2) select and present potent reinforcers at the appropriate time, (3) design and impose, with consistency, an intervention technique based on the principles of reinforcement, and (4) monitor and evaluate the effectiveness of the intervention. These steps in the behavior change process are presented in detail in Chapter 3.

Public Law 94-142

On November 29, 1975, President Ford signed Public Law (PL) 94-142, which in a bipartisan effort was passed by both the House of Representatives and the Senate. This landmark legislation, the *Education for All Handicapped Children Act of 1975,* mandates throughout the United States *a free, appropriate public education for all handicapped children.*

Congress emphasized the key elements of the act in its use of the words *free, appropriate, public,* and *all.* It is the intention of Congress that *all* handicapped children receive an education regardless of race, religion, sex, or the characteristics of their particular handicaps. They are to receive an education that is *appropriate* to their individual needs. This education is to be *free* (without cost) to the child and the parents or guardian. Finally, the handicapped child's *free, appropriate* education is to be provided by the *public* school system rather than in private school or institutional settings (Shea and Bauer, 1987).

The Education for All Handicapped Children Act of 1975 is having and will continue to have a significant impact on the structure and operation of the total educational establishment in the nation for many years to come. Its provisions will affect education from the preschool to the university level in general and special education programs. It will affect regular elementary and secondary education teachers as well as special education teachers. It will have a significant impact on both handicapped and nonhandicapped individuals.

Among the provisions of PL 94-142, of greatest significance to the topics presented in this text are (Abeson & Weintraub, 1977):

1. Each handicapped individual needing special education and related services is to have an individualized education program (IEP) written in response to his or her individual educational needs.
2. Parents are to be involved in the child's IEP. As partners with professionals in the child's education, parents have several important functions. They participate in the child's assessment, the IEP development process, the approval of the IEP and educational placement, and the evaluation of the IEP. Parents may participate directly in the child's educational program.
3. The regular and special classroom teachers are to be fully participating members of the IEP decision-making team. As the professionals primarily responsible for the delivery of services to the handicapped individual, the teacher—general or special —has full and active involvement in the IEP development, implementation, and evaluation.
4. Handicapped children are to be placed in the least restrictive environment necessary to meet their unique educational needs. This provision requires that the handicapped child be placed in an educational environment that is as close to a normal or regular school program as feasible, yet one that is responsive to the child's individual educational needs. A child's special educational needs *only* are to be met in a special education service program. The child's normal childhood needs are to be met in the regular classroom and school setting. This concept is frequently referred to as *mainstreaming*, an often misunderstood term.

Mainstreaming is defined as

> . . . a belief which involves an educational procedure and process for exceptional children, based on the conviction that each such child should be educated in the least restrictive environment in which his educational and related needs can be satisfactorily provided. This concept recognizes that exceptional children have a wide range of special educational needs, varying greatly in intensity and duration; that there is a recognized continuum of educational settings which may, at a given time, be appropriate for an individual child's needs; that to the maximum extent appropriate, exceptional children should be educated with non-exceptional children; and that special classes, separate schooling, or

other removal of an exceptional child from education with non-exceptional children should occur only when the intensity of the child's special education and related need is such that they cannot be satisfied in an environment including non-exceptional children, even with provisions of supplementary aides and services. (Council for Exceptional Children, Delegate Assembly, 1976, p. 3)

Individualized Education Programs

A key provision of PL 94-142 is the individualized education program (IEP) to be written for each child who is declared eligible for special education services, whether service is provided in the general or special education setting. The IEP is developed in response to each child's educational needs.

In PL 94-142 the IEP is described as

... a written statement for each handicapped child developed in any meeting by a representative of the local educational agency or an intermediate educational unit who shall be qualified to provide, or supervise the provision of, specially designed instruction to meet the unique needs of handicapped children, the teacher, the parents or guardian of such child, and, whenever appropriate, such child, which statement shall include (A) a statement of the present levels of educational performance of such child, (B) a statement of annual goals, including short-term instructional objectives, (C) a statement of the specific educational services to be provided to such child, and the extent to which such child will be able to participate in regular educational programs, (D) the projected date for initiation and anticipated duration of such services, and (E) appropriate objective criteria and evaluation procedures and schedules for determining, on at least an annual basis, whether instructional objectives are being achieved. (Public Law 94-142, Section 4)

As noted previously, the law specifically requires the direct participation of parents, teachers, and, when appropriate, the child in the IEP development process. In addition, PL 94-142 mandates that the child be integrated into the regular school programs for educational activities unless such integration is detrimental to child's overall educational progress.

Analysis of the preceding description of the IEP suggests the following minimum requirements under the law:

1. The child's educational performance must be assessed and the resulting data included in the written IEP.
2. The results of the assessment must be translated into annual goals and short-term instructional objectives. These annual goals and short-term instructional objectives form the basis for which the child's educational program is designed.
3. The educational program must be written in response to the child's individual needs as stated in the goals and instructional objectives.
4. An objective evaluation procedure must be designed and implemented to ascertain the effectiveness of the instructional program.

A correlation can be made between the IEP process and the steps in the behavior change process, described in detail in Chapter 3. Briefly, the behavior change process requires the following steps:

☐ Collection of baseline data (IEP assessment phase)
☐ Selection of objectives for the behavior change program (IEP short-term instructional objectives phase)
☐ Design and implementation of a specific behavior change intervention or strategy (IEP instructional or educational program phase)
☐ Collection of intervention data to evaluate the effectiveness of the behavior change intervention (IEP evaluation phase)

These similarities are demonstrated on the sample IEP in Figures 1.5 and 1.6.

It appears that both regular and special education teachers trained in behavior modification procedures will find this training a valuable asset in their efforts to develop meaningful IEPs.

SUMMARY

In this introductory chapter, an effort is made to prepare the reader for the discussion of behavior management strategies presented in Chapters 2 through 7.

First, a definition of behavior management and several behavior management guidelines are presented and discussed.

Next, the relationship between models of human behavior (conceptual frameworks) and behavior management interventions evolving from these models are discussed. Four models of behavior are discussed in detail. These are psychodynamic, biophysical, environmental, and behavioral. It is suggested that each of the models contributes to our understanding of human behavior.

Several important components of PL 94-142 (Education for All Handicapped Children Act of 1975) having bearing on the role and function of general and special educators and parents are presented. The major components of the IEP are reviewed and exemplified. The similarities between the IEP and the behavior change process are discussed.

In Chapters 2 through 5, the reader's attention is turned to processes and techniques associated with the behavioral model. Chapters 2 and 3 present the principles of reinforcement and the steps in the behavior change process, respectively. Chapters 4 and 5 present several behavior modification techniques applied to change behavior.

Individualized Education Program

Student's name: *E.J. Jolpe*
IEP manager's name: *T.J. Waller*

Planning conference date: *May 12, 1987*
Date for review/revision: *May, 1988*

PRESENT LEVELS OF PERFORMANCE

Academics: *One year below grade level in reading and spelling, as noted on PIAT, Botel, and a teacher informal assessment*

Speech/Language: *Age appropriate as noted on Utah and district speech and language therapist using portions of ITPA*

Motor: *Below age level in visual perception on DTVP and Beery. Below age level in auditory discrimination on Wepman. Visual and hearing tests negative.*

Social Behavior: *Inattentative and hyperactive as observed by teacher, district psychologist, and speech and language therapist.*

Prevocational/Vocational: *Not applicable*

Self-Help: *Not applicable*

Extent of Participation in Regular Education: *All activities except 1 hour daily in resource room*

Type of Physical Education Program: *Regular physical education*

Services to be provided for current year

Type	Initiation date	No. minutes per week	No. weeks
Resource room	Aug. 23, 1987	300	36
Second grade teacher consultation	Aug. 23, 1987	150	36

Placement: *Special Education Resource Room, 2nd grade with consultation on behavior problem*

Justification for Placement: *Needs assistance in visual perception and auditory discrimination which cannot be provided in regular 2nd grade classroom*

FIGURE 1.5
Sample IEP statement.
(*Modified from Illinois primer on individualized education programs.* Springfield, Ill.: State Board of Education, Department of Specialized Educational Services and Regional Resource Center, 1981.)

Students name: E.J. Jolpe
Implementer's names:
 T.J. Waller, resource room
 J.J. Topel, second grade

Instruction areas:
1. Visual perception
2. Auditory discrimination
3. a. Inattentiveness
 b. Hyperactivity

SHORT-TERM INSTRUCTIONAL OBJECTIVES

Condition	Behavior	Criteria	Special media and materials	Evaluation/Schedule	Date objective mastered
1. Visual perception	Cannot discriminate between b/d, d/p, etc.	100% accuracy	Kephart (1960)	Teacher on-going evaluation with formal evaluation every 9 weeks	
2. Auditory discrimination	Cannot discriminate between "was/saw", etc.	100% accuracy	Valett (1974)	As above	
3. a. Inattentive	a. Attends to teacher directions and ongoing group activities less than 20% of time	Increase attend behavior to 60%	Token economy	Count and chart daily; summary weekly; reevaluate at 9 weeks	
b. Hyperactive	b. On an average, during seat work, is in seat less than 30% of time	Increase in-seat behavior to 70%	Token economy and time-out by exclusion Communication via token economy card carried by child to all special and regular school activities	As above	

FIGURE 1.6 Sample IEP short-term objectives. (Modified from Illinois primer on individualized education programs. Springfield, Ill.: State Board of Education, Department of Specialized Educational Services and Regional Resource Center, 1981.)

EXERCISES

Quiz

1. Define behavior management.

   _____

   _____

   _____

   _____

   _____

2. List five of the behavior management guidelines presented in this chapter.

   a. _____

   b. _____

   c. _____

   d. _____

   e. _____

3. Briefly discuss one of the guidelines you listed in the previous question.

4. The desired result of all behavior management interventions is:

5. In addition to personal traits, the effective teacher must have specific knowledge and skills to successfully lead children. Four of these work characteristics are:

   a. _____

   b. _____

   c. _____

   d. _____

6. "According to Hewett and Forness (1984), there are four historical determiners of our behavior toward ourselves and others." These determiners are:

   a. _____

   b. _____

   c. _____

   d. _____

7. List the four *model* explanations of human behavior:

   a. _____

   b. _____

   c. _____

   d. _____

8. A belief in the existence of a dynamic intrapsychic life reflects on the _____ model.

9. Organic origins of human behavior refer to the _____ model.

10. Anomie, social disorganization, cultural transmission, and labeling theory all refer to the

    _____model.

11. The _____ model refers to learned behavior an individual exhibits that is unacceptable and inappropriate.

12. The _____ model differs from the other models in that it attempts to answer the question "how" behavior occurs instead of "why."

13. PL 94-142 is known as _____

    _____of _____ .

14. What does PL 94-142 mandate?

    _____

    _____

15. What does the abbreviation IEP mean?

    _____

16. List the minimum requirements of an IEP.

    _____

    _____

    _____

    _____

    _____

    _____

    _____

    _____

Projects
1. Conduct a class discussion of the definition of behavior management presented in the text.
2. Using the professional literature, locate three definitions of behavior management. Compare these definitions with that presented in the text.

3. Using the professional literature, write a five- or six-page paper on one of the models of human behavior discussed in this chapter.
4. Discuss the impact of the four historical determiners (survival, superstition, science, and service) on contemporary human behavior.
5. Invite to class for a presentation or conduct an interview with a special education administrator or teacher to discuss the impact of PL 94-142 on general and special education.
6. Discuss the sample IEP presented in the text. Write an IEP using a child who is familiar to you or your instructor.

REFERENCES

Abeson, A., & Weintraub, F. (1977). Understanding the individualized education program. In S. Torres (Ed.), *A primer on individualized education programs for handicapped children* (pp. 3–8). Reston, VA: The Foundation for Exceptional Children.

Algozzine, B. (1980). The disturbing child: a matter of opinion. *Behavioral Disorders, 5*(2), 112–115.

Algozzine, B., Mercer, D. C., & Countermine, T. (1977). The effects of labels and behavior on teacher expectations. *Exceptional Children, 44*(2), 131–132.

Bandura, A. (1969). *Principles of behavior modification.* New York: Holt, Rinehart & Winston.

Beez, W. V. (1972). Influence of biased psychological reports on teacher behavior and pupil performance. In A. Morrison & D. McIntyre (Eds.), *The social psychology of teaching* (pp. 324–332). Baltimore: Penguin Books.

Berkowitz, P., & Rothman, E. (1960). *The disturbed child.* New York: New York University Press.

Berne, E. (1964a). *Games people play.* New York: Grove Press.

Berne, E. (1964b). *Principles of group treatment.* New York: Oxford University Press.

Bower, E. M. (1961). *The education of emotionally handicapped children: A report to the California Legislature.* Sacramento: California State Department of Education.

Caplan, G. (1963). Opportunities for school psychologists in the primary prevention of mental disorders in children. *Mental Hygiene, 47,* 525–540.

Chetkow, G. H. (1964). Discipline problems in camp. *Recreation, 57*(3), 136–137.

Council for Exceptional Children, Delegate Assembly. (1976). Mainstreaming. *CEC Update, 7*(4) 3.

Cruickshank, W., Bentzen, F., Ratzenburg, F., & Tannhauser, M. (1961). *A teaching methodology for brain-injured and hyperactive children.* New York: Syracuse University Press.

Des Jarlais, D. C. (1972). Mental illness of social deviance. In W. C. Rhodes and M. L. Tracy (Eds.), *A study of child variance: Vol. 1. Conceptual project in emotional disturbance* (pp. 259–322). Ann Arbor: The University of Michigan Press.

Dreikurs, R., & Grey, L. (1968). *Logical Consequences: A new approach to discipline.* New York: Hawthorn Books.

Durkheim, E. (1951). *Suicide.* New York: Free Press.

Erikson, E. H. (1963). *Childhood and society.* New York: W. W. Norton & Co.

Erikson, E. H. (1974). *Dimensions of a new identity: The 1973 Jefferson lectures in the humanities.* New York: W. W. Norton & Co.

Eysenck, H. J. (1960). *Behavior therapy and the neuroses.* New York: Pergamon Press.

Fernald, G. (1943). *Remedial techniques in basic school subjects.* New York: McGraw-Hill Book Co.

Freud, S. (1949). *An outline of psychoanalysis.* New York: W. W. Norton & Co.

Frostig, M., LeFever, W., & Whittlesey, J. R. B. (1961). *Developmental test of visual perception.* Palo Alto, CA: Consulting Psychologists Press.

Getman, G. N. (1962). *How to develop your child's*

intelligence. Luverne, MN: Announcer Press.

Glasser, W. (1965). *Reality therapy.* New York: Harper & Row.

Haring, N. G., & Phillips, E. L. (1962). *Educating emotionally disturbed children.* New York: McGraw-Hill Book Co.

Hawley, A. (1950). *Human ecology: A theory of community structure.* New York: Ronald Press Co.

Hewett, F. M. (1968). *The emotionally disturbed child in the classroom: A developmental strategy for educating children with maladaptive behavior.* Boston: Allyn & Bacon.

Hewett, F. M. & Forness, S. R. (1984). *Education of exceptional learners* (3rd ed.). Boston: Allyn & Bacon.

Hewett, F. M. & Taylor, F. D. (1980). *The emotionally disturbed child in the classroom.* Boston: Allyn & Bacon.

Hobbs, N. (1966). Helping disturbed children: Psychological and ecological strategies. *American Psychologist, 21*(12), 1105-1115.

Hull, C. L. (1943). *Principles of behavior.* New York: Appleton-Century-Crofts.

Illinois primer on individualized education programs. (1981). Springfield, IL: State Board of Education, Department of Specialized Educational Services and Regional Resource Center.

Kauffman, J. M., Pullen, P. L., & Akers, E., (1986). Classroom management: Teacher-child-peer relationships. *Focus on Exceptional Children, 19*(1), 1–10.

Kavale, K., & Hirshoren, A. (1980). Public school and university teacher training programs for behaviorally disordered children: Are they compatible? *Behavior Disorder, 5*(3), 151-155.

Kephart, N. (1971). *The slow learner in the classroom.* Columbus, OH: Charles E. Merrill.

Morse, W. C. (1964). Intervention techniques for the classroom teacher of the emotionally disturbed. In P. Knoblock (Ed.), *Educational programming for emotionally disturbed children: The decade ahead.* Syracuse, NY: Division of Special Education and Rehabilitation, Syracuse University.

Morse, W. C. (1965). The crisis teacher. In N. Long, W. C. Morse, and R. Newman (Eds.), *Conflict in the classroom* (1st ed.). Belmont, CA: Wadsworth Publishing Co.

Morse, W. C. (1985). *The education and treatment of socioemotionally impaired children and youth.* Syracuse, NY: Syracuse University Press.

Munroe, R. L. (1955). *Schools of psychoanalytic thought: An exposition, critique, and attempt at integration.* New York: Holt, Rinehart & Winston.

National Foundation-March of Dimes. (1975). *Birth defects: The tragedy and the hope.* White Plains, NY: The Foundation

Nichols, P. (1984). Down the up staircase: The teacher as therapist. In J. Grosenick, S. Huntze, E. McGinnis, & C. Smith (Eds.). *Social/affective intervention in behavioral disorders* (pp. 43–66). Des Moines: State of Iowa Department of Public Instruction.

Orme, M. E. J., & Purnell, R. F. (1970). Behavior modification and transfer in an out-of-control classroom. In G. Fargo, C. Behrns, & P. Nolen (Eds.). *Behavior modification in the classroom* (pp. 116–138). Belmont, CA: Wadsworth Publishing Co.

Park, R. E., & Burgess, E. W. (1925). *The city.* Chicago: University of Chicago Press.

Parsons, T. (1951). *The social system.* New York: Free Press.

Redl, F., & Wineman, D. (1951). *Children who hate.* New York: Free Press.

Redl, F., & Wineman, D. (1952). *Controls from within.* New York: Free Press.

Rhodes, W. C., & Paul, J. L. (1978). *Emotionally disturbed and deviant children: New views and approaches.* Englewood Cliffs, NJ: Prentice-Hall.

Rhodes, W. C., & Tracy, M. L. (Eds.). (1972a). *A study of child variance: Vol. 1. Conceptual project in emotional disturbance.* Ann Arbor: The University of Michigan Press.

Rhodes, W. C., & Tracy, M. L. (Eds.). (1972b). *A study of child variance: Vol. 2. Interventions.* Ann Arbor: The University of Michigan Press.

Rimland, B. (1969). Psychogenesis versus biogenesis: The issues and evidence. In S. C. Plog & R. B. Edgerton (Eds.). *Changing perspectives in mental illness* (pp. 702–735). New York: Holt, Rinehart & Winston.

Roberts, T. B. (1975). *Four psychologies applied to education: Freudian-behavioral-humanistic-transpersonal.* Cambridge, MA: Schenkman Publishing Co.

Rosenthal, D. (Ed.). (1963). *The Genain quadruplets: A case study and theoretical analysis of heredity and environment in schizophrenia.* New York: Basic Books.

Rosenthal, R. & Jacobson, L. (1966). Teacher's expectancies: Determinants of pupils' IQ gains. *Psychological reports, 19,* 115–118.

Rubin, R., & Balow, B. (1971). Learning and behavior disorders: A longitudinal study. *Exceptional children, 38,* 293–298.

Sarason, I. G., Glaser, E. M., & Fargo, G. A. (1972). *Reinforcing productive classroom behavior.* New York: Behavioral Publications.

Schroeder, S. R. & Schroeder, C. (1982). Organic factors. In J. L. Paul and B. Epanchin (Eds.). *Emotional disturbance in children.* Columbus, OH: Charles E. Merrill.

Shea, T. M. & Bauer, A. M. (1987). *Teaching children and youth with behavior disorders (2nd Ed.).* Englewood Cliffs, NJ: Prentice-Hall.

Skinner, B. F. (1953). *Science and human behavior.* New York: Macmillan Publishing Co.

Skinner, B. F. (1971). *Beyond freedom and dignity.* New York: Alfred A. Knopf.

Swap, S. M., Prieto, A. G., & Harth, R. (1982). Ecological perspective of the emotionally disturbed child. In R. L. McDowell, G. W. Adamson, & F. H. Wood (Eds). *Teaching emotionally disturbed children.* Boston: Little, Brown & Co.

Thorndike, E. L. (1932). *The fundamentals of learning.* New York: Teachers's College Press.

Tisdale, P. C. (1985). The teacher's ten commandments. *The Directive Teacher, 7*(1), 6–8.

Wagner, M. (1972). Environmental interventions in emotional disturbance. In W. C. Rhodes & M. L. Tracy (Eds.). *A study of child variance: Vol. 2. Intervention.* Ann Arbor: The Unversity of Michigan Press.

Wolpe, J. (1961). The systematic desensitization treatment of neuroses. *Journal of nervous and mental disease, 132,* 189–203.

Wood, F. H. (1978). Punishment and special educators: Some concluding comments. In F. H. Wood & K. C. Lakin, (Eds.). *Punishment and aversive stimulation in special education: Legal, theoretical and practical issues in their use with emotionally disturbed children and youth* (pp. 119–122). Minneapolis: University of Minnesota.

CHAPTER TWO

Basic Principles of Behavior Modification

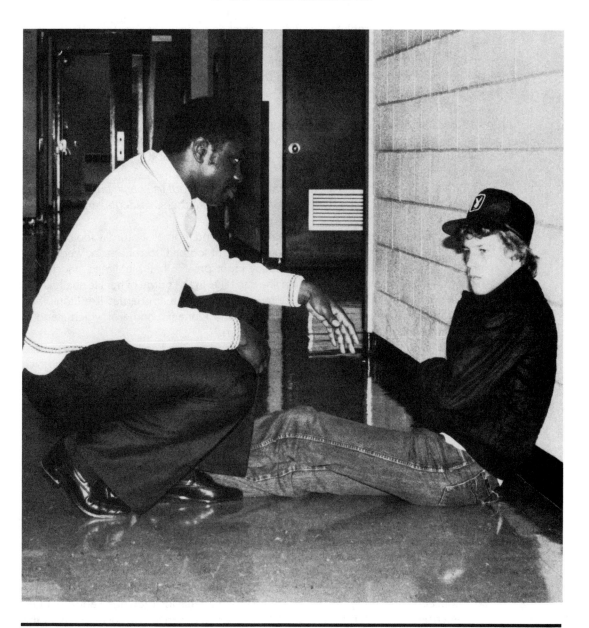

Mr. Rodrigues has completed his first semester as principal of San Jose Mission High School. It has been a challenging semester for the new principal, but something is not going right among the faculty and staff. The morale of the office staff is low; teachers are not motivated; students are going through the motion of learning; and the community acts as if it doesn't know the school exists. Mr. Rodrigues wonders how he might create a more positive, exciting educational atmosphere. Conversations among staff and teachers suggest that Mr. Rodrigues is an administrator who believes that if a person is being paid for a job, that should be ample reward. The teachers and staff think their efforts are not appreciated. The students appear to reflect the attitudes of the staff and teachers.

Maybe if Mr. Rodrigues were taught something about the basic principles of behavior modification, his relations with his staff, teachers, students, and the community would improve.

Linda has about had it with her husband, Bob, and football. Saturday football, Sunday football, Monday night football, Tuesday night football from Canada, Wednesday night college football highlights, Thursday night pro football highlights, and Friday night football forecasts are more than she can take. In the prime of her life she has lost Bob to oversized giants who wear funny uniforms with team names like Lions, Falcons, Raiders, Bears, Fighting Irish, Trojans, and Pioneers, some of which stand in front of television cameras and wave, "Hi, Mom."

Linda has attended workshops for football widows. She has gone so far as to have the name and number of Bob's favorite player printed on a very "naughty" nightgown and dance seductively in front of the television, only to be told, "Linda, would you please move; I can't see the game."

Is it possible that Linda could change Bob's behavior? Perhaps if Linda knew something about the basic principles of behavior modification, she could become the football player in Bob's life.

Most persons go through life unaware of the many factors in their lives and the influences these factors have on the way they behave. They appear unaware of the fact that as "normal" *Homo sapiens* they tend to be attracted to those experiences which are pleasurable and avoid those which are not pleasurable. Most persons receive pleasure from smiles, positive comments, a pat on the back, an excellent grade in a course, and a bonus in their paychecks. They avoid situations where physical or mental pain is inflicted, and they avoid associating with persons they don't like to be around.

"What you do is influenced by what follows what you do" (Sarason et al., 1972). The consequences and probable consequences of behavior, more than any other factor, determine the behavior that an individual exhibits (Shea & Bauer, 1987). In the field of behavior modification the consequences of behavior are called *reinforcers*. These reinforcers may increase or decrease behavior (Axelrod, 1983; Morris, 1985).

Reinforcers can be classified in a number of ways. Basically, they are classified as tangible or primary reinforcers (food, drinks, and tokens) and social or secondary reinforcers (praise, smiles, and other signs of approval).

For example, why does a child attend school? What reinforces school-attending behavior? A child may go to school because:

1. It is warmer in the school than in the home.
2. The people at school give the child more attention than the people at home or in the neighborhood.
3. The child plans after-school activities with friends during the morning recess.
4. The child eats the hot meal provided each noon by the school.

It can be understood, then, that a child attends school for both tangible (heat and food) and social (attention and friends) rewards.

Reinforcers may be positive (rewarding, pleasure giving) or negative (aversive, punishing). Tangible and social reinforcers may be positive reinforcers, that is, desirable consequences for which appropriate behavior is exhibited. Or they may be negative, that is, undesirable consequences for which behavior is not exhibited.

A child who considers school an aversive stimulus might exhibit inappropriate behavior in an attempt to avoid school. If the child were successful in this attempt, the inappropriate behavior would increase; thus school-attending behavior would decrease. For example, two situations that would result in an increase in school-avoiding behavior are:

1. The child is allowed to remain at home during the school day because he or she complains of being ill.
2. The child is allowed to remain at home because a homework assignment is not completed.

If the child were not allowed to avoid school by exhibiting these behaviors, they would probably decrease.

Punishment would also be effective in getting a child to attend school. Among the punishments that could be employed are (1) a spanking from the child's father, (2) a reprimand from the child's mother, (3) loss of allowance or the use of a bike, (4) loss of privileges, such as watching television or attending the movies, and (5) the threat of being sent to juvenile court or a detention center.

The consequences of behavior, then, are the determiners of behavior. Human beings tend to repeat behaviors that are, in their perception, rewarded or praised. They tend not to repeat behaviors that are, in their perception, punished.

In the remainder of this chapter the basic principles of behavior modification are presented and exemplified. These principles can be systematically applied by the teacher in the classroom and by the parents in the home.

The effective and efficient application of behavior modification techniques involves more than the simple memorization and application of the principles of reinforcement. For effective implementation it is necessary that the teacher or parent be intuitive, creative, and empathetic.

Principles of Reinforcement

The principles of reinforcement are a set of rules to be applied in the behavior change process. The successful behavior modifier relies heavily on these principles when planning and implementing a behavior change program.

Principle 1: Reinforcement Is Dependent on the Exhibition of the Target Behavior

If we are attempting, via a planned intervention, to change a specific behavior in an individual, we must reinforce *only* the behavior we are planning to change and only after that behavior is exhibited. In planning and implementing an intervention, we must *take caution to ensure that nontarget behaviors are not reinforced unwittingly.*

EXAMPLES
■ Ms. Jones was attempting to decrease Bill's out-of-seat behavior in her classroom. It had been ascertained through systematic observation that Bill received attention from her for out-of-seat behavior. When Bill was out of his seat, Ms. Jones proceeded to yell or otherwise reprimand him. Although Bill was receiving negative attention (in Ms. Jones' perception), his attempts to receive attention—positive or negative—were apparently being met in this situation. Bill's inappropriate behavior (being out of his seat) kept increasing as Ms. Jones's behavior (yelling or scolding) kept increasing. ■

■ Ms. Long was faced with a problem similar to Ms. Jones'—Jerry's out-of-seat behavior. She was reported to have said that she had to dust Jerry's chair every morning because he never used it.

At first she applied Ms. Jones' technique, that is, yelling. Then she planned a behavior modification intervention. She would totally ignore Jerry's out-of-seat behavior. She would in *no* way reinforce inappropriate behavior. However and whenever Jerry's overactive bottom hit his assigned seat, she would immediately reward him. She would praise him in front of the whole class, if necessary, and pat his shoulder.

As a result of this intervention, Jerry not only learned to sit in his seat, but Ms. Long discovered she liked him. ■

In the second example the approach was effective in bringing about the desired behavior. In the first example, however, Ms. Jones is still yelling and Bill is still high on all the attention he is receiving.

In conclusion, Principle 1 suggests that if we desire to modify a specific behavior, we must reinforce *only* that behavior and *only* after it is exhibited.

Principle 2: The Target Behavior Is to be Reinforced Immediately after It Is Exhibited

The importance of presenting the reinforcer immediately after the target behavior is exhibited cannot be overstressed. This principle is especially true during the initial stages of the behavior change process, when we are attempting to establish a new behavior. Inappropriate and nonfunctional behaviors occur from time to time in every individual's behavioral repertoire. If reinforcers are delayed in a planned intervention program, nontarget behaviors (rather than the target behavior) may be accidentally or unwittingly reinforced, thus increasing the probability that a nontarget behavior will be exhibited in the future.

EXAMPLE ■ Mr. Flamer was attempting to increase the number of problems Pat completed during math period. He planned to reward Pat immediately after he completed each assigned group of problems. The number of problems in each group would be increased on a weekly basis if Pat responded to the intervention as predicted.

Mr. Flamer was very inconsistent in the presentation of the reinforcer (tokens). As a result, Pat spent considerable time waiting at his desk and waving his hand frantically to gain Mr. Flamer's attention.

After a few weeks it was found that the intervention program was ineffective in increasing the number of completed problems. However, Pat now sat at his desk for much longer periods of time with a bored expression.

Mr. Flamer became aware of Pat's behavior and of his own personal inconsistency. He began to reinforce Pat immediately after Pat had completed each group of problems. Within a short time Pat was completing his problems and had doubled his production. ■

When attempting to establish a new behavior or increase the frequency of an existing behavior, we must reinforce that behavior as soon as it occurs.

Principle 3: During the Initial Stages of the Behavior Change Process the Target Behavior Is Reinforced Each Time It Is Exhibited

If newly acquired behavior is to be sustained at the appropriate frequency rate, the reinforcer must be administered each time the behavior is exhibited. Frequently beginning behavior modifiers reinforce new, but not yet habituated, behaviors with such inconsistency and so infrequently that the child becomes confused and the target behavior does not become an established part of the child's behavioral repertoire.

EXAMPLES ■ Ms. Traber worked several months with Matt, rewarding approximations of a desired behavior (in this case, a complete sentence). Finally, after 6 months Matt said a complete sentence: "I want a candy." Matt was immediately rewarded with a candy, and for the next several weeks he consumed many candies; he was given many opportunities to receive the reward. In addition, during this phase of the behavior change process Matt increased his variety of complete sentences to include "I want a glass of milk," "I want some juice," "I want some soda," "I want a puzzle," and the like. ■

■ Russell never requested any materials or assistance in the junior high school classroom without whining, screaming, or both. He would yell, "I want my paper," or "Give me some help." Mr. Hicks had taken about as much of this behavior as he could tolerate. He decided to ignore all whining and screaming from Russell. Russell's initial reaction to being ignored dramatically increased his inappropriate behavior, but Mr. Hicks stuck to the plan.

After 2 weeks of mutual frustration Russell raised his hand one day during social studies. He politely requested Mr. Hicks' assistance. He immediately received the assistance, verbal praise, and a pat on the back. Mr. Hicks was very pleased with Russell (and himself). A mutual admiration society developed and continued very consistently for a few days.

Mr. Hicks then focused his attention on the problem of another boy in the class. As a result, Mr. Hicks became an inconsistent reinforcer and Russell began whining and screaming anew.

Mr. Hicks forgot that Russell's inappropriate behavior had been learned over 12 or 13 years and could not be changed overnight and after only a few successes. ■

A newly acquired, unconditioned, or not fully habituated behavior cannot be sustained if it is not reinforced each time it occurs. Consistent reinforcement during the initial stages of the behavior change process is essential.

Principle 4: When the Target Behavior Reaches a Satisfactory Frequency Level, It Is Reinforced Intermittently

Although this principle may appear to be a contradiction of Principle 3, it is not. The behavior modifier must be consistent in the application of inconsistent (intermittent) reinforcement *after* the target behavior is established. This practice appears to be the only way in which a newly acquired behavior can be firmly established and become self-sustaining.

Once a target behavior has been established at a satisfactory level, the presentation of the reinforcer is changed from continuous to intermittent. This change in the reinforcer presentation increases the probability that the behavior will be maintained at a satisfactory level. It appears that if the child whose behavior is being changed does not know exactly when the reinforcer will be given *but does know reinforcement will occur,* the target behavior will continue to be exhibited at a satisfactory level.

EXAMPLES   ■ Ms. Williams wished to increase Phil's frequency of voluntary responses during current events discussions. In this situation poker chips were used as a reinforcer. The chips could be saved and cashed in at the end of the discussion period for a tangible reward from the class store.

Initially Ms. Williams reinforced Phil each time he volunteered a response during the discussion. After several weeks Phil's frequency of responses was at a satisfactory level; that is, it was equal, or nearly equal, to the average frequency of responses of the other members of the discussion groups. At this point in the behavior modification process Ms. Williams changed from giving continuous to intermittent reinforcement.

With intermittent reinforcement Phil's behavior remained at a high level. Phil became aware that he would be rewarded when he responded, but not every time. It also became evident to Ms. Williams that Phil was enjoying his participation in the class discussions. ■

■ Mr. Jones and Ms. Walker had similar problems in their classroom groups. In Mr. Jones' room Jared would not participate in class discussions. In Ms. Walker's room Herman presented the same problem.

Mr. Jones wished to increase the frequency of Jared's responses during group discussions. He introduced an intervention similar to the one used by Ms. Williams in the previous example. However, once Jared had attained an acceptable level of performance, Mr. Jones discontinued all reinforcement. Because of the lack of reinforcement, Jared's newly acquired behavior decreased.

Ms. Walker also initiated an intervention program to increase Herman's level of participation. Ms. Walker kept Herman on the continuous reinforcement schedule until he became bored with the tokens and the tangible rewards he could purchase with them. Like Mr. Jones' program, Ms. Walker's was ineffective. Herman's participation decreased to its original level. He remained an infrequent participant in group discussions. ■

The reinforcement schedules most commonly applied in behavior modification intervention are discussed later in this chapter.

Principle 5: Social Reinforcers Are *Always* Applied with Tangible Reinforcers

All reinforcement, even during the initial phases of the behavior change process, must include the presentation of social and tangible reinforcers simultaneously, if a tangible reinforcer is used. The purpose of the behavior change process is to help the child perform the target behavior, not for a tangible reward but for the satisfaction of personal achievement.

If tangible reinforcers, such as tokens, chips, candy, stars, smiling faces, or checks, are presented, they must always be accompanied by a social reward, such as a smile, a pat on the back, praise, or a wink. In this way the child associates the social reinforcer with the tangible reinforcer. As the behavior change process progresses, the tangible reinforcer is extinguished (phased out) and the target behavior is maintained by social reinforcers alone. If the change process is effective, behavior is maintained by self-satisfaction, occasional unplanned social reinforcers, and delayed tangible rewards.

EXAMPLES   ■ When Ms. Williams was initially attempting to increase Phil's discussion group participation (see example in previous section), she provided Phil with verbal praise and a token each time he exhibited the desired behavior. However, when Phil was placed on an intermittent schedule, Ms. Williams continued to provide consistent social reinforcement but only occasional token reinforcement. During the final phase of the behavior change process Phil was provided only intermittent social reinforcement to maintain the desired behavior. ■

■ Mr. Whiteface wanted to modify George's hand-raising behavior. A Sugar Smack was given to George every time he raised his hand. The reward was delivered by a dispenser affixed to George's desk. When George raised his hand, Mr. Whiteface would push a button to activate the dispenser and release a Sugar Smack.

In this way, Mr. Whiteface rewarded George consistently. In addition, he gave George social reinforcers for the new behavior. He would say, "That was very good, George"; "I like the way you are raising your hand, George"; or "Fine," "Great," "Good."

After 6 months on the program George functioned with intermittent social reinforcement only. The dispensing of Sugar Smacks had been terminated, and George's hand-raising behavior remained at a high rate. ■

Beginning behavior modifiers are cautioned to apply this important principle when using reinforcers: *always apply tangible and social reinforcers simultaneously, if tangible reinforcers are used.*

An extensive list of potentially effective reinforcers, both tangible and social, is presented in Chapter 3.

Consequences of Behavior

Behavioral consequences (results) have a direct influence on the behavior a child exhibits. Behavior can be modified, that is, increased, decreased, initiated, or extinguished by systematic manipulation of its consequences. The possible consequences of human behavior are classified as positive reinforcement, extinction, negative reinforcement, and punishment.

In Table 2.1 are several examples of (1) classification of the consequence, (2) appropriate and inappropriate behavior, (3) the consequence of that behavior *(not necessarily a planned intervention)*, and (4) the probable effect of the consequence on the behavior in the future. The reader is encouraged to study Table 2.1 carefully.

Positive Reinforcement

Positive reinforcement is the presentation of a pleasurable reinforcer after a behavior has been exhibited. These reinforcers, or consequences of behavior, tend to increase or sustain the frequency with which the behavior is exhibited in the future. Everyone receives positive reinforcement throughout each day. The process of positive reinforcement involves increasing the probability of a behavior recurring by reinforcing it with a reinforcer that is appropriate and meaningful to the individual.

Remember, a reinforcer is reinforcing only if it is perceived as reinforcing to the individual.

EXAMPLES   ■ Kevin has received a superior report card and is praised by his parents and siblings. As a result of the positive reinforcer (praise), the probability of Kevin's continuing to study hard and receive superior report cards in the future is increased. If Kevin's report card were ignored or severely criticized because of a single poor grade, the probability of his continuing his efforts and receiving superior report cards in the future would be decreased. ■

■ Ms. Pompey has identified stars as positive reinforcers with her classroom group. She puts a star on Cynthia's paper because Cynthia has successfully completed her homework

Basic Principles of Behavior Modification

TABLE 2.1
Behavior: Consequence, probable effect, and classification

Classification	Original Behavior Exhibited	Consequence	Probable Effect on the Original Behavior in the Future
Positive reinforcement	Jane cleans her room	Jane's parents praise her	Jane will continue to clean her room
Positive reinforcement	Shirley brushes her teeth after meals	Shirley receives a nickel each time	Shirley will continue to brush her teeth after meals
Extinction	Jim washes his father's car	Jim's car-washing behavior is ignored	Jim will stop washing his father's car
Positive reinforcement	Alton works quietly at his seat	The teacher praises and rewards Alton	Alton will continue to work quietly at his seat
Punishment	Gwenn sits on the arm of the chair	Gwenn is spanked each time she sits on the arm of the chair	Gwenn will not sit on the arm of the chair
Negative reinforcement	Bob complains that older boys consistently beat him up, and he refuses to attend school	Bob's parents allow him to remain at home because of his complaints	Bob will continue to miss school
Punishment	Elmer puts Elsie's pigtails in the paint pot	The teacher administers the paddle to Elmer's posterior	Elmer will not put Elsie's pigtails in the paint pot
Extinction	Shirley puts glue on Joe's seat	Shirley is ignored	Shirley will stop putting glue on students' seats
Negative reinforcement	Jason complains of headaches when it is time to do homework	Jason is allowed to go to bed without doing his homework	Jason will have headaches whenever there is homework to do

assignment. Cynthia enjoys receiving the stars. By placing a star on Cynthia's paper, Ms. Pompey knows she is increasing the probability of Cynthia's completing her homework assignments in the future. ■

Extinction

Extinction is the removal of a consequence that is sustaining or increasing a behavior. Extinction is an effective method for decreasing undesirable behaviors exhibited by individuals. Unplanned and unsystematically applied extinction techniques have been naturally applied throughout history. For example, parents tend to *ignore* many unacceptable behaviors exhibited by children, such as roughhousing, arguing, and showing reluctance to go to bed, in the hope that these behaviors will decrease in frequency. The ineffectiveness of ignoring as an unplanned intervention is frequently a result of the inconsistency of its application rather than its inadequacy as a behavior change technique. We insist that there be no roughhousing or arguing and that the children be in bed at the designated time one day but do not insist on these rules the next day. This inconsistency on our part, as a teacher or parent, tends to confuse children and reinforce the unacceptable behavior.

Extinction involves the removal or withdrawal of the reinforcer responsible for maintaining the inappropriate behavior. In the classroom setting the target behavior will be extinguished once the reinforcer has been withdrawn for a sufficient period of time.

EXAMPLES ■ John, a ninth grader, was always making funny sounds with his mouth in Mrs. Rawlin's class. These activities not only got him a lot of attention from his peers but from Mrs. Rawlin. She usually stopped the class and told John how immature he was behaving for his age and that he was making a fool of himself. The class responded with laughter. John laughed the loudest. After several meetings with the school counselor about John's classroom behavior, Mrs. Rawlin agreed to implement another approach.

The next time John made a funny sound, Mrs. Rawlin told the class to ignore him and those students that did would be rewarded with free time. John continued to make sounds for a few days, but because of the lack of attention from peers and teacher, the behavior began to change. Over the course of 7 school days John's behavior was extinguished. Mrs. Rawlin was able to conduct her class without disruptions. John is now receiving attention from his peers and Mrs. Rawlin for appropriate behavior. ■

■ Eight-year-old Robin was constantly tattling on every child who committed the slightest transgression within his purview. Robin's teacher, Ms. Fye, was reinforcing Robin's behavior by responding and attending to him when he tattled on others. Finally, she planned an intervention program employing extinction to decrease Robin's behavior. She would ignore all of his tattling.

Each time Robin approached her to tattle on a classmate, Ms. Fye did one of the following:

Intervened before Robin had an opportunity to tattle and focused his attention on another topic, picture, book and so on;

Turned her back on him and attended to another child who was performing appropriately;

Turned her back on him and walked away without any sign of recognition.

During the initial phase of the behavior change process, Robin's tattling increased for a brief period. As the program continued, the behavior decreased and was extinguished (Figure 2.1). ■

During the extinction process there are two behavior response phases. During the intitial phase, immediately after the reinforcer sustaining the behavior has been re-

FIGURE 2.1.
Frequency of Robin's tattling behavior a week before the removal of the reinforcer and 2 weeks afterward.

moved, the target behavior usually increases or decreases dramatically. During the second phase the target behavior changes systematically.

The response during the initial phase is a natural, human one that occurs when an individual is suddenly confronted with a situation wherein established methods of gaining desirable goals become nonfunctional. It is natural to become confused under such conditions and continue to try the previously effective method of attaining a goal.

It is during this initial phase that beginning behavior modifiers frequently throw up their hands in frustration and abandon a project. However, if they will persist, the behavior will in all probability extinguish.

Robin's rate of tattling before and during the extinction process is presented in Figure 2.1. The reader should note that Robin's tattling behavior increased on the first 3 days of extinction, then decreased dramatically during the next 7 days.

The teacher or parent should be patient and consistent; the behavior will change.

Negative Reinforcement

Negative reinforcement is one of the most difficult concepts in behavior modification to explain and exemplify. Consequently, several examples of this process are presented. The reader is urged to study this section and Tables 2.1 and 2.2 carefully.

Negative reinforcement is the removal of an already-operating aversive stimulus (negative reinforcer). As a consequence of the removal of the aversive stimulus, the target behavior is strengthened.

TABLE 2.2
Effects of consequences

	Positive Reinforcer	*Aversive Stimulus*
Add	Positive reinforcement (behavior increases)	Punishment (behavior decreases)
Remove	Extinction (behavior decreases)	Negative reinforcement (behavior increases or decreases)

Axelrod (1983) has described the technique of negative reinforcement in the classroom setting as "an operation in which a student performs a behavior and the teacher removes something the student dislikes" (p. 8).

As stated earlier, negative reinforcement is the removal of an aversive stimulus in an effort to change the frequency of a desired behavior. In contrast, punishment is the addition of an aversive stimulus or the subtraction (taking away) of a pleasurable item or activity in an effort to change the frequency of a behavior.

Axelrod provides two excellent examples.

EXAMPLE
■ A group of students are working very diligently at their desks *after* the teacher has stated that they will not be required to do homework assignments that evening if their classroom assignments are completed during the allotted time during the school day. ■

In this example the homework assignment, which was already given by the teacher, is the aversive stimulus (most students perceive homework as aversive). It is removed, and as a result the students' in-classroom work is increased.

EXAMPLE
■ Jimmy is in the process of twisting Tommy's arm. This situation is causing Tommy considerable pain. Jimmy says. "Say Uncle Dudley-Do-Good, and I'll let you go." Tommy, in agony, screams, "Uncle Dudley-Do-Good." Jimmy with a smile on his innocent face releases Tommy's arm, and the pain ends. ■

In this example the arm twisting, which was already giving Tommy pain (and Jimmy pleasure), is the aversive stimulus. It is removed, and as a result Tommy's comfort level is increased.

The following examples are provided to offer additional clarification of negative reinforcement.

EXAMPLES
■ The Reynoldses have a 2-year-old daughter, Alice, who wakes up crying (aversive stimulus) in the middle of the night. She wants to sleep with Mommy and Daddy. In an effort to get their sleep and stop Alice from crying, the parents permit her to sleep with them (thus removing the aversive stimulus of crying). By allowing Alice to sleep in their bed, the parents are increasing both their and Alice's sleeping behavior.

However, the parents' method of stopping Alice's crying (allowing Alice to sleep with them) actually reinforces the frequency of the crying. ■

■ Bobby was absent 141 of 180 days during the school year. He gave no reason for his nonattendance except that he simply did not want to come to school. After several hours of discussion, it was discovered that Bobby remained away from school so his mother would not die, disappear, or become ill. Bobby's mother unconsciously reinforced his staying-at-home behavior. Many times each day she would say, "Bobby, I always feel safe when you're with me," or "I hope I will be here when you get home," or "I am not well, you know."

Bobby, a very sensitive and concerned son of 11 years, applied the following logic to this predicament: "I love my mother and want her to remain with me. If I leave her to go to school, she may die, become ill, or have an accident. Thus I will not attend school; I will remain with her, and she will be OK."

During the discussion that followed this discovery of why Bobby stayed home, his mother was made aware of her statements and their probable effect. She was asked to cease making these and similar comments (aversive stimulus). After a reasonable time Bobby returned to part-time and eventually full-time attendance at junior high school. ■

In this example Bobby's mother used her concerns of becoming ill, dying, or having an accident to keep him home. Each time his mother complained of being afraid to be at home alone, Bobby would stay with her, thereby reinforcing the mother's inappropriate behavior as well as Bobby's inappropriate behavior.

Punishment

Punishment appears to be the most familiar and frequently used behavior change technique. Although it is frequently used on children by a majority of parents and teachers, punishment is perhaps the least effective of the behavior modification interventions discussed in this text. Those using punishment have been reinforced by its immediate result; however, it is has been determined that the long-term effects of punishment are limited. McDaniel (1980) points out that punishment tends to *suppress* the undesirable behavior rather than extinguish it. This suppression is of short duration, and frequently the behavior recurs in the absence of the punisher.

Punishment is viewed by the behavior modification practitioner as two distinct operations. Punishment is accomplished by the *addition* of an aversive stimulus to the environment. Examples of this operation are paddling, electric shock, additional homework, and the like. Punishment may also be seen as the *subtraction* (taking away) of a pleasurable item or activity. Examples of this operation include loss of extracurricular activities, recess, and the like. Punishment is not to be confused with extinction (see earlier section).

EXAMPLES ■ Anita, one of Mr. Cooper's fifth-grade pupils, constantly talks in class. She disturbs her classmates when she should be completing her assignments. To stop Anita's inappropriate behavior, Mr. Cooper scolds her, shakes her, and has her stand in the corner of the classroom with a dunce cap on her head.

These techniques are very effective while Mr. Cooper is in the room. However, when Mr. Cooper leaves the classroom for whatever reason, the long-term ineffectiveness of punishment becomes apparent. On these occasions Anita goes around the room yelling and screaming, to the glee of her classmates. ■

■   Joe is in Mr. Dee's junior high school class for the socially maladjusted. Joe enjoys using four-letter words. In addition, he takes great pleasure in the expression on Mr. Dee's face when he tosses a few well-chosen words at him. Mr. Dee believed he could eliminate this behavior via the 3-P method, that is a punishing paddle on the posterior. He designed the following intervention, which he explained to Joe:

"Each time you swear in my presence, you will assume the hands-on-ankle position and receive four swats."

Mr. Dee's intervention has had the following results:

1. Joe's language has improved in Mr. Dee's presence but not in his absence (according to a burnt-eared substitute).
2. Mr. Dee has a very tired arm.
3. Joe continues to use his vocabulary on Mr. Dee to gain attention, especially when there are visitors in the classroom.
4. Others in the class encourage Joe to curse so that they can enjoy the circus.
5. Mr. Dee has tried to prove that might is right.   ■

It can be seen that *some punishments will remove some unacceptable behaviors* (Wood & Lakin, 1978). It has been found, however, that when a punished behavior recurs, it usually does so at a rate higher than before the punishment was originally imposed. Another concern associated with punishment is its potential and actual effect on the emotional health of the child. In some cases punishment may cause emotional problems. The fact that the punished child identifies the punishment with the punisher rather than with the inappropriate behavior should be of great concern to teachers and parents. The results of punishment do not appear sufficient to justify its use as a behavior change agent.

Effects of Consequences

A thorough understanding of the relationships among the four basic consequences of behavior is a primary requisite for the effective application of behavior modification principles and techniques. The reader is encouraged to study Table 2.2 carefully and compare it with Table 2.1.

In general, positive reinforcement *increases* the target behavior; punishment and extinction *decrease* the target behavior. Negative reinforcement may increase or decrease behavior depending on the particular target behavior.

Generalization

Generalization, or the transfer of learning, is the process by which a behavior reinforced in the presence of one stimulus will be exhibited in the presence of another stimulus. The generalization process is an important element of learning. If the process of generalization did not occur, each response would have to be learned in every specific situation. "Transfer of behavior does not occur automatically, but needs to be planned and programmed as part of the training process" (Vaughn, Bos, & Lund, 1986).

EXAMPLES

■ A young child learns the name of an animal (dog). He calls a specific dog "dog" and will soon generalize the name "dog" to all four-legged animals within this classification. He will at times label other four-legged animals, such as cats, cows, and crawling brothers and sisters, with the name "dog." ■

■ A toddler is reinforced for calling her father "Daddy." She will generalize and call all male figures "Daddy" at an early stage of her development. She may call the mailman, milkman, and others "Daddy." This may result in considerable stress between husband and wife. ■

If we wish to function successfully in the environment, we must apply the concepts learned in one situation to many and varied situations. For example, as young children we learn honesty, respect for authority, and the basic principles of computation. It is hoped that each year we can generalize this learning to the completion of our income tax returns.

Stokes and Baer (1977) and Baer (1981) make several suggestions for teaching students to generalize. They suggest that natural contingencies facilitate the learning of generalization. Natural contingencies are those which commonly occur in the environment as a consequence of a behavior. In addition, training more exemplars may help students to generalize. Reinforcing generalization and self-reports of the target behavior assists in generalization. It is important to remember that just because a student behaves in a desired way in one situation does not mean that generalization of that behavior to other settings has occurred. At least initially, generalization should be programmed.

Vaughn, Bos, and Lund (1986) recommend several practical strategies for teachers wishing to help their students develop generalization skills. The recommended strategies include:

1. Varying the amount, power, and type of reinforcers applied to students, such as fading reinforcers, changing from tangible to social reinforcers, or using the same reinforcers in different settings.
2. Varying the instructions given to students, such as using alternative and parallel directions, rewording directions, and using photographs and pictures.
3. Varying the medium and the media of the instructional materials used by students to complete tasks. In the written medium, this could mean varying things such as paper size and color, writing instruments, and inks. The teacher may use other instructional media, such as films or computers.
4. Varying the response modes students use to complete tasks, for instance, changing from written to oral responses, or using a variety of test question formats.
5. Varying the stimulus provided to students, such as changing the size, color, and shape of illustrations, or using concrete objects.
6. Varying the instructional setting, such as changing the work location, or changing

from individual to small group study.
7. Varying instructors, such as using aides, peers, or parents.

Vaughn, Bos, and Lund recommend that teachers carefully plan, monitor, and evaluate the effects of generalization instruction on students.

Discrimination

Discrimination is another important learned behavior. Through discrimination we learn that we act one way in one situation and another way in a different situation (Axelrod, 1983). If it were not for the process of discrimination, we would generalize behaviors to a variety of situations in which they would be inappropriate.

EXAMPLE
■ We behave differently in church than we do at a cocktail party (most of us) and differently in class than we do at a football game (although some classes are stimulating and some football games are boring). Our behaviors in these situations are reinforced by the rewards we receive. ■

Discrimination is the result of differential reinforcement. Reinforcing a behavior in the presence of one stimulus and not reinforcing it in the presence of another stimulus is differential reinforcement.

EXAMPLE
■ Teaching a young child to discriminate between the words *cat* and *rat* may be accomplished by listening and reacting to the child's responses. The child is reinforced for the appropriate response only. In this way the child discriminates between the words *rat* and *cat* when they are presented in the future. ■

Schedules of Reinforcement

A schedule of reinforcement is the pattern with which the reinforcer is presented in response to the exhibition of the target behavior. The schedule of reinforcement that is applied has a significant effect on the behavior change process. The six most common types of reinforcement schedules are continuous ratio (CR), fixed ratio (FR), variable ratio (VR), continuous interval (CI), fixed interval (FI), and variable interval (VI).

The primary distinctions among these schedules are related to the timing and frequency with which the reinforcer is presented. The ratio schedules, fixed and variable, focus on the *completion of specific tasks* before the reinforcer is presented to the child. Reinforcer presentation on the interval schedules, fixed and variable, depends on the exhibition of specific behaviors for *definite periods of time.* The continuous schedule is applicable to both ratio and interval data.

Table 2.3 summarizes the various schedules discussed in the following sections.

TABLE 2.3
Relationships among the common reinforcement schedules

	Ratio	Interval
Continuous	Child is reinforced after each problem	Child is reinforced after each time period
Fixed	Child completes 20 problems to receive 10 minutes of free time	Child is rewarded for remaining in seat for 5 minutes
Variable	Teacher rewards child, on an average, every third time child raises hand	Teacher gives child individual attention, on an average, every 15 minutes in response to acceptable behavior during the time period

Continuous Schedule

The continuous schedule of reinforcement requires the presentation of the reinforcer immediately after each occurrence of the target behavior or after each time period during which the target behavior is exhibited. The continuous schedule is most often applied during the initial stage of a behavior change program. Frequently, its use will change the behavior rapidly in the desired direction. It is not recommended for long-term or continuous use, however, because individuals tend to satiate on this schedule and initial behavior change gains may be lost.

EXAMPLES
■ Ms. Bantle wished to increase Deanna's hand-raising behavior during history. To do this she decided, at least initially, to reinforce Deanna each time she raised her hand. Application of this continuous ratio schedule rapidly increased the target behavior to an acceptable level. ■

■ Mr. McCloud was disturbed by Bobby's out-of-seat behavior. He planned an intervention to increase Bobby's in-seat behavior. During the initial intervention, he reinforced Bobby's in-seat behavior each time it occurred. This continuous interval schedule quickly increased Bobby's in-seat behavior. ■

Fixed Ratio Schedule

When a fixed ratio schedule is applied, the reinforcer is presented after a specific number of appropriate responses are emitted by the child.

EXAMPLES
■ Every time John answers 15 social studies questions correctly, he is given 10 minutes to read a comic book. John's reward (comic book reading) is based on his successful completion of a fixed number (15) of social studies questions. ■

■ Every time Sheila reads five brief passages in her reading workbook with 80% accuracy, she is allowed to listen to her favorite record album for 5 minutes. In this case Sheila is on a fixed ratio schedule. ■

The fixed ratio schedule usually results in a high rate of response. Consequently it is most effectively and appropriately applied during the initial phase of the behavior change process.

Variable Ratio Schedule

The variable ratio schedule is designed to sustain the level of response to reinforcement once the acceptable level of behavior has been attained by means of the continuous or fixed ratio schedule. When the variable ratio schedule is applied, the ratio of the reinforcer presentation varies around a response mean or average. This variability is instrumental in sustaining the appropriate level of response.

EXAMPLES ■ Mr. Davis has Kerry raising his hand and participating in class discussions. He accomplished this via a fixed ratio schedule. He now wishes to change to a variable ratio schedule. Kerry is placed on a variable ratio schedule of 5 (the reinforcer is presented around a response mean of 5). Kerry may be reinforced the seventh time he raises his hand, the sixth time, the third, the fourth, or the fifth. If this schedule (7, 6, 3, 4, and 5) is averaged, the response mean or variable ratio is 5. The fact that Kerry does not know when Mr. Davis will call on him to respond (but does know that he will be called on) maintains his hand-raising behavior at a high level. ■

■ Las Vegas slot machines (in our experience) operate on a variable ratio schedule. The gambler puts quarters in the slot and is occasionally reinforced with small rewards. This occasional reinforcement keeps the person playing until he or she is broke, but the loser always has the hope that the next pull of the arm will result in the super jackpot. ■

Inexperienced behavior modifiers are cautioned not to change from a continuous or fixed ratio to a variable ratio schedule too early in the behavior change process. The desired behavior must be adequately established on a fixed ratio schedule before it can be changed to a variable ratio schedule. Many behavior change programs have failed as a result of the practitioner's impatience in making this transition.

Fixed Interval Schedule

On the fixed interval schedule a specified period of time must elapse before the reinforcer is presented. The reinforcer is presented immediately *after the first response after* the specified time has elapsed. The following examples should clarify this seeming confusion.

EXAMPLES ■ Debbie does not remain in her seat during language lessons. Mr. Quick has decided to reinforce Debbie on a fixed interval schedule of 10. Thus every time Debbie remains in her seat for 10 minutes during language lessons, she is rewarded. ■

■ Most people work on a fixed interval (1 week, 2 weeks, or 1 month) pay schedule. They receive their paychecks after the pay period has elapsed. ■

With fixed interval schedules, the longer the time interval between reinforcements, the lower will be the level of performance. This would suggest that initially during an intervention reinforcers should be presented at frequent intervals.

Variable Interval Schedule

The variable interval schedule is similar to the variable ratio schedule. However, the presentation of the reinforcer is based on a behavioral response mean or average. The individual whose behavior is being modified is not aware of when reinforcement will occur. However, the individual does know that he or she will be reinforced for exhibiting a certain behavior.

EXAMPLE   ■ Mr. Quick has decided to place Debbie on a variable interval schedule of 10. On this schedule Debbie will continue to be reinforced for in-seat behavior. She may be reinforced the first time after only 9 minutes of appropriate behavior, the second time after 4 minutes, the third time after 9 minutes, the fourth time after 15 minutes, and the fifth time after 13 minutes. This is a reinforcement schedule of 9, 4, 9, 15 and 13. It is based on a variable interval with a mean or average of 10 minutes. ■

Again, the behavior modifier should be cautious when changing from fixed ratio or fixed interval to variable ratio or variable interval schedules. If this is done too early or too late in the behavior change process, the newly acquired behavior may be extinguished.

The specific schedule to be applied varies with the behavior being changed. For example, if the concern is to keep an individual in his or her seat for a period of time, an interval schedule would be the most appropriate. However, if the behavior is related to the completion of specific numbers or kinds of tasks, a ratio schedule should be applied. The selection and application of the appropriate schedule is part of the art of behavior modification. Knowing when and how to apply a specific schedule of reinforcement becomes less confusing with experience.

SUMMARY

The basic principles of behavior modification are presented in this chapter, followed by a discussion of the concepts of positive and negative reinforcement, extinction, and punishment. An understanding of these operations and their effects on behavior is essential. To use the aforementioned operations, the reader must understand how they are different as well as how they are interrelated.

The concepts of generalization and discrimination are discussed. Generalization increases the probability that a behavior reinforced in the presence of one stimulus will be exhibited in the presence of another stimulus. Discrimination is the process by which we learn to behave differently in different situations.

A discussion of the schedules of reinforcement is also presented. A schedule of reinforcement is the pattern with which the reinforcers are presented in response to the exhibition of a behavior. Six of the most common types of schedules are continuous ratio, continuous interval, fixed ratio, fixed interval, variable ratio, and variable interval. It is essential that the new practitioner of behavior modification have a thorough knowledge of these schedules.

EXERCISES

Quiz

1. One of the basic principles of reinforcement states that, when building new behavior, the teacher or parent should reinforce the behavior _____.

2. When the new behavior has been established to a degree of satisfaction, the best schedule of reinforcement to use is a _____ schedule.

3. The decrease in the strength of a response when it is no longer reinforced is called _____.

4. The addition of an aversive stimulus or the subtraction of something pleasurable is known as _____.

5. The process of reinforcing behavior in the presence of one stimulus situation and not reinforcing it in the presence of other stimulus situations is called _____ _____.

6. _____ is the occurrence of a response in the presence of other stimuli following its response in the presence of one stimulus situation.

7. The process of removing an aversive stimulus is known as _____ _____.

8. Consequences that strengthen or increase behavior are called _____.

9. _____ and _____ schedules of reinforcement are dependent on the number of responses.

10. _____ and _____ schedules of reinforcement are dependent on the passage of time and a specific response.

Projects

1. Explain the five basic principles of reinforcement.
2. Give examples of how positive reinforcement, extinction, negative reinforcement, and pun-

ishment can be used to change the behavior of children.
3. List several factors involved in the use of punishment as a behavior change technique.
4. Describe two examples for each of the following: continuous, fixed ratio, fixed interval, variable ratio, and variable interval schedules of reinforcement as applied in the classroom or home setting.
5. Compare the concepts of generalization and discrimination.

REFERENCES

Axelrod, S. (1983). *Behavior modification for the classroom teacher.* New York: McGraw-Hill Book Co.

Baer, D. M. (1981). *How to plan for generalization.* Austin, Texas: Pro-Ed.

Gardner, W. I. (1977). *Learning and behavior characteristics of exceptional children and youth.* Boston: Allyn and Bacon.

McDaniel, T. (1980). Corporal punishment and teacher liability: Questions teachers ask. *The Clearing House, 54* (1) 10–13.

Morris, R. J. (1985). *Behavior modification with exceptional children: Principles and practices.* Glenview, Illinois: Scott, Foresman & Co.

Sarason, I. G., Glaser, E. M., & Fargo, G. A. (1972). *Reinforcing productive classroom behavior: A teacher's guide to behavior modification.* New York: Behavioral Publications.

Shea, T. M. & Bauer, A. M. (1987). *Teaching children and youth with behavior disorders.* Englewood Cliffs, NJ: Prentice-Hall.

Stokes, T. F., & Baer, D. M. (1977). An implicit technology of generalization. *Journal of Applied Behavior Analysis, 10* (2), 349–67.

Vaughn, S., Bos, C. S., & Lund, K. A. (1986). . . . But they can do it in my room: Strategies for promoting generalization. *Teaching Exceptional Children, 18* (3), 176-180.

Wood, F. H., & Lakin, K. C. (1978). *Punishment and aversive stimulation in special education: Legal, theoretical and practical issues in their use with emotionally disturbed children and youth.* Minneapolis: University of Minnesota, Advanced Training Institute.

CHAPTER THREE

Steps in the Behavior Change Process

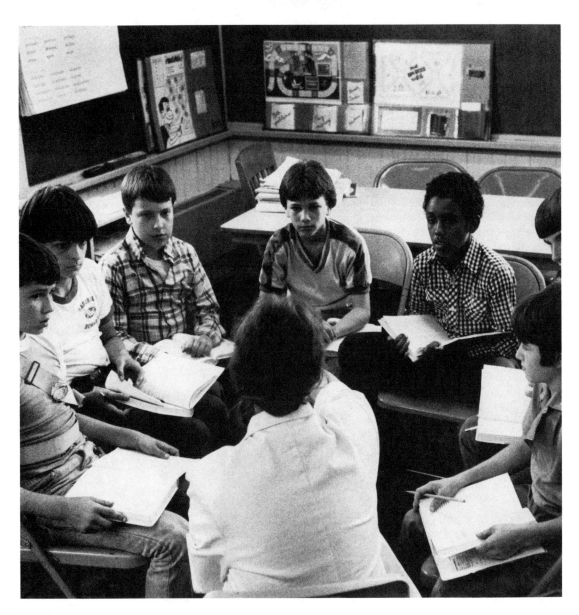

George, a junior high school student at the John T. Belfast School, appears to be having problems in school. Mrs. Chung, a social studies teacher, notices that George does not participate in class discussions, associate with other students, or take part in cocurricular activities. Mrs. Chung wishes there were some way she could help George become involved with his peers. She feels guilty about George's isolation and believes that she has in some manner let him down. The one thing Mrs. Chung has noticed about George is that he likes to draw.

One day, out of frustration, Mrs. Chung refers George for placement in a special class. However, the school psychologist's report reveals that George has an IQ of 144 with no signs of learning disabilities. Next she decides to show some of George's drawings to the school art teacher. Mr. Bonetti, the art teacher, is impressed by the creative quality of George's efforts. He shows the drawings to an art professor at the university. He agrees that the drawings are the work of a genius.

Perhaps if we could teach Mrs. Chung the steps in the behavior change process, George, her young genius, may become more involved with other students.

Mrs. Anderson teaches algebra and geometry at the Thomas Edison High School. She enjoys teaching and is a conscientious instructor. Her students respect her; she is admired by her colleagues; and the principal refers to her as "my perfect teacher." Mrs. Anderson has been presented the "Outstanding Teacher of the Year" award twice by the school board. She was voted "Teacher of the Year" by the state education association. However, Mrs. Anderson has a serious problem. It is not at school, but at home.

Mrs. Anderson is a single parent. She is head of a household that includes three teenagers, ages 13, 15, and 17. Her children take little responsibility for caring for themselves or the house. After Mrs. Anderson has taught school, attended faculty meetings, corrected papers, called parents, changed her bulletin board, prepared monthly reports, and planned for the next day, she goes home to her other job. At home she must prepare meals, wash and iron, clean the house, do the yardwork, take out the garbage, wash and fuel the car, shop for food and clothing, care for the dog, and finally care for three teenagers.

Perhaps if we could teach Mrs. Anderson the steps in the behavior change process, she could change her home situation.

In this chapter the specific steps and procedures applied during the behavior change process are discussed and exemplified in detail. Teachers and parents should follow these steps closely: (1) selecting a target behavior, (2) collecting and recording baseline data, (3) identifying reinforcers, (4) implementing the intervention and collecting and recording intervention data, and (5) evaluating the effects of intervention.

Selecting a Target Behavior

The initial step in the behavior change process is the identification of the target behavior. The target behavior is the behavior to be changed or modified. A target behavior may be an existing behavior that the teacher or parent desires to increase or decrease or a nonoccurring behavior, that is, a behavior that is not observable in the individual's behavioral repertoire but one to be developed.

In most classroom situations it is not difficult for the teacher to identify a variety of behaviors needing change (target behaviors). The teacher may recognize the following:

1. Percy does not communicate verbally.
2. Jake should increase his reading skills.
3. Mary should stop yelling in the classroom.
4. Joseph needs to learn to listen to instructions before he begins an assignment.
5. Ellis should improve his table manners in the lunchroom.

All of the aforementioned are potential target behaviors that the teacher could identify in the classroom.

It should be remembered that whenever an individual or a group is singled out for observation and study for the purpose of initiating a behavior change program, it is inevitable that several individual and group target behaviors will be identified. All children and adults manifest behaviors that are unacceptable to some other individuals or groups of individuals under certain conditions.

Decisions leading to the selection of a behavior for modification should be governed by the following considerations, among others:

☐ Type of behavior.
☐ Frequency of the behavior.
☐ Duration of the behavior.
☐ Intensity of the behavior.
☐ Overall number of behaviors needing modification.

It is generally recommended that the beginning behavior modifier not attempt to change more than one individual or group behavior at a time. Implementing several behavior change programs simultaneously frequently results in inefficiency, and otherwise useful interventions prove ineffective. Therefore, we advocate that individual and group behaviors needing modification be ranked in priority (Morris, 1985). The teacher then systematically works down the priority list from the most important to the least important of the potential target behaviors. The importance of a specific behavior should be determined on the basis of its effect on the child's functioning. Schopler, Reichler, and Lansing (1980) suggest the following order of priorities be applied to changing the behaviors of severely developmentally disabled children:

1. Problems that risk the child's life.
2. Problems that risk the child's continuing to live with the family.
3. Problems that limit the child's participation in special education.
4. Problems that limit the child's adaptation to the community outside home and school.

EXAMPLE ■ Peter, an autistic-like child, manifests a variety of unacceptable behaviors. Among the behaviors of greatest concern to his teacher, Mr. Wise, are (1) withdrawal from group activities, (2) unacceptable eating habits, (3) inability to communicate with his classmates and Mr. Wise via speech, and (4) unsatisfactory gross motor skills.

Mr. Wise recognizes that a program cannot be initiated to modify all of Peter's potential target behaviors at a single time. Because of the nature of the behaviors, the proposed interventions could be in conflict with one another. Mr. Wise must respond to the following question: "Is it more important for Peter, at this time, to participate in the luncheon discussion [behaviors 1 and 3 would be targets], or is it more important to improve his gross motor skills and eating habits [behaviors 2 and 4 would be targets]?"

In reponse to this question, Mr. Wise develops the following priority list for Peter's program:

□ First priority: to increase participation in group activities.
□ Second priority: to increase verbalization with others.
□ Third priority: to increase gross motor skills.
□ Fourth priority: to increase acceptance of a variety of foods. ■

With an increase in experience and skill in the behavior change process, the teacher or parent may wish to program more than one individual or group target behavior simultaneously. However, the beginning practitioner should refrain from multiple programming.

When selecting a target behavior, the practitioner must consider the frequency of the behavior. Some behaviors occur so infrequently that they do not necessitate or respond to a formal behavior modification intervention. Of course, the reverse is also true; some behaviors occur so frequently that they obviously require a behavior change program.

EXAMPLE ■ Ms. Lochman was very concerned about Martin, a member of her class, and on many occasions she became very angry with him. Six-year-old Martin appeared to be constantly out of his assigned seat. When out of his chair, he would grab other children's work, work tools, and lunches. Using a time-sampling technique (see p. 65), Ms. Lochman collected baseline data on Martin's out-of-seat behavior for 1 hour a day for 5 days. She found that during these observation periods Martin was out of his seat 17 times an hour on an average.

This behavior was so frequent and so obtrusive that it usually brought all productive classroom activity to a halt until Ms. Lochman could corral Martin and return him to his seat. ■

Teachers and parents are confronted daily with behaviors that are responsive to behavior change intervention. Such behaviors include lack of attention to tasks, incomplete assignments, fighting, not cleaning their room, tardiness to and from school, weight loss, excessive television watching, neglecting music or dance practice, and independent reading, to name a few.

EXAMPLE
- ■ Ms. Derry, like many of her peers, does not approve of chewing gum in school. Johnny, a member of her classroom group, was seen chewing gum on the second day of school this year. Ms. Derry grabbed him, removed the gum from his mouth, and stuck it on his nose, where it stayed for the remainder of the day. Ms. Derry then proceeded to make plans for a formal behavior change program. After several hours of planning, she was satisfied with her elaborate scheme for gathering baseline data and applying the chosen intervention. Unfortunately (or fortunately), Johnny never chewed gum in school again (that she observed). ■

There are many behaviors like Johnny's that appear so infrequently that they do not require a formal behavior change program. Examples of such behaviors are:

- ☐ George's annual 2-minute tantrum
- ☐ Barbara's occasional reading reversal
- ☐ Don's infrequent falling out of his seat
- ☐ Judy's monthly bus-missing behavior

If a proposed target behavior is both obtrusive and occurs frequently, the teacher should next consider the duration of the behavior.

EXAMPLES
- ■ For several weeks Gerald was very nervous in school. His teacher, Ms. Farley, noted that he was frequently out of his seat, irritable, and ready to burst into tears. She had never seen Gerald in this condition. She attempted to discuss the situation with him but was rebuffed.

Ms. Farley decided to establish a formal behavior modification program to decrease the behaviors. However, before initiating the program, she discussed the situation with Gerald's mother. During the conversation the mother indicated that she had observed similar behavior at home and was attempting to help Gerald regain his old composure. She thought the behavior was the result of the recent death of Gerald's grandfather. Gerald and his grandfather had been pals; they had always been together in the evenings. The death left a great void in Gerald's daily life. Gerald's mother said that her husband was rescheduling his evening activities so that he and Gerald could spend more time together.

Ms. Farley decided to hold the intervention program in abeyance for another few weeks. Within a short time Gerald was his normal self. The program was never implemented. ■

- ■ Mr. Parker is Maryann's kindergarten teacher. He thoroughly enjoys his work with Maryann and her 16 classmates. The kindergarten is an interesting and exciting learning place for the children.

During the first few weeks of the school year Mr. Parker observed that Maryann, although involved in the classroom activities, seldom if ever spoke to him, the aide, or her classmates. He decided to collect some baseline data on the frequency of Maryann's verbal behavior. In cooperation with the kindergarten aide, an observation schedule was set up to obtain some objective data. Using a time-sampling technique, they observed Maryann's behavior on an average of 1 hour a day for 10 days. Data indicated that Maryann spoke only 4 times a day, on an average, while in school. She directed all her verbalizations to one classmate.

Although Mr. Parker was very concerned about the behavior, he did not implement a behavior change program at this time. He had worked with kindergarten children in the past who were shy and quiet and did not begin to interact verbally in the classroom until just before Christmas vacation.

The aide continued to collect data 1 day each week until mid-December. No change was noted in Maryann's behavior.

Mr. Parker concluded that the behavior had endured too long and that a behavior change program was needed to help Maryann. He conferred with the school's language therapist, who evaluated Maryann. He also discussed the problem with Maryann's mother, who agreed to participate in a home-school behavior change program. The intervention was implemented immediately after the Christmas holidays. ■

The teacher or parent must also consider the intensity of the behavior. Some behaviors, although unacceptable, are relatively mild and unobtrusive. They do not generally interfere with the classroom process or the individual child's overall functioning. Of course, other behaviors, although infrequent, are so intense that they are extremely obtrusive. Not only do they adversely affect the individual's overall functioning, but they also interfere with the classroom program and group process. Such behaviors must be modified.

EXAMPLES ■ Ricky is 7 years old and in a special class for emotionally handicapped children. Ricky has temper tantrums that are totally unpredictable, frequent, and analogous to all of the Fourth of July fireworks in all the towns of the United States igniting simultaneously. These tantrums involve lying on the floor with feet and arms flying and verbalizations that are interesting but disturbing combinations of four-letter words. The tantrums last up to 45 minutes, averaging about 25 minutes.

These tantrums destroy the classroom program, frighten the other children, and interfere with Ricky's overall functioning. This behavior must be changed. ■

■ Keith is 13 years old and in the seventh grade. Occasionally he manifests some behaviors, normal for his age-group, that are bothersome, such as know-it-all behavior, big-shotism, and negativism. These behaviors are of minimal intensity. They are manifested by a wise remark at the termination of a conversation, his saying "No, I won't" before beginning a task, and the like. The behaviors are generally ignored by others and have little effect on either the classroom process or Keith's overall functioning. ■

The final characteristic to be considered in the selection of a target behavior is the type of behavior. Some behavior that is disturbing to some adults and children is really quite normal from a child development point of view. In fact, a child who did not manifest such behavior might be considered abnormal.

EXAMPLES ■ Paul is a sixth grader and a straight-A student. When he is asked if he likes school, his teacher, or the like, he says "No, I hate it." In addition, he insists on having long hair, wearing jeans and sneakers to school, and other equally "obnoxious" things.

As most teachers realize, these behaviors are quite normal for sixth-grade boys. The behavior manifested by Paul is within normal limits and of a kind that does not necessitate a formal intervention program. ■

■   Russell is 12 years old and in a junior high school special class. He has an uncontrolled temper and frequently tells his teacher to "go to hell" or "drop dead" (among other things). Russell gets into occasional fights with his classmates. These fights are extremely vicious. On two occasions he has inflicted severe injury on his opponent.

Russell's behavior is of a type that cannot simply be ignored. An intervention must be implemented for both his benefit and the safety of his peers.   ■

After all of these variables have been considered and a target behavior selected, the teacher must decide the direction of the behavior change process. There are three possible directions a behavior may follow as a consequence of an intervention. The behavior may (1) increase, (2) decrease, or (3) remain unchanged (be maintained). Table 3.1 presents these behavior change directions and examples of each.

The majority of behavior change programs are implemented to increase acceptable behaviors or decrease unacceptable behaviors. Teachers can easily select behaviors they wish to increase or decrease. However, the implementation of behavior modification programs to maintain behaviors has been largely neglected. In most instances the practitioner takes the child's manifestation of acceptable behaviors for granted and does not systematically reward such behaviors. More effort should be made to prevent unacceptable behaviors from developing, via the systematic rewarding and maintenance of existing acceptable behaviors. Such efforts could reduce the need to design interventions to either decrease or increase behaviors in the future.

TABLE 3.1
Behavior change directions

Direction	Example
Increase	Group participation
	In-seat behavior
	Interaction with peers
	Typing skills
	Reading rate
	Number skills
	Visual-perceptual skills
Decrease	Verbal outbursts
	Inattentiveness
	Use of four-letter words
	Food intake
	Smoking
	Talking in study period
	Spelling errors
Maintain	Language skills
	Reading skills
	School attendance
	Independent study habits
	Writing skills
	Motor skills
	Group participation

Two other important characteristics of the target behavior are observability and measurability. The behavior must be readily observable by an observer in the environment in which it occurs.

EXAMPLES
■ Ernest, in Ms. Moral's words, is "an unhappy child." Ms. Moral would like to decrease his unhappiness (and increase his happiness). However, when she attempted to observe and quantify Ernest's unhappiness, she abandoned the behavior change program before the baseline data were collected. ■

■ Brian seldom participated in organized group activities on the playground. Mr. Spencer wished to increase his level of activity. He recorded Brian's group participation rate on the playground during morning recess. Mr. Spencer easily established Brian's baseline of activity; he could thus directly observe and quantify the frequency and duration of Brian's participation in group activities. ■

■ Roy is in Mr. Watson's fourth-grade class. He has perfect school attendance during the first 7 months of the school year. Mr. Watson would like to have Roy maintain his present level of attendance for the remaining 2 months of the school year. Roy is the only student in his class with a perfect attendance record. Mr. Watson and the class praise Roy for his attendance. If Mr. Watson and Roy's classmates have anything to do with it, Roy's perfect attendance will be maintained. ■

Statements describing the target behavior, the precise intervention, and the criteria for success or acceptability of performance should be written or otherwise communicated in objective and specific terminology. The following objectives are written so that the target behavior and the result of the intervention can be observed, quantified, and evaluated:

☐ Maintain the number of times Jack volunteers to answer questions during social studies class discussions.
☐ Increase the number of pages Susan reads during each 15-minute study period.
☐ Decrease the number of times Marion yells during the first hour of the morning.
☐ Maintain the number of times Ken uses the reference books on the science table.
☐ Decrease the amount of time Sharon sucks her thumb during the school day.
☐ Increase Benji's skill in recognizing and naming the letters of the alphabet during language development class.

Program objectives should be written as instructional objectives, whether the target behavior is in the cognitive, affective, or psychomotor learning domain. The instructional objective in its written form should respond to the following guidelines:

1. What is the child or group of children whose behavior is being modified expected to do or not to do?
   a. Use action verbs to denote the behavior change process.

     b. List the specific resources and materials to be used by the child during the behavior change process.

     c. Indicate specifically the desired interaction between the child and the environment, including persons and objects.

2. What is the level of performance (in terms of accuracy, duration, and skill) expected of the child?

3. What percentage of time or what percentage of occurrences of the desired behavior is the child expected to perform at the criterion level?

4. How will the anticipated changes in behavior be measured for evaluative purposes? What instrumentation is needed for the evaluation?

5. How long will the proposed intervention program be in force before its effectiveness is evaluated?

Further information on the writing of specific instructional objectives may be found in Mager (1984).

The following guidelines summarize the process of selecting a target behavior:

1. Select only one individual or group target behavior to change at a time.

2. Analyze the potential target behavior for its frequency, duration, intensity, and type. The importance and pertinence of these variables vary with the characteristics of the specific target behavior under consideration.

3. Consider the direction or course the behavior is to take during the change process. Is the behavior to be maintained, decreased, or increased?

4. Determine whether the behavior is observable.

5. Determine whether the behavior is measurable in numeric terms.

6. Describe the target behavior in precise, descriptive terminology in all verbal and written communications.

The beginning behavior modifier is advised to use the checklist in Figure 3.1 to assist in the target behavior selection process. An additional copy of this checklist is provided in the back of the text.

Collecting and Recording Baseline Data

Information collected before the behavior change intervention has been implemented is referred to as *baseline data*. Baseline data provide the foundation on which the behavior change process is established. These data are also used to determine the effectiveness of the intervention during the evaluation phase of the behavior change process.

EXAMPLE   ■ The behavior change program Mr. Dixon selected for Jean concerned increasing the amount of time Jean remained in her seat during history class. Mr. Dixon collected baseline data for 1 week. The data demonstrated that Jean usually remained in her seat an average of

---

Target Behavior Selection Checklist

1. What is the target behavior to be modified? _____

_____

_____

_____

2. Each characteristic of the behavior that should be considered in the target behavior selective process is listed below. An X should be marked by each characteristic as it is considered. The pertinency of these characteristics varies with the specific target behavior under consideration.

(X)	Characteristic	Comment
( )	1. Frequency	
( )	2. Duration	
( )	3. Intensity	
( )	4. Type	
( )	5. Direction	
( )	6. Observability	
( )	7. Measurability	

3. Restate the target behavior in precise and specific terminology. _____

_____

_____

_____

_____

FIGURE 3.1
Sample checklist to assist in the selection of a target behavior.

10 minutes at a time before she was up and about the classroom. This information provided Mr. Dixon with the data he needed to determine the kind and characteristics of the reinforcement schedule to be implemented. In order to be sure Jean received immediate reinforcement for staying in her seat, a fixed interval schedule of 7 minutes was used.

The selection of the fixed interval 7 schedule was not a haphazard choice. It was based on the fact that Jean had demonstrated that she could, on the average, remain in her seat for 10 minutes without interference. Therefore it was reasonable to select a 7-minute interval because that was a level of performance that Jean could easily attain. Consequently she could be frequently reinforced for appropriate behavior.

If Mr. Dixon had not collected baseline data but had proceeded on a hunch, he might have selected a fixed interval schedule of 11 minutes. With this interval there would be a strong possibility that Jean would be infrequently rewarded and that her behavior would not change significantly.   ■

Reinforcement is initiated at a level of performance either above or below the baseline depending on whether the behavior is to be increased or decreased. For instance, you want to work with a student on increasing the number of words he can read per minute. You know that the student can read 75 words per minute. To start at baseline or above baseline will usually mean waiting too long to get the appropriate behavior, and your behavior change program may not be effective. If, however, you start your reinforcement at a level below baseline, in this case, for example, at 65 words per minute, you have then established a level at which you can provide immediate success for the student and can begin the program on a positive note.

EXAMPLE   ■ Ms. Waters has a little terror in her class who responds occasionally to the name of Emmet. Emmet is constantly yelling in the classroom, to the annoyance of Ms. Waters and the other members of the group. Ms. Waters initiated a behavior change program but did not collect baseline data, since Emmet appeared to yell constantly. She withdrew attention from Emmet each time he yelled and praised him when he was not yelling.

After 2 weeks, Ms. Waters was convinced that no change had occurred in the frequency of the behavior. Emmet seemed to yell in class more frequently. Ms. Waters concluded that "this behavior modification stuff" only works in textbooks, and she abandoned the project. Emmet is still yelling in class.   ■

It should be stressed here that behavior modification *always* works. The failure of an intervention does not lie in the principles of behavior modification but in the application of those principles by the practitioner. In the preceding example Ms. Waters would have been wise to collect baseline data. She would have been able to evaluate the effectiveness of the behavior change process. Baseline data would have revealed that Emmet yelled in class on an average of 21 times a day. When the intervention was abandoned, the behavior was occurring only 18 times a day (Figure 3.2). The behavior was, in fact, changing in the desired direction. However, without appropriate data, 18 yells a day sound very much like 21 when you are immersed in a situation, as in the case of Ms. Waters.

There are a variety of methods for observing and recording baseline data behavior. The efficiency of a particular technique varies with the expertise of the practitioner, the characteristics of the behavior, and the setting in which the behavior occurs.

To obtain meaningful baseline data, the behavior modifier must engage in two activities: counting the behavior and charting or graphing the behavior. Counting the behavior means enumerating the number of times the behavior occurs in a given period of time. Charting or graphing the behavior means preparing a visual display of the enumerated behavior in graphic form.

Steps in the Behavior Change Process

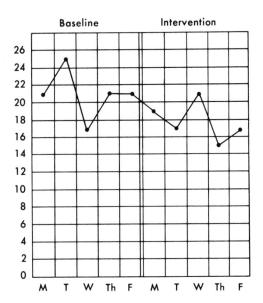

FIGURE 3.2
Frequency of Emmet's yelling behavior before and during the intervention.

These two processes are of paramount importance in the behavior change process. When the number of occurrences or the average duration of the occurrences of a behavior in a temporal framework are known, the behavior modifier can select an efficient reinforcement schedule before implementing an intervention. Equally important is the application of the baseline data to the intervention evaluation process. By comparing baseline data with intervention data, the teacher can determine the effectiveness of the reinforcer and the reinforcement schedule. Judgments can be made regarding the responsiveness of the target behavior to the intervention; that is, is the behavior increasing, decreasing, or being maintained?

The recommended method of collecting baseline data is direct observation of the child in the environment in which the behavior occurs. The beginning behavior modifier is well advised to obtain observation data by means of a time-sampling technique.

A trained observer realizes that it is impossible to observe *all* of the behavior occurring within the environment; neither is it possible to efficiently observe all of the occurrences of a single behavior over an extended period.

With the time-sampling technique the teacher first selects the behavior to be observed and then selects the periods of time that can be devoted to observing that behavior each day during the baseline phase. Each occurrence of the target behavior during the observation period is tallied or recorded.

EXAMPLE   ■ Joshua's teacher, Mr. Cates, wished to modify Joshua's hitting behavior during the 2-hour language arts period. With all his other teaching duties, he could not observe Joshua the full 2 hours for the 5 days required to collect reliable baseline data. Thus Mr. Cates used a time-sampling technique; he observed Joshua's behavior during two 10-minute periods for each hour of the language arts period for 5 days. He designed a behavior-tallying sheet to record his observations (Table 3.2).

Mr. Cates noted several things as a result of his data-collecting efforts:

1. Joshua hit other children a total of 32 times during the observation periods.
2. Mr. Cates only observed one third of the total language arts period, that is, 20 minutes out of each 60 minutes. Thus, in all probability, Joshua hit others approximately 96 times during language arts that week.
3. Joshua hit others, on an average, approximately 6 times a day. However, he hit others less on Friday than on any other day of the week.
4. Joshua hit others more frequently with the passing of each observation period of the day.

During the intervention phase of the behavior change program, Mr. Cates would isolate Joshua for 2 minutes each time he hit another child.

Before initiating the intervention, Mr. Cates transferred the baseline data to a graph to improve his visual image of the behavior (Figure 3.3).

Mr. Cates first made a chart for a 2-week period. His baseline data was entered in the section of the chart reserved for the first week. The remainder of the chart would be used for intervention data; he would enter the number of occurrences of hitting behavior during his observations each day of the intervention phase.

Mr. Cates used the horizontal axis of the chart for the days of the week and the vertical axis for the frequency of the behavior. He plotted the behavior and drew lines between the daily occurrences. ■

Although the same basic methods of counting and charting behavior are applied in all cases, certain modifications may be necessary, depending on the behavior under consideration.

In the example of Joshua's hitting behavior, we were primarily concerned with the frequency of the behavior. The behavior itself was instantaneous; thus the duration of the occurrences was not germane to the primary objective of the behavior change program.

However, if we were concerned with the duration of Bucky's tantrums, for example, we would focus our observation on both the frequency of occurrence and the dura-

TABLE 3.2
Baseline data: Joshua's hitting behavior

Time	Day					Time Total
	Mon.	Tue.	Wed.	Thur.	Fri.	
9:00-9:10	/	/		/	/	4
9:30-9:40	/	/	//	/	/	6
10:00-10:10	//	///	/	//	/	9
10:30-10:40	///	/	////	///	//	13
DAY TOTAL	7	6	7	7	5	32

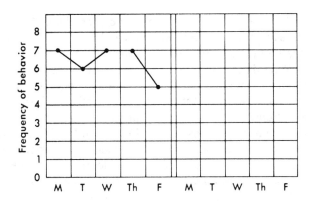

FIGURE 3.3
Joshua's hitting behavior (frequency).

tion of each occurrence. In this case we would collect raw observation data in the manner shown in Table 3.3

Table 3.3 is a tally log for Monday only, but the tally logs for the remaining 4 days of the baseline period are similar. The teacher, Mr. Wagner, is interested in decreasing both the frequency of the behavior and the duration of the behavior when it does occur.

Mr. Wagner has noted in the comments column that the tantrums occur when a change in group activity is taking place, such as at the end of reading period, at the beginning of science, at the beginning of lunchtime, and when it's time for preparing to go home.

The planned intervention is:

1. Intervene before an activity change and assist Bucky through the potential tantrum period.
2. If a tantrum does occur, isolate Bucky immediately until 2 minutes after the tantrum ceases.

TABLE 3.3
Bucky's tantrums (duration and frequency)

Time Begin	End	Total Minutes	Comments
9:31	9:38	7	End of reading
11:03	11:12	9	Beginning of science
12:07	12:17	10	Lunchtime
2:30	2:39	9	Preparing-to-go home time

Total occurrence for day: *4*
Average duration: *9* minutes
Day: *Monday*

As a result of this data-collecting procedure, Mr. Wagner designed two graphs to visually display the behavior. Figure 3.4 is concerned with the number of tantrums a day. Figure 3.5 represents the average duration of the tantrums.

Regardless of the specific target behavior being charted, the practitioner should remember that the ordinate points are generally located on the vertical axis of the chart and the abscissa points on the horizontal axis. Ordinate points represent the behavior's frequency, duration, and percent of occurrence. Abscissa points represent the hours, days, and sessions of observation (Axelrod, 1983).

The methods of counting and charting behavior presented in this section are the ones used most frequently in the field, probably because of the ease with which the practitioner can visually perceive and evaluate the data and thus determine the status of the behavior at a given point in time.

Observer Reliability

Successful application of the behavior change process is dependent on the reliability with which target behaviors are observed or measured. If unreliable measurement procedures are used, then (1) behaviors which change may be recorded as stable, and (2) behaviors which are stable may be recorded as changed (Hall & Houten, 1983).

To increase confidence in their skills as observers, it is recommended that teachers conduct interobserver reliability checks. To do this, a second observer should be invited to observe and record the target behavior. This should be done occasionally during both the baseline and intervention phases of the behavior change process. It is important that the second person observe the target behavior at the same time, under the same circumstances, and use the same definition of the behavior as the first observer.

By comparing the results of the two observations, using the following formula, an interobserver reliability percent or quotient can be calculated. The closer to 100% the

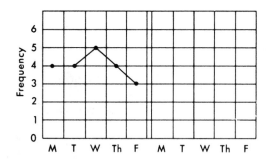

FIGURE 3.4
Bucky's tantrums (frequency).

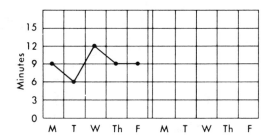

FIGURE 3.5
Average duration of Bucky's tantrums.

quotient is, the greater the confidence the practitioner has in the observation data. Hall and Houten (1983) suggest calculating interobserver reliability for interval data by dividing the number of intervals during which two observers agree by the total number of intervals they observed and multiplying the result by 100.

For example, Mrs. Sims and Mr. Horner observed Darlene's behavior together for a total of 20 five-minute intervals. Mrs. Sims observed the target behavior 20 times; Mr. Horner observed it 18 times. Using the preceding formula, their interobserver reliability quotient is:

$$\frac{18}{18 + 2} \times 100 = 90\%$$

To obtain an interobserver reliability quotient for frequency data, divide the frequency reported by the observer with the "lower" frequency by the frequency reported by the observer with the "higher" frequency and multiply the results by 100. For example, Mr. Luther and Ms. Shanks were both observing Angel's frequency of cursing. They observed during the same time period. Mr. Luther recorded 12 curses; Ms. Shanks recorded 11. Using the formula, their interobserver reliability quotient is:

$$\frac{11}{12} \times 100 = 91.66\%$$

Identifying Reinforcers

A behavior modification intervention is only as effective as its reinforcer. Regardless of the intervention applied in any behavior change program, if the exhibition of the behavior is not reinforced, the behavior will in all probability not change. In a behavior change program all factors may be carefully planned and the intervention precisely implemented, but if the child is not reinforced by the result of his or her behavior, little probability exists for a permanent behavior change.

Remember, a reinforcer is not necessarily a desirable or undesirable consequence for a child merely because the child's teacher or parent believes it should be (Hall & Hall, 1980; Shea & Bauer, 1987). Likewise, a reinforcer is not necessarily desirable to John simply because it is desirable to Mary, Herm, or Lucinda. The *only* true test of the effectiveness of a specific reinforcer with a specific child is implementation.

How can the teacher or parent identify potential reinforcers for the child whose behavior is to be modified? There are several procedures recommended for identifying reinforcers having a high probability of changing behavior in the desired direction. Among the available procedures are (1) reinforcement preference scales, (2) reinforcement lists, (3) interview with the child, (4) parent or teacher interview about the child, and (5) direct observation.

Reinforcement Preference Scales

Commercially available reinforcement preference scales are designed to assist the practitioner in eliciting and ranking the child's preferences. By means of pictures and questions the teacher or parent presents the child with a variety of objects and activities, both tangible and social. The child selects from these reinforcers. The teacher or parent systematically guides the child through the process of selecting, comparing, and ranking the reinforcers. With these materials, however, the possibility exists that the child will not respond to the selected reinforcers during the behavior change process.

The Children's Reinforcement Survey Schedule (CRSS) (Cautela, 1977) is a reinforcement preference scale. The CRSS includes three parts or forms. Forms A and B are parallel short forms for application with children in kindergarten through third grade. Form C is applied with children in grades four through six. Form A consists of 25 items; the individual is asked to indicate how much he or she likes a certain material object, organism (animals, people), or activity. The choice categories are "dislike," "like," and "like very much." Form B consists of 25 similar items scored in the same manner. Form C consists of 75 items scored as in Forms A and B and 5 open-ended questions concerning other possible reinforcers. The three forms of the CRSS are presented in Figures 3.6–3.8.

The child's interpersonal skills may prohibit communication of his or her real desires to the teacher. It is also possible that the reinforcers suggested in the scale are not desirable to the child or are not appropriate for the child's age. Of course, the possibility always exists that the child does not know or simply cannot articulate what is desirable to him or her.

Another problem with commercially prepared materials is that they are both costly and time consuming to administer.

Reinforcement Preference Lists

Reinforcement lists, such as the following one, are frequently helpful to the teacher or parent who is having difficulty thinking of reinforcers. The list may be used in a manner similar to the reinforcement preference scale discussed previously. The disadvantages of the reward list are similar to those of the preference scale.

The reinforcement list's greatest practical value to the practitioner is that it stimulates consideration of a broad spectrum of potential reinforcers; new reinforcers can be added to the list as the teacher or parent becomes aware of them.

Sample Tangible and Social Reinforcers.   The reinforcers listed are suggestions for classroom use. Each child has unique personal likes and dislikes. The reinforcers must be selected and decided on in consultation with and by observation of the child whose behavior is to be changed. A list for home use is presented in Chapter 8.

CRSS—Part A

Directions:

This is a list of many different things or activities. Explain how much you like each choice by making an "X" in the appropriate box.

If you dislike the choice, make an "X" in the box under *Dislike:*

Dislike	Like	Like Very Much
X		

If you like the choice, make an "X" in the box under *Like:*

Dislike	Like	Like Very Much
	X	

If the choice is something which you like very, very much, make an "X" in the box under *Like Very Much:*

Dislike	Like	Like Very Much
		X

	Dislike	Like	Like Very Much
1. Do you like candy?			
2. Do you like raisins?			
3. Do you like milk?			
4. Do you like stuffed toy animals?			
5. Do you like coloring?			
6. Do you like making things out of clay?			
7. Do you like listening to music?			
8. Do you like animal stories?			
9. Do you like playing on swings?			
10. Do you like kickball?			
11. Do you like going on field trips at school?			
12. Do you like being the teacher's helper?			
13. Do you like going to the library?			
14. Do you like people to tell you that you did a good job?			

FIGURE 3.6 *Children's Reinforcement Survey Schedule.*

CCRS—Part A, cont'd

	Dislike	Like	Like Very Much
15. Do you like your teacher to buy materials that you especially like?			
16. Do you like teaching things to other people?			
17. Do you like watching trucks, bulldozers, and tractors?			
18. Do you like to go shopping?			
19. Do you like to eat out in a restaurant?			
20. Do you like going to a circus or a fair?			
21. Do you like playing with dogs?			
22. Do you like to play with some children younger than you?			
23. Do you like to play with some special grown-ups?			
24. Do you like people to take care of you when you are sick?			
25. Do you like taking care of pet animals?			

FIGURE 3.6, *continued*
(Reprinted with permission of authors and publisher from: Cautela, J.R., and Brion-Meisels, L. A children's reinforcement survey schedule. Psychological Reports, *1979, 44, 327-338.)*

Consumable food reinforcers

Apples
Grapes
Oranges
Raisins
Crackers
Cookies
Popcorn
Potato chips
Peanuts
Gumdrops

Jelly beans
Small candies
Mints
Juice
Fruit-flavored drink
Milk
Soda
Ice cream
Lollipops
Sugarless gum

CRSS—Part B

Directions:

This is a list of many different things or activities. Explain how much you like each choice by making an "X" in the appropriate box.

If you dislike the choice, make an "X" in the box under *Dislike:*

Dislike	Like	Like Very Much
X		

If you like the choice, make an "X" in the box under *Like:*

Dislike	Like	Like Very Much
	X	

If the choice is something which you like very, very much, make an "X" in the box under *Like Very Much:*

Dislike	Like	Like Very Much
		X

	Dislike	Like	Like Very Much
1. Do you like apples?			
2. Do you like breakfast cereals?			
3. Do you like fruit juice?			
4. Do you like to play with toy cars?			
5. Do you like painting?			
6. Do you like making things out of wood?			
7. Do you like to sing?			
8. Do you like cartoons and comic books?			
9. Do you like swimming?			
10. Do you like riding a bike?			
11. Do you like outdoor recess?			
12. Do you like to be the winner of a contest?			
13. Do you like arithmetic and working with numbers?			
14. Do you like being better than everyone else at something?			

FIGURE 3.7 *Children's Reinforcement Survey Schedule.*

CRSS—Part B, cont'd

	Dislike	Like	Like Very Much
15. Do you like saving your school papers to show to other people?			
16. Do you like your parents to ask you what you did in school today?			
17. Do you like to watch television?			
18. Do you like traveling to different, far-away places on vacation?			
19. Do you like to go to the movies?			
20. Do you like playing with cats?			
21. Do you like to go to the zoo?			
22. Do you like playing with some children older than you?			
23. Do you like being alone rather than being with other people?			
24. If your friend is sick, do you like to take some things to your friend's house to make your friend feel happier?			
25. Do you like someone to take care of you when you are scared?			

FIGURE 3.7, *continued*
(From: Cautela, J.R., Behavior analysis forms for clinical interventions. *Champaign, Ill.: Research Press Co., 1977.)*

Reinforcing activities in relation to the above-listed consumables
Distributing reinforcers
Cleaning the area after reinforcers have been distributed
Popping popcorn
Scooping ice cream
Baking cookies
Preparing snacks

Tangible reinforcers other than food
Tickets to games, movies
Personal grooming supplies
Toys, games, and so on, from the class store
Special materials such as colored chalk, pencils, or felt-tipped pens

CRSS—Part C

Directions:

This is a list of many different things or activities. Explain how much you like each choice by making an "X" in the appropriate box.

If you dislike the choice, make an "X" in the box under *Dislike:*

Dislike	Like	Like Very Much
X		

If you like the choice, make an "X" in the box under *Like:*

Dislike	Like	Like Very Much
	X	

If the choice is something which you like very, very much, make an "X" in the box under *Like Very Much:*

Dislike	Like	Like Very Much
		X

	Dislike	Like	Like Very Much
1. Do you like candy?			
2. Do you like fruit?			
3. Do you like cooking?			
4. Do you like to drink soda?			
5. Do you like to make models?			
6. Do you like to play with model cars and trains?			
7. Do you like to draw and paint?			
8. Do you like to do crafts?			
9. Do you like carpentry and woodworking?			
10. Do you like making things out of clay?			
11. Do you like working with motors?			
12. Would you like to have sports equipment of your own?			
13. Do you like to play on playground equipment?			
14. Do you like to go bike riding?			

FIGURE 3.8 *Children's Reinforcement Survey Schedule.*

CRSS—Part C, cont'd

	Dislike	Like	Like Very Much
15. Do you like to go swimming?			
16. Do you like to go skiing?			
17. Do you like hockey?			
18. Do you like baseball?			
19. Do you like football?			
20. Do you like basketball?			
21. Do you like kickball?			
22. Do you like camping?			
23. Do you like listening to music?			
24. Do you like singing?			
25. Do you like learning how to play musical instruments?			
26. Do you like cartoons and comic books?			
27. Do you like fairytales?			
28. Do you like science fiction?			
29. Do you like mysteries?			
30. Do you like biographies (stories about peoples' lives)?			
31. Do you like having field trips at school?			
32. Do you like outdoor recess?			
33. Do you like puzzles?			
34. Do you like being a leader in your class, such as being a class officer?			
35. Do you like giving reports in front of the class?			
36. Do you like creative writing (making up stories or poems)?			
37. Do you like science?			
38. Do you like math?			
39. Do you like spelling?			

FIGURE 3.8, *continued*

CRSS—Part C, cont'd

	Dislike	Like	Like Very Much
40. Do you like go-carts?			
41. Do you like mini-bikes?			
42. Do you like to sell things?			
43. Do you like to go shopping?			
44. Do you like to watch television?			
45. Do you like to go to different, far-away places on vacation?			
46. Do you like to eat out in a restaurant?			
47. Do you like to go to the movies?			
48. Would you like to go to a circus or a fair?			
49. Do you like playing with dogs?			
50. Do you like playing with cats?			
51. Do you like to go to the zoo?			
52. Do you like to play with some children younger than you?			
53. Do you like to play with some children older than you?			
54. Do you like to play with some special grown-ups?			
55. Do you like being alone rather than being with other people?			
56. Would you like to talk to a sports' star you know about?			
57. Would you like to talk to a TV or movie star you have seen?			
58. Do you like going to parties?			
59. Do you like to stay overnight at a friend's house?			
60. Do you like earning money?			
61. Do you like it when your teacher buys materials that you especially like?			

FIGURE 3.8, *continued*

CRSS—Part C, cont'd

	Dislike	Like	Like Very Much
62. Do you like to be praised for your good work?			
63. Do you like your parents to ask you what you did in school today?			
64. Do you like to be the winner of a contest?			
65. Do you like to have your teacher ask you to help?			
66. Do you like getting the right answer?			
67. Do you like to show your good work to other people?			
68. Do you feel good when you have just finished a project or job you had to do?			
69. Do you like it when all the other kids think you are terrific?			
70. Do you like taking care of pet animals?			
71. Do you like fixing broken things?			
72. Do you like having a birthday party and getting presents?			
73. If your friend is sick, do you like to take some things to your friend's house to make your friend feel happier?			
74. Do you like someone to take care of you when you are scared?			
75. If you are sick, do you like people to take care of you?			

76. What do you think is the best thing about you?

_____

_____

_____

FIGURE 3.8, *continued*

CRSS—Part C, cont'd

77. What do you daydream about?

_____

_____

78. What do you do for fun?

_____

_____

79. What would you like for your birthday?

_____

_____

80. Do you have any collections? _____ If so, what do you collect?

_____

_____

FIGURE 3.8, *continued*

(From: Cautela, J.R., Behavior analysis forms for clinical interventions. *Champaign, Ill.: Research Press Co., 1977.)*

Token reinforcers

Check marks and points
Happy faces and stars
Behavior and achievement charts
Individual behavior and achievement
   cards and bankbooks
Rubber stamp marks of various designs
Gold stars next to child's name on the
   class chart
Trading stamps
Conservation stamps
Good citizen tags and certificates

Game activity reinforcers

Checkers
Dominoes
Puzzles
Dot-to-dot
Color-print-draw

Blockhead™
Spill and Spell™
Throw and Add™
Coloring books
Tip-It™
Beanbags
Jacks
Bingo
Blocks
Lincoln Logs™
Lego™
Dolls and dollhouses
Matchbox cars
Frisbees™
Gliders
Jump ropes
Kites
Marbles
Modeling clay

Monopoly™
Tops
Yo-yos
Tinker Toys™
Chess
Sorry™
Tiddlywinks
Cards
Life™
Word games
Number games
Crossword puzzles
Number puzzles
Circle games

Reinforcing activities

Reading books, magazines, and comic books
Writing on the chalkboard with white or colored chalk
Getting free time for self-selected projects
Making things, such as kites, model cars, and airplanes
Participating in creative drama
Participating in creative dance
Making bead jewelry
Playing in water or sand
Singing
Finger painting
Playing with puppets
Drawing with colored pens, pencils, or paints
Reading or studying with a friend
Being group leader
Bringing pets to school
Using a computer
Tutoring younger children
Eating lunch at a restaurant
Being excused from a test
Decorating a designated area of the room in own style
Taking field trips or walks

Going on outdoor walks
Watching a movie
Watching television
Listening to music
Doing project of own interest
Using the tape recorder, phonograph, or radio
Roller skating
Having access to the playroom
Getting extra recess
Going home early
Taking a class pet home for the weekend
Going on a trip to a fair or museum
Using a typewriter
Doing "special," "the hardest," or "impossible" teacher-made arithmetic problems
Reading the newspaper
Reading or drawing a road map
Going to the library
Doing a science experiment
Weighing or measuring various objects in the classroom

Social reinforcers

Receiving verbal praise
Having photograph displayed
Getting personal time with the teacher, aide, counselor, or principal
Participating in small-group discussions
Having work and projects displayed
Participating in show and tell
Demonstrating a skill
Clapping and cheering by others when successful
Being leader or organizer of an event
Getting a hug, handshake, or pat on the back
Sitting next to the teacher at lunch
Playing with a classmate of choice
Sitting and talking with a friend (child or adult)

Job reinforcers

Conducting an auction in class
Passing out paper, pencils, and so on
Taking a note to the office
Erasing the chalkboard
Helping the teacher with a project
Conducting a class raffle
Being teacher for a lesson
Managing the class store
Shopping for the class store
Being messenger for the day
Helping in the cafeteria
Assisting the custodian
Cleaning the erasers
Watering the plants
Running the ditto machine
Stapling papers together
Feeding the fish or other animals
Giving a message over the intercom
Picking up litter on the school grounds
Cleaning the teacher's desk

Taking the class roll
Carrying messages to other teachers
Serving as secretary for class meetings
Raising or lowering the flag
Emptying the wastebasket
Carrying the wastebasket while other
 children clean out their desks
Distributing and collecting materials
Operating a slide, filmstrip, or movie
 projector
Using the overhead projector
Recording own behavior on a graph
Teaching another child
Helping the librarian
Telling the teacher when it is time to go
 to lunch
Sharpening the teacher's pencils
Opening the teacher's mail
Sweeping the floor of the classroom
Adjusting the window shades

Interview with Child

Interviewing a child to determine what he or she finds reinforcing is frequently productive. The interview should be structured, and the reinforcement list may be used to stimulate discussion. The child is encouraged to express and discuss desires; he or she is asked questions such as "What kinds of things do you like to do?" "What are your favorite toys?" "What do you like to do more than anything else?" The child's responses will be of great help in attempting to pinpoint those items and activities to be used as reinforcers. Also, the interviewer has an opportunity to thoroughly explain the behavior change program and answer the child's questions.

There is evidence to indicate that when a child is involved in decision making concerning important ingredients of his or her program, the overall quality and rate of the program are enhanced (Raschke, 1979). Thus involving the child in the selection of reinforcers enhances the probability that the intervention will be successful.

The use of the interview technique provides the child with an opportunity to learn to select reasonable and positive reinforcers. Many children initially have difficulty making reasonable selections because of a lack of experience in decision making. In this situation the interview is in itself a learning experience for the child.

The interview technique can be used with small groups as well as individuals. The disadvantage of the technique is that it is time consuming and its success is dependent on (1) the child's or group's ability to communicate with the interviewing adult and (2) the adult's skill as an interviewer.

In the interview situation the following steps should be used as guidelines (Shea et al., 1974a, 1974b):

1. Establish rapport with the child or group.
2. Explain the purpose of the meeting.
3. Define and explain the meaning of individual and/or group reinforcers.
4. Elicit suggestions for individual and/or group rewards.
   a. Ask the child or group which rewards could be used as individual reinforcers. Record these suggestions. If working with a group, ask the individuals which suggested rewards could be used as group rewards.
   b. Give the child or group an opportunity to add to the list of rewards.
   c. Request that the child or each member of the group choose three rewards and rank them according to their desirability. If working with a group, determine the group's ranking of the rewards. Have the members vote to decide on the reward.
   d. Make arrangements for another meeting at which the child or group may choose to add to or change the reinforcers. It is useful to record the reinforcers suggested by the child or group on the chalkboard.

Raschke (1981) published a procedure for designing reinforcement surveys which permit a child to choose personal reinforcers. The procedure is responsive to the needs and interests of the child and teacher in a specific instructional setting. To develop a survey the teacher follows four steps: select content items, design a survey inventory, administer the inventory, and summarize the results.

The content of the inventory reflects not only the child's likes and dislikes but what is practical and possible in the specific instructional setting. To assist in the selection of the survey's content, the teacher is encouraged to consult the list of potential reinforcers presented in the previous pages.

The survey itself may take one of several forms, an open-ended format, multiple choice format, or a rank-order format. Examples of the open-ended format and multiple choice format are presented on the following pages.

The administration of the survey includes very specific instructions which emphasize the confidentiality of responses and the fact that there are no right or wrong answers. From the information obtained, the teacher develops individual and group preference lists.

REINFORCEMENT ASSESSMENT: OPEN-ENDED FORMAT

1. If I had 10 minutes free time during this class, I would most like to . . .
2. The favorite type of activity that I wish we would do more often in this class is . . .
3. My favorite seating arrangement in this class is . . .

4. My favorite place to sit in this class is ...
5. My favorite way to learn new information in this class is ...
6. My favorite instructional equipment to use in this class is ...
7. The special jobs I like to help the teacher with the most in this class are ...
8. If I could change one class rule for 1 hour in this class, the rule I would change would be ...
9. If I were to choose two students in this classroom to do a fun activity with, I would select ...
10. If I went to the store and had 50 cents to spend on whatever I wanted, I would buy ...
11. The person in this school I like most to praise me when I do good work is ...
12. In this class, I feel proudest of myself when ...
13. The thing that motivates me the most to do well in this classroom is ...
14. The nicest thing that has ever happened to me in this class for doing good work is ...
15. The very best reward in this class that the teacher could give me for good work is ...[1]

REINFORCEMENT ASSESSMENT: MULTIPLE CHOICE FORMAT

1. The way I best like to learn about something new in this class is:
   a. Lecture
   b. Books
   c. Pamphlets
   d. Films
   e. Tapes
   f. Language master
   g. Small-group work
   h. Guest speakers
2. My favorite writing tool to use in this class is:
   a. Magic Markers™
   b. Felt pens
   c. Colored pencils
   d. Colored chalk
3. My favorite seating arrangement in this class is:
   a. Desks in rows
   b. Chairs at tables
   c. Desks randomly scattered
   d. Study carrels randomly scattered
4. The special job I like to help the teacher with the most in this class is:
   a. Handing out papers
   b. Putting away supplies
   c. Decorating a bulletin board

---

[1]From "Designing Reinforcement Surveys—Let the Students Choose the Reward" by D. Raschke, 1981, *Teaching Exceptional Children, 14,* p. 93. Copyright 1981 by The Council for Exceptional Children. Reprinted by permission.

    d. Running the filmstrip projector

    e. Writing the assignment on the chalkboard

    f. Straightening up cupboards and bookcases

5. The best privilege I could earn in this class for good work would be to:

    a. Sit anywhere I want in the class

    b. Help the teacher grade papers

    c. Put an assignment on the chalkboard

    d. Give the class announcements

    e. Pick a partner to work with

6. When I do well in this class, I like it most when the teacher:

    a. Smiles at me

    b. Informs the class of my good work

    c. Writes a note on my paper

    d. Tells me privately in words

    e. Draws a big happy face on my paper

    f. Puts my good work on the bulletin board

7. When I do good work in this class, I would most like to earn:

    a. Free time

    b. Praise from the teacher

    c. A favorite activity with a friend

    d. A favorite activity with a teacher

    e. Good work displayed on a bulletin board

8. My favorite free-time activity in this class is:

    a. Playing checkers or a card game

    b. Listening to radio or playing records

    c. Working a puzzle or doing a craft

    d. Visiting with a friend

    e. Reading a favorite book

    f. Playing a computer game

9. The nicest thing that could happen to me for doing good work in this class would be:

    a. Receiving an award in front of the class

    b. Receiving an A+ on a project

    c. A phone call to my parents describing my good work

    d. Having my work displayed in the hallway

    e. Earning free time for the whole class

10. The best tangible reward I could earn in this class would be a:

    a. Gold star

    b. Happy gram

    c. Good work badge

    d. Certificate of achievement

    e. Scratch-n-sniff sticker

    f. Spacemen stamp

11. If I had 50 cents to buy anything I wanted, I would buy:

    a. A yo-yo

    b. A Frisbee™

    c. A poster

    d. Some Silly Putty™

    e. A comic book

12. Something really different I would work hard for in this class would be:
    a. A warm fuzzy
    b. A monster tattoo
    c. Some space dust
    d. A creepy spider
    e. Some monster teeth
    f. A vampire fingernail
    g. A squirt ring[2]

Parent or Teacher Interview

The parent or teacher interview can also be used in an effort to obtain and rank the child's reinforcers. Although less desirable than a direct interview with the child, the parent or teacher interview can be helpful in determining which reinforcers have been applied successfully and unsuccessfully by others. It may also be used to determine the range of successful reinforcers within the child's response repertoire.

The parent or teacher interview is especially valuable to the consultant who is trying to determine the level of understanding and acceptance of behavior change techniques by the individual who works directly with the child.

The obvious disadvantage in applying this technique is that the parent's or teacher's level of sophistication as an objective observer is unknown. It should be recognized that the parent or teacher may not be of real assistance in the selection of potent rewards because of a distorted perception of the child's likes and dislikes. However, the use of the technique can be an excellent learning experience for parents and teachers; frequently it can sensitize them to the importance of meaningful reinforcers for children.

This topic is discussed in detail in Chapter 6.

Direct Observation

The most productive strategy for identifying effective reinforcers is direct observation. According to an old saying, "If you want to see a person do something well, observe him doing something he enjoys."

Direct observation requires the teacher to observe the child's self-selected activities in a variety of situations, such as on the playground, in the classroom, during structured time, and during free time, and to list those activities the child chooses. These self-selected activities and items can be used during the intervention as reinforcers.

EXAMPLES　■　Ms. Maron observed that Marvin liked to congregate with his friends during recess to trade baseball cards. She decided to allow the boys to have an additional trading time after

---

[2]From "Designing Reinforcement Surveys—Let the Students Choose the Reward" by D. Raschke, 1981, *Teaching Exceptional Children, 14,* p. 93. Copyright 1981 by The Council for Exceptional Children. Reprinted by permission.

they finished their arithmetic lesson. The total arithmetic period was 40 minutes. After 30 minutes the boys who had finished the assignment could go to a special area of the room and quietly trade cards. The longer Marvin took to complete the lesson, the less time he had to trade cards. ◼

◼ Mr. Dee knew that all 8-year-old boys like to play baseball. Mr. Dee wished to improve Jamie's performance in spelling. He told Jamie that each day that he got 80% of his spelling words correct, he could play baseball for 20 minutes on the playground. Mr. Dee was astonished when Jamie did not respond to this reward.

There were several reasons why Jamie did not respond, and Mr. Dee had failed to take them into consideration. Jamie had not only a visual-perceptual handicap but also a gross motor handicap, and these problems interfered with his skill in large muscle activities. It was far more difficult to play baseball than to flunk spelling. Mr. Dee's fundamental error was that he did not include Jamie in the reinforcer selection process. ◼

Additional Suggestions

Different children value different consequences. It is nearly impossible to identify any event or item that will serve as a positive reinforcer for all children.

In the end the potency of a reinforcer selected as a result of using any technique can only be determined by implementation. Many reinforcers, thought to be highly potent, fail to be effective with some children; whereas some reinforcers, discovered only on a teacher's hunch, prove to be most powerful in changing behavior.

A few additional suggestions for the selection and use of positive reinforcers may be useful.

1. Except for a few basic items such as food and water, no item or activity can be identified with certitude as an effective reinforcer before it has been demonstrated to be effective for a specific child. What is highly reinforcing for one child may not be for another.
2. When satiation occurs, even the most powerful reinforcer will lose strength and must be replaced. The teacher should provide a variety of reinforcers, not only to prevent satiation but also to satisfy the individual and his ever-changing preferences. Many teachers provide a "menu of reinforcers" for their children. On any given day a variety of items or activities are available to satisfy the diverse needs and interests of the children. They are permitted to select from this menu.
3. The task of observing the effects of existing reinforcers and searching for new reinforcers is a continuous process. A good reinforcement system is an ever-changing blend of established and potential reinforcers.
4. Reinforcers should not be thought of only in terms of tangible items. There are many activities and privileges that are potent reinforcers. Frequently teachers use a tangible reinforcer (with a social reinforcer) initially during the behavior change program. Later they change the reward from the tangible reinforcer to a special ac-

tivity or privilege (always keeping the social reinforcer). In the final stages of the behavior change process, the social reinforcer used alone should be adequate.

Although several methods for identifying reinforcers are discussed in this section, the two procedures most recommended are direct observation and a direct interview with the child. Both have proved effective for identifying reinforcers (Karraker, 1977).

The fact that a child is motivated by a specific reinforcer today does not necessarily mean the child will respond to that particular reinforcer next week. A change in performance may be the signal to initiate a new reward. The fact that Lisa correctly completed 25 addition problems on Monday to play with a puzzle, 27 problems on Tuesday to play with a puzzle, and 28 problems on Wednesday for the same privilege does not mean she will respond in a similar fashion on Thursday. To avoid this situation, a reward menu, as discussed in Chapter 4, is recommended. The menu allows the practitioner to systematically vary the rewards a child can work for on different days. With proficiency gained through practice in the techniques for changing behavior, the practitioner can predict when it is time to change reinforcers.

Schedules of reinforcement are discussed in Chapter 2; however, it should be reemphasized that the schedule on which the reinforcement is delivered has considerable influence on the behavior change process.

Phasing Out Reinforcers

As stated previously, a goal of the behavior change process is to train an individual to respond to appropriate and occasional social reinforcers *only*. Consequently it is necessary that the behavior modification practitioner focus particular attention to phasing out the reinforcers over a period of time. This difficult task is accomplished primarily by changing from a fixed interval or ratio reinforcement schedule to a variable interval or ratio reinforcement schedule and by the systematic attenuating of the average frequency of reinforcer presentation. It must be remembered that a social reinforcer is always presented concurrently with a tangible reinforcer, if tangible rewards are used.

Procedures applied to phasing out reinforcers are:

Step 1: Social and tangible reinforcers are presented simultaneously to the individual on a fixed reinforcement schedule. This statement assumes that tangible reinforcers are needed initially in the particular situation.

Step 2: Social reinforcers are continued on a fixed schedule, and tangible reinforcers are presented on a variable schedule. Tangible reinforcers are attenuated over time and are finally extinguished. Social reinforcers are presented simultaneously with tangible reinforcers during this step.

Step 3: Social reinforcers are presented on a variable schedule. They are attenuated over time and are finally extinguished as the formal behavior change program is terminated.

Implementing the Intervention and Collecting and Recording Intervention Data

The next step in the behavior change process is selecting and implementing the intervention and collecting and recording intervention data. Chapters 4 and 5 are devoted to a detailed description of interventions applied to increase and decrease target behaviors.

Intervention data involve information collected on the effects of the intervention during the implementation phase. Equally as important as baseline data, intervention data provide a yardstick for comparing baseline behavior with new behavior. By comparing baseline data with intervention data, the teacher can determine the changes that have occurred as a result of the intervention. Figure 3.9 presents a comparison of Joshua's hitting behavior before and during the intervention.

In this graph the target behavior shows an increase during the initial 2 days of intervention. The behavior then decreases to zero over the remaining days of the program.

The initial increase in the behavior (days 6 and 7) was probably a result of Joshua's testing of the teacher's response to his original behavior. In all probability Joshua was confused by the fact that his previously effective response was no longer effective. Of course, this increase might also have been a result of the initial inefficiency of either the reinforcer or the practitioner. However, the initial increase in behavior, as discussed in Chapter 2, is normal and should be anticipated during the beginning days of the intervention.

The importance of continuing to count and chart the target behavior during the intervention can be readily seen on Joshua's graph. This procedure provides the practitioner with a visual image to be used in comparing the baseline and intervention behaviors. The data alerts the teacher to the child's response to the intervention and thus to the overall effectiveness of the program at a particular point in time.

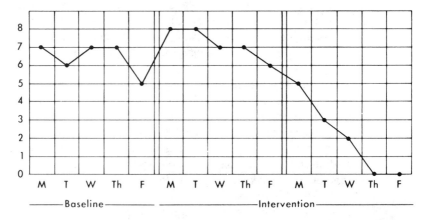

FIGURE 3.9
Frequency of Joshua's hitting behavior before and during the intervention.

Evaluating the Effects of Intervention

Once the new behavior has been established at the acceptable level, the practitioner may question whether the observed changes were a result of the intervention or of an unknown intervening variable. This query cannot be responded to with exactitude. However, there is a procedure to test the effectiveness of the intervention. This is the process of extinction, or of reestablishing the baseline (Baseline 2). The process of reestablishing the baseline in this situation is as follows: If a behavior is thought to be maintained at a specific level by a reinforcer, the practitioner can evaluate the effectiveness of the reinforcer by withdrawing it.

EXAMPLE

■ Mr. Curtain had established Shirley's hand-raising behavior at an acceptable level. He then wondered if the reinforcer applied in the intervention phase was the *factor* that had resulted in her change in behavior. The reinforcer was a smile and verbal praise each time Shirley raised her hand in class.

To check the potency of the reinforcer, Mr. Curtain withdrew it; that is, he ceased smiling at Shirley and praising her when she raised her hand in class. Within a few days, as demonstrated in Figure 3.10, Shirley's hand-raising response began to be extinguished. Because of the decrease in Shirley's hand-raising behavior, Mr. Curtain could assume that the reinforcer (smiles and verbal praise) was instrumental in increasing the hand-raising behavior. He had evaluated the effect of reinforcement on the behavior. ■

Reestablishing the baseline is not always an effective means of evaluating the potency of a reinforcer. If a behavior has been firmly habituated into the child's behavioral repertoire, it will not respond to extinction.

Establishing and extinguishing a behavior is *not* a standard procedure applied in the behavior change process. However, this technique may assure new students of behavior modification that their efforts are effective in changing behaviors.

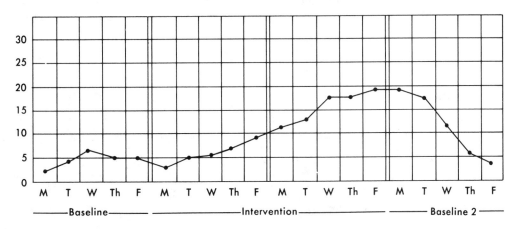

FIGURE 3.10
Frequency of Shirley's hand-raising behavior before and during the intervention and as a result of reestablishing the baseline (Baseline 2).

The use of Baseline 2 in an intervention is at the discretion of the practitioner. However, once a teacher or parent has determined that the reinforcer was instrumental in the behavior change program, it would be a disservice to the child not to reinstate it or not to return to the intervention state.

SUMMARY

In this chapter the steps for changing behavior are discussed. They are (1) *selecting a target behavior*, (2) *collecting and recording baseline data*, (3) *identifying reinforcers*, (4) *implementing the intervention and collecting and recording intervention data*, and (5) *evaluating the effects of the intervention.*

When selecting a target behavior, the practitioner should choose only *one* individual or group behavior to change at a time. The practitioner should analyze the potential target behavior in relation to its frequency, duration, intensity, and type; determine the direction the behavior is to take (whether it is to increase, decrease, or be maintained); determine whether the behavior is observable and quantifiable; and finally, describe the behavior in precise, descriptive terminology. Collecting and recording baseline data allow an analysis of the changes in behavior that occur during the intervention.

A list of tangible and social reinforcers for application in the classroom and school are presented. Consideration is given to consumable rewards, tangible and token rewards, games, activities, social rewards, and jobs. The two most effective methods of identifying reinforcers are direct observation and an interview with the child.

Comparison of baseline and intervention data provides the practitioner with an evaluation technique for determining changes occurring in the target behavior as a result of intervention.

It is highly recommended that the new practitioner of behavior modification carefully follow each step in the behavior change process presented in this chapter.

EXERCISES

Quiz

1. The steps in the behavior change process are:

    a. Selecting a _____ behavior.

    b. _____ and _____ baseline data.

    c. Identifying _____ reinforcers.

    d. Implementing the _____ and collecting and recording

    _____ data.

    e. Evaluating the effects of intervention.

2. Decisions concerning the selection of a target behavior should be governed by the following four characteristics of the behavior:

   a. _____   c. _____

   b. _____   d. _____

3. The directions a behavior may take as a result of an intervention are:

   a. _____   c. _____

   b. _____

4. List three of the techniques available for collecting baseline data.

   a. _____

   b. _____

   c. _____

5. a. Counting means enumerating the _____ that the behavior occurs.

   b. _____ means presenting a visual display of the enumerated behavior.

6. Three techniques for obtaining a list of potential reinforcers are:

   a. _____

   b. _____

   c. _____

7. The best method available to demonstrate the effectiveness of a reinforcer

   is _____.

8. Collecting and charting data should continue throughout the _____

   _____ phase.

9. In most cases immediately after the implementation of an intervention to change a behavior, the practitioner can anticipate a brief dramatic _____ in the behavior.

10. One method of evaluating the effectiveness of a reinforcer during the behavior change

    process is to withdraw it. This is the process of _____.

Projects

1. Select five potential target behaviors and observe them. After observing the behaviors, discuss their characteristics in terms of frequency, duration, intensity, and type.
2. Collect and record accurate baseline data on two of the behaviors observed.
3. List 25 reinforcers that may be useful in modifying the behavior of children in your present teaching situation. Classify these as tangible or social reinforcers. At least 12 of the 25 reinforcers should be classifiable as social rewards.
4. Observe a child and develop a list of potential reinforcers for this child. Observe the child in a variety of situations.

5. a. As outlined in the text, interview the same child and develop another list of reinforcers.
    b. Interview the child's parent or teacher and develop a third list of reinforcers.
6. Conceptualize and write a detailed description of an intervention to be applied to one of the behaviors observed in Project 1.

REFERENCES

Axelrod, S. (1983). *Behavior modification for the classroom teacher.* New York: McGraw-Hill Book Co.

Cautela, J. R., & Meisels, L. B. (1977) Children's reinforcement survey schedule. In J. R. Cautela (Ed.), *Behavior analysis forms for clinical intervention* (pp. 53–62). Champaign, IL: Research Press Co.

Hall, R. V., & Hall, M. C. (1980). *How to select reinforcers.* Austin, TX: Pro-Ed.

Hall, R. V., & Houten, R. V. (1983). *The measurement of behavior.* Austin, TX: Pro-Ed.

Karraker, R. J. (1977). Self versus teacher selected reinforcers in a token economy. *Exceptional Children, 43*(7), 454–455.

Mager, R. F. (1984). *Preparing instructional objectives* (2nd rev. ed.). Belmont, CA: Pitman Learning Press.

Morris, R. J. (1985). *Behavior modification with exceptional children: Principles and practices.* Glenview, IL: Scott, Foresman & Company.

Raschke, D. (1979). The relationship of internal-external control and operant reinforcement procedures with learning and behavior disordered children. *Dissertation Abstracts International, 40,* 4533. (Unpublished doctoral dissertation, University of Wisconsin, Madison).

Raschke, D. (1981). Designing reinforcement surveys—let the students choose the reward. *Teaching Exceptional Children, 14,* 92–96.

Schopler, E., Reichler, R. J., & Lansing, M. (1980). *Individualized assessment and treatment for autistic and developmentally disabled children; Vol. II. Teaching strategies for parents and professionals.* Austin, TX: Pro-Ed.

Shea, T. M., & Bauer, A. M. (1987). *Teaching children and youth with behavior disorders* (2nd ed.). Englewood Cliffs, NJ: Prentice-Hall.

Shea, T. M., Whiteside, W. R., Beetner, E. G., & Lindsey, D. L. (1974a). *Psychosituational interview.* Edwardsville: Southern Illinois University.

Shea, T. M., Whiteside, W. R., Beetner, E. G., & Lindsey, D. L. (1974b). *Selecting reinforcers.* Edwardsville: Southern Illinois University.

CHAPTER FOUR

Methods of Increasing Behavior

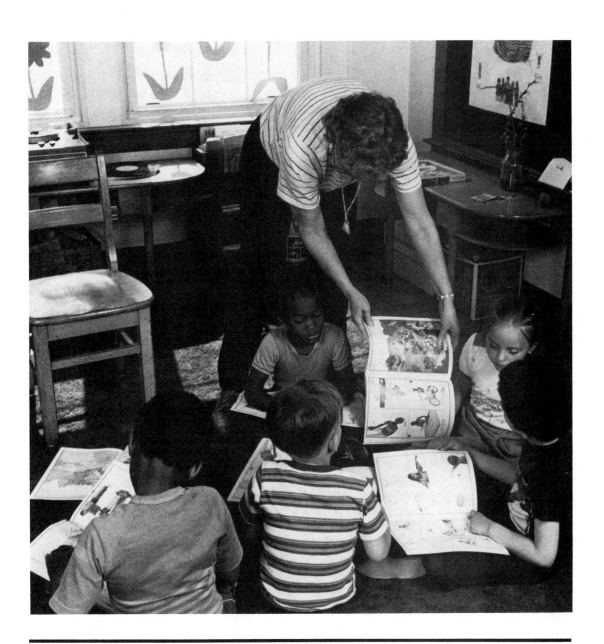

Judy, a second grader, is more socially mature than her peers. This social maturity is a result of her close association with her sister Joanne, who is a fifth grader. The girls spend most of their time playing together and with Joanne's friends. Judy thinks that second graders are babies and therefore does not associate with them at recess; she associates with them only when necessary in the classroom. Judy is not only socially mature for her age but intellectually mature as well.

Behavior problems are developing for Judy among her peers, as well as among Joanne's friends. Joanne's friends often invite her to their homes for parties or to the movies. They do not invite Judy because they think she is too young. As Joanne gets older, Judy is finding herself alone more and more frequently. Not having anyone to play with upsets her greatly.

Maybe if Judy's parents knew more about behavior management, they might increase Judy's socialization with her peers.

Mr. Peterson is a basketball coach at William Tolbert Community College. Over the past 2 years he has developed a winning basketball team and an excellent reputation as a coach. Mr. Peterson is employed by the college part-time to coach and recruit basketball players. He is a full-time employee of a local high school where he teaches physical education. Because of over-staffing and declining budgets, the college is unable to offer Coach Peterson a full-time position.

Mr. Peterson is worried that additional budget cuts will eliminate his position at the college. He fears he will be replaced by the former basketball coach, who is teaching full-time in the physical education department. If so, he believes he is developing a winning basketball team for another coach. He is so paranoid about the former basketball coach taking his team away from him that it is affecting his coaching and his relationship with the college faculty. Mr. Peterson dwells on one topic in all conversations: "I'm working day and night to build a team for someone else."

Maybe if the physical education department chairperson knew more about increasing behaviors, he would be able to help Coach Peterson be more positive toward his part-time position.

The five most common techniques applied in behavior modification interventions for increasing a target behavior are (1) positive reinforcement, (2) shaping, (3) modeling, (4) contingency contracting, and (5) the token economy. These basic methods should be of assistance to the beginning practitioner attempting to establish acceptable behaviors in children. The techniques are applicable with both individual and group behaviors.

Positive Reinforcement

Positive reinforcement, which is discussed in some detail in Chapter 2, is reviewed in this section. Positive reinforcement is known by various other labels, such as positive attention, approval, social reinforcement, and rewarding. Here it is defined as the process of rewarding an appropriate target behavior in order to increase the probability that the behavior will recur. The advantages of positive reinforcement are (1) it is responsive to the child's natural need for attention and approval and (2) it decreases the probability that the child will exhibit inappropriate behavior in an effort to obtain needed attention.

Two rules are essential for the effective application of positive reinforcement. First, when a child is initially exhibiting a new appropriate behavior, it must be positively reinforced each time it occurs. Second, once the target behavior is established at a satisfactory rate, the child should be reinforced intermittently.

To apply positive reinforcement, the teacher should (Shea and Bauer, 1987):

1. Carefully select a target behavior (do not attempt to reinforce every positive behavior a child exhibits).
2. Observe the child's behavior to ascertain when he or she engages in the behavior.
3. During the initial stage, reinforce the behavior immediately after it is exhibited.
4. Specify for the child the behavior that is being reinforced ("I like the _____," or a similar comment).
5. When reinforcing, speak with enthusiasm and show interest in the child's behavior.
6. When appropriate, the practitioner may become involved in the child's behavior, that is, give the child help.
7. Vary the reinforcer.

A note of caution: Public reinforcement is unwelcome to some children under some circumstances. They may be embarrassed by positive reinforcement in the presence of peers, teachers, parents, and others.

EXAMPLES ■ Michael has extremely poor table manners. He not only eats with his hands and fingers, but he eats very rapidly. His teacher, Ms. Vandan, is attempting to improve the boy's table manners by positively reinforcing Michael's use of a fork and placement of the fork on the plate between each bite of food.

Michael is pleased with the extra attention, and over a period of several weeks his table manners have dramatically improved. Ms. Vandan used first a continuous reinforcement schedule, and then a variable schedule to help Michael. ■

■ Fourteen-year-old George, a member of the "Wild and Crazy Bunch," likes his math teacher, Ms. Chinn, very much. He enjoys receiving her attention, but sometimes it is a little annoying. This is especially true when Ms. Chinn makes a big show in front of the whole class of his successfully completing a difficult problem. It seems the other members of the "Bunch" hassle him after class when this occurs. ■

Shaping

To initiate an intervention for the purpose of increasing a behavior, the teacher or parents need only wait until the target behavior is emitted by the child. When the behavior occurs, it must be immediately rewarded with a potent reinforcer.

However, suppose a situation arises in which the level of performance of the behavior is at zero or near zero. What can the teacher or parent do to establish the behavior? There are two alternatives:

1. Wait an undetermined length of time (in some cases, forever) for the behavior to naturally occur.
2. Use a behavior-shaping technique.

Shaping is the systematic, immediate reinforcement of successive approximations of the target behavior until the behavior is established (Panyan, 1980; Shea & Bauer, 1987). It is primarily used to establish behaviors that have not been previously manifested in the individual's behavioral repertoire. Just as the sculptor shapes and molds an object of art from clay, the behavior modifier shapes and molds a new behavior from an undifferentiated behavioral response (Neisworth and others, 1969). This technique is applicable to both behavioral and academic problems.

The behavior-shaping process includes the following steps:

Step 1: Selecting a target behavior.
Step 2: Obtaining reliable baseline data.
Step 3: Selecting potent reinforcers.
Step 4: Reinforcing successive approximations of the target behavior each time they occur.
Step 5: Reinforcing the newly established behavior each time it occurs.
Step 6: Reinforcing the behavior on a variable reinforcement schedule.

Many of these steps are explained in Chapters 2 and 3. However, some of them require additional comments here for clarification.

The behavior selected for shaping must be carefully specified. The teacher or parent must be positive that the selected behavior is meaningful to the child in terms of the child's present life situation and developmental level.

If the performance level of the target behavior is at zero, the teacher or parent must initiate the shaping process from the child's undifferentiated behavioral manifestations.

EXAMPLES   ■ Tommy's teacher, Ms. Allen, wishes to establish intelligible verbal responses in Tommy's behavioral repertoire. However, the child enunciates no understandable words. His entire verbal behavior consists of vocal noises such as screeches, howls, and gutteral sounds. The teacher must begin the shaping process with the manifested behavior, that is, vocal noise. She must reinforce successive approximations of intelligible verbal responses. ■

■ Jeff, a severely handicapped child, was having great difficulty interacting appropriately on the playground during circle or ball games requiring running from one specific location to another. When he was required to engage in a game of this type, he ran about at random, dashing here and there, jumping up and down, and in general confusing himself and his playmates.

Mr. Speer, the physical education teacher, wished to modify this behavior. He realized he had to start the change process with the behavior presently being manifested by Jeff. He determined that Jeff did attend to the action of the game and attempted to play by the rules. In his effort to help Jeff, Mr. Speer modified the rules of the game; he established a "new rule" in which all team members ran hand-in-hand in pairs from one location to another. Jeff was Mr. Speer's partner until he was conditioned to the new running pattern. The game was played by the traditional rules after Jeff developed acceptable skills. ■

During the behavior-shaping process, the teacher or parent reinforces only those behavioral manifestations that most approximate the desired behavior.

EXAMPLE ■ Mr. Jackson designed a shaping intervention to increase the number of assigned math problems that Robert would successfully complete in his workbook during independent study. Robert never completed the 20 problems given for practice. However, baseline data revealed that Robert consistently solved the first 9 problems successfully in each practice section. He simply did not attempt the remaining 11 problems.

During the shaping process, Mr. Jackson reinforced Robert for *improvements* over his baseline of 9. Robert was rewarded for successfully completing 10 problems, 11 problems, 12 problems, and so on. Robert was *never* rewarded for completing a quantity of problems below his highest level of accomplishment. Within a short time Mr. Jackson's intervention data confirmed the fact that Robert was consistently completing the 20 problems successfully. The reinforcer was phased out. ■

Reinforcing less than the existing baseline results in rewarding behavior in a direction of change that is the reverse of the proposed direction. Remember, *only* the *highest* approximation of the target behavior should be reinforced.

Another important consideration in the shaping process is the teacher or parent's knowledge of how long to provide reinforcement at one level of performance before moving to the next level. Such a movement increases the demands on the child. Determining when to move on is the teacher or parent's greatest dilemma. If reinforcement continues too long at a given performance level, the child's behavior may become so rigidly established that further progress will be difficult. However, if the practitioner insists that the child progress too rapidly from one level to the next, there is a great possibility that the new behavior will be extinguished.

Knowing when to progress from one level of performance to the next is of utmost importance. Unfortunately, this knowledge is part of the skill needed for behavior modification, and developing it is not easy. The teacher or parent develops this needed sensitivity and skill only with practice and experience in behavior shaping and through knowing the individual child.

The following two examples are presented to clarify the steps in the behavior-shaping process.

EXAMPLES
■ Ms. Simpkins wished to increase Jim's letter identification skills. Jim could identify 7 of the 26 letters of the alphabet consistently. Before implementing a shaping intervention, Ms. Simpkins determined that gumdrops were an effective reinforcer for Jim.

During the intervention phase of the behavior change program, Jim was exposed to one new letter of the alphabet at a time. He was to learn each new letter before another letter was presented. Jim was only reinforced with a gumdrop if he identified the new letter and all previously identified letters. The new letter was always presented last in the daily sequence of letters. After he had learned a letter, it was presented randomly with all the other previously learned letters in the daily session.

This procedure was continued until Jim successfully identified all the letters in the alphabet. ■

■ Mr. Behe wished to increase Barry's in-seat behavior. Baseline data revealed that on an average, Barry remained in his seat approximately 6 minutes. Mr. Behe had determined through observation that Barry enjoyed listening to story records. This activity was selected as a reinforcer for acceptable in-seat behavior.

During the intervention a timer was placed on Barry's desk. He was told that each time he remained in his seat until the timer bell sounded, he would be allowed to go to the reinforcement area of the classroom and listen to his favorite story record for a specified number of minutes. The reinforcement schedule Mr. Behe used to shape the in-seat behavior is presented in Table 4.1.

Barry's behavior was shaped with little difficulty. However, during the 20-minute interval between reinforcement Barry became bored. As a consequence, he remained at the 20-minute interval longer than the teacher had anticipated. At Barry's suggestion, Mr. Behe changed the reinforcer from story records to jigsaw puzzles. ■

According to Panyan (1980), there are two distinct types of behavior-shaping interventions: progressive and chain.

TABLE 4.1
Reinforcement schedule for in-seat behavior

Minutes of In-seat Behavior	Minutes in Reinforcement Area
5	2
5	2
7	2½
8	2½
10	2½
15	3
20	3
25	3
30	3½
45	4
60	4
90	5
120	7½
150	10

In the progressive shaping intervention, the child is required to engage in a series of steps, each of which is a continuation and progression of the previously learned step or steps. Examples of this intervention are bathing, hand-washing, putting on a sweater or socks, and so on. (See the example of Marie below.)

A chain intervention is composed of two or more separate and distinct steps or skills that are learned and combined sequentially to complete a specific task. Examples of this intervention are tying shoes, polishing shoes, eating, buttoning clothing, and so on.

To summarize this discussion of the behavior-shaping process, the following example and conceptual model are presented.

EXAMPLE ■ Five-year-old Stephen was nonverbal. His speech teacher selected the initiation of verbal exchanges with his preschool teacher as the target behavior. Baseline data revealed that Stephen's only verbal behavior consisted of babbling, yelling, and screaming. This behavior was frequent when he was in the company of adults he knew. However, he did not consistently emit this behavior in response to queries from others.

Stephen was observed by the speech teacher, who determined that he consistently responded to four tangible reinforcers: pickles, potato chips, prunes, and Popsicles.

The behavior-shaping intervention was initiated on a daily basis for 30 minutes during the preschool sessions that Stephen attended at a local school. The effectiveness of the intervention was to be evaluated by means of direct observation of the behavior-shaping sessions and the boy's activities in the preschool classroom with his teacher and playmates.

Shaping began with undifferentiated, inconsistent verbal responses. Within a single school year Stephen had progressed to initiating some verbal exchanges with others in both the shaping sessions and the preschool class. By the end of the year he would ask his teacher for milk, juice, cookies, toys, and the like. Although he seldom played with his classmates, he did verbally object to their attempts to confiscate his toys and snacks.

Stephen's ascent up the behavior-shaping ladder is presented in Figure 4.1. The steps of the ladder are self-explanatory with the possible exception of steps 3 and 4. During these steps Stephen consistently used specific verbal noises in place of words. For example, "ah" was used for the word "milk," "eh" was used for the word "no," and the like. Emphasis here was put on converting these emissions into meaningful words. ■

Prompting

Children often need special assistance during the behavior change process. This special assistance may be manual or verbal and is called *prompting*. Prompts may include such activities as guiding a child's hand or foot in the completion of a task, moving the child's head to gain his or her attention, talking a child through a task by repeated precise verbal instruction, providing a verbal model for imitation, and providing printed or three-dimensional material that structures a task (Schloss, 1986). Prompts are used to increase the probabilities of success in a task. Although discussed here as it is applied in shaping, prompting is applicable with several behavior change interventions discussed in this chapter and Chapter 5.

Initiates verbal exchange with teacher	10	← Target behavior
Initiates verbal exchamge with therapist	9	
Initiates two or more–word exchanges	8	
Initiates one-word exchange	7	
Gives two or more–word responses	6	
Gives one-word response	5	
Gives second-level approximations	4	
Gives first-level approximations	3	
Emits undifferentiated consistent verbal noise	2	
Emits undifferentiated inconsistent verbal noise	1	← Baseline behavior

(Left margin: Direction of desired behavior ↑)

FIGURE 4.1
Behavior-shaping model (Stephen's verbal behavior).

Although prompts of various kinds may be a necessary component of the behavior change intervention initially, they must eventually be eliminated; the child must learn to complete the task independently. The gradual elimination of prompts is called *fading* (Panyan, 1980). Fading includes the reduction of the amount and quality of manual guidance, verbal assistance, and/or printed or three-dimensional material used to structure an activity.

EXAMPLE
■ Marie, a 6-year-old child, was enrolled in a motor therapy program in an effort to remediate her physical coordination problems. One of the objectives of her program was walking a 10-foot balance beam without assistance.

During the therapy program's assessment phase, Marie fell off the balance beam seven times in her effort to walk its length unaided. It was decided that during the initial stages of her motor therapy Marie would be manually guided by a therapist. He would hold her right hand as she walked the beam.

With manual guidance Marie learned to walk the 10-foot beam with efficiency within a few days. The therapist decided to fade the prompt (manual guidance) and applied the following schedule during the fading process:

1. The therapist reduced the firmness of his grasp on Marie's right hand.
2. The therapist grasped only one finger of Marie's hand.
3. The therapist positioned his hand in progressive steps approximately 6, 9, and 12 inches from Marie's right hand.
4. The therapist walked beside Marie with his hands at his side.
5. The therapist withdrew to the position he normally assumed to observe a person's efficiency on the balance beam. ■

An example of the use and elimination of a prompt can also be seen in the previous example of Jeff (p. 97).

Contingency Contracting

When one considers contemporary emphasis on deferred payment purchasing and organized crime in modern communications media, one believes that every child should have some idea of the meaning of a contract. A *contract* is an agreement, written or verbal, between two or more parties, individuals, or groups that stipulates the responsibilities of the parties concerning a specific item or activity. Contingency contracting in behavior modification parlance was well defined by Becker (1979) when he stated, "Arrange the conditions so that the child gets to do something he wants to do following something you want him to do."

We are all parties to contracts in daily living. Some of us are fortunate enough to have a written contract stating the terms of employment. This contract explains what duties we are to perform, for what period of time, and for what compensation. If we perform as specified in the contract, we cannot be fired under normal circumstances. A verbal contract exists between spouses. The terms of the contract state that they will love, honor, and respect one another until death (or divorce) does them part.

There are many lesser contracts in American society, such as home loans, loans on new automobiles, boats, and the like. Contracts such as these are indispensable to the efficient operation of the business system.

There are some contracts, seldom written, that are often taken for granted but nevertheless are indispensable in a complex urban society. Among these unwritten contracts are trust arrangements with the sanitation service that the rubbish will be collected on certain mornings, the lights will go on when we turn a switch, or the water will flow when we open a faucet.

The use of contingency contracting as a behavior modification technique is based on a principle developed by Premack (1965). Premack's principle states: "A behavior that has a high rate of occurrence can be used to increase a behavior with a low rate of occurrence." What Premack stated was a very ancient and frequently used principle. For centuries people have applied this principle to raising their children, teaching their students, and supervising their employees. *If you do X, then you can do or get Y.* This principle has often been referred to as "Grandma's law." Most persons remember the power of this law from childhood:

☐ "Eat your spinach; then you can have some ice cream."
☐ "Clean your room; then you can go to the movies."
☐ "Cut the lawn; then you can use the car."

This same principle carries over to adult life:

☐ "Write 27 articles and 10 books; then you will be promoted to professor."

☐ "Don't join the union; then you will retain your job."
☐ "Don't make waves on the bureaucratic sea of calm; then you will be granted tenure."

Table 4.2 presents a series of *X* and *Y* statements found in the classroom.

Within the last two decades teachers and parents have recognized the significance of individual differences caused by such factors as maturation, general knowledge, locus of control, and experience. Various instructional programs have been developed in response to these differences. Contingency contracting is one method that can be used to individualize instruction and behavior control to respond to the child's interest, needs, and abilities; it can be applied to the cognitive, affective, and psychomotor domains of learning.

The advantages of contingency contracting are many. The method is positive; that is, the child takes an active role in deciding the type and amount of work required. Consequently personal responsibilities are understood by the child. At regular intervals the contract is reviewed for the child's reaffirmation. Accountability factors are built into this intervention. The teacher collects empirical data that indicate where the child was, where the child has progressed, and the child's current needs. The teacher can use this information to develop the program, instructional objectives, and developmental objectives with the child.

The teacher serves as contract manager, providing facts and explaining the principles. The teacher encourages the child to choose realistic goals and desirable reinforcers and keeps the ratio of task to reinforcer within realistic limits. The teacher ensures that both the task and the reinforcer are fair to both parties of the contract (child and teacher).

When contingency contracting is first used with a child, small tasks and small reinforcers are most effective because they encourage frequent reinforcement. Lengthy or complex tasks and small reinforcers are unfair and defeat the motivational factors inherent in this intervention. If the task is more demanding than the reinforcer is desirable, the learner is not sufficiently motivated to perform. Likewise, the reinforcer should not be greater than the task warrants; otherwise the instructional objective established for the child is difficult to obtain.

Initially contracts may encourage and reward approximations of desired behavior. Short work periods are desirable because they permit frequent reinforcement. Low-achieving children usually require immediate reinforcers; consequently short-term

TABLE 4.2
X, then Y, statements

X	Then	Y
Sit in your seat 2 hours		Get a 10-minute recess
Complete your term paper		Get an A
Be a "good" student		Receive a good report card
Volunteer for the football team		Receive recognition from the cheerleaders
Learn a letter of the alphabet		Immediately receive a gumdrop

contracts (daily) are appropriate. Higher-achieving children can usually delay reinforcements; therefore long-term contracts (1 or 2 weeks) are feasible.

Some practitioners believe it is beneficial to separate the locations for task performance and reinforcer delivery. In this way the learner equates the task performance as a means to a desirable end, that is, going to the reinforcement area. This also broadens the type and variety of reinforcers that can be made available to the students. Teachers are encouraged to establish a reinforcement area in their classroom. The establishment of reinforcement areas is discussed later in this chapter.

The teacher must encourage the child to adhere to the contract for the designated period of time. The child should be cautioned that if the agreed-on task is not performed, the child will not receive the reinforcer. However, if the original contract is too difficult, a new contract must be written for the learner to perform successfully. However, every effort should be made to ensure the success of the original contract.

The underlying principle of contingency contracting is constant: the learner, by making decisions concerning personal productivity, develops critical thinking skills, self-control, and the independence that increases productivity (Hall & Hall, 1982).

There are two types of contracts applicable in the classroom setting: verbal and written. Educators have generally found verbal contracts more useful than written contracts. The following are examples of verbal contracts that can be used in the classroom:

- ☐ "John, when you have completed 8 addition problems correctly, you may play with the puzzles."
- ☐ "Mary, if you remain in your seat for 5 minutes, you may work in your coloring book."
- ☐ "James, if you come to school on time tomorrow, you may be first in line for lunch."
- ☐ "Tom, if you don't hit anyone this morning, you may have an extra milk at lunch."
- ☐ "Mike, if you complete your seat work, you may watch 'Sesame Street' on television."

Verbal contracts such as these are made daily in the classroom. They work effectively for both the teacher and the child.

Written contracts are more elaborate than verbal contracts. The elaborateness of the written contract depends on the child for whom it is designed. Contracts frequently lose their effectiveness when they include pseudolegal jargon such as "the parties of the first part," "the party of the second part," or "henceforth and forevermore." It is recommended that the teacher or parent use the contract format in Figure 4.2 or a similar one. An additional copy of the contract is provided in the back of the text.

Homme and others (1979) have suggested ten basic rules for writing a contract for classroom use. These rules are:

1. The contract payoff (reinforcer) should be immediate.
2. Initially contracts should call for and reinforce approximations of target behavior.

Date _____

Contract

This is an agreement between _____
Child's name

and _____. The contract begins on
Teacher's name

_____ and ends on _____. It will be re-
Date   Date

viewed on _____ .
Date

The terms of the agreement are:

Child will _____

_____

_____

_____

Teacher will _____

_____

_____

_____

If the child fulfills his or her part of the contract, the child will receive the agreed-on reward from the teacher. However, if the child fails to fulfill his or her part of the contract, the
rewards will be withheld.

Child's signature _____

Teacher's signature _____

FIGURE 4.2
Contingency contract.

3. The contract should provide for frequent reinforcers in small amounts.
4. The contract should call for and reinforce accomplishments rather than just obe-
   dience.
5. The performance should be reinforced after it occurs.
6. The contract must be fair to both parties.
7. The terms of the contract must be clear.

8. The contract must be honest.
9. The contract must be positive.
10. Contracting must be used systematically as an integral part of the on-going class-room program.

In addition to the preceding rules, the practitioner should consider the following factors when developing and implementing a contract:

1. The contract must be negotiated and freely agreed on by both child and teacher.
2. The contract must include the target achievement or production level.
3. The reinforcer must be consistently delivered in accordance with the terms of the contract.
4. The contract must include the date for review and renegotiation.

One of the major functions of contingency contracting is to get children to the level of development at which they will initiate a contract instead of waiting for suggestions from the teacher.

The key to successful contracting is a negotiation session during which (1) the system of contracting is explained and discussed, (2) the contract is written, and (3) the contract is signed by the child and the teacher.

Negotiation should be systematic and precise. The teacher, as manager, has an obligation to ensure that the session is productive. It is recommended that the new practitioner use the following negotiation procedure (Shea et al., 1974):

1. Teacher establishes and maintains rapport with the child.
2. Teacher explains the purpose of the meeting by saying something such as, "I know you've been working hard on your schoolwork [reading, writing, spelling, arithmetic], and I'd like to help you."
3. Teacher gives a simple definition of a contract, explaining that a contract is an agreement between two people.
   a. Teacher gives an example of a contract such as: "When your mother takes your TV to the repair shop, the clerk gives her a ticket. The ticket is a contract between your mother and the repairman. He will repair and return the TV, and your mother will pay him."
   b. Teacher asks the child to give an example of a contract.
   c. If child cannot respond, the teacher gives another example and repeats 3b, above.
4. Teacher explains to the child that they are going to write a contract.
5. Teacher and child discuss tasks.
   a. Child suggests tasks for the contract.
   b. Teacher suggests tasks for the contract.
   c. Child and teacher discuss and agree on the specific task.
6. Teacher and child discuss reinforcers.
   a. Teacher asks the child which activities the child enjoys doing and which things he or she likes (see Chapter 3). The teacher may also suggest reinforcers.

   b. Teacher writes a reinforcer menu of child-suggested reinforcers.

   c. Child selects reinforcers for which he or she would like to work.

   d. Teacher and child rank the reinforcers in the child's order of preference.

7. Teacher and child negotiate the ratio of task to reinforcer.

8. Teacher and child agree on the time to be allotted for the child to perform the task; for example, the child works 10 addition problems in 15 minutes to receive the reinforcer, or the child completes a unit of science and does the laboratory experiments in 2 weeks to receive an A.

9. Teacher and child identify the criteria for achievement; that is, the child will work the 10 addition problems in 15 minutes with at least 80% accuracy.

10. Teacher and child discuss evaluation procedures.

   a. Teacher discusses various types of evaluations with the child.

   b. Teacher and child agree on a method of evaluation.

   c. Teacher asks the child to explain the method of evaluation. If the child appears confused, the teacher clarifies the evaluation procedure.

11. Teacher and child negotiate delivery of the reinforcer.

12. Teacher and child agree on a date for renegotiation of the contract.

13. Teacher or child writes the contract. If feasible, the child should be encouraged to write it. Teacher gives a copy of the contract to the child.

14. Teacher reads the contract to the child as the child follows on his or her own copy.

15. Teacher elicits the child's verbal affirmation to the contract terms and gives affirmation.

16. Child and teacher sign the contract.

17. Teacher congratulates the child for making the contract and wishes the child success.

A properly conducted negotiating session is complex and time consuming, particularly if the teacher has not previously introduced the concept of contracting in the classroom. As an aid to reducing confusion on the part of the teacher or the child and in an effort to facilitate the negotiation process, a contract work sheet is provided (see Figure 4.3). A copy of the work sheet is provided in the back of the text.

The left-hand column of the work sheet should be checked as the practitioner and child complete each of the specified tasks. The tasks to be accomplished are specified in the middle column. The tasks are presented in logical order. It is strongly recommended that the order of presentation be followed during the session. The right-hand column of the work sheet is reserved for comments and notations.

Three examples of contracts drawn from classroom experience are found in Figures 4.4–4.6.

Contracts need not be as formal as suggested by the above procedures. Many home and school situations are responsive to less formal contracts. Examples of less formal contracts, developed by Kaplan and Hoffman (1981), are shown in Figures 4.7–4.11.

Contract Work Sheet

Child _____

Teacher _____ Date _____

(X)	Tasks	Comments
( )	1. Establish and maintain rapport.	
( )	2. Explain the purpose of the meeting.	
( )	3. Explain a contract.	
( )	4. Give an example of a contract.	
( )	5. Ask the child to give an example of a contract; if there is no response, give another example.	
( )	6. Discuss possible tasks.	
( )	7. Child-suggested tasks: _____ _____ _____ _____	
( )	8. Teacher-suggested tasks: _____ _____ _____ _____	
( )	9. Agree on the task.	
( )	10. Ask the child what activities he or she enjoys and what items he or she wishes to possess.	
( )	11. Record child-suggested reinforcers.	
( )	12. Negotiate the ratio of the task to the reinforcer.	

FIGURE 4.3
Sample work sheet for contract negotiation.

Contract Work Sheet—cont'd		

(X)	Tasks	Comments
( )	13. Identify the time allotted for the task.	
( )	14. Identify the criterion or achievement level.	
( )	15. Discuss methods of evaluation.	
( )	16. Agree on the method of evaluation.	
( )	17. Restate and clarify the method of evaluation.	
( )	18. Negotiate the delivery of the reinforcer.	
( )	19. Set the date for renegotiation.	
( )	20. Write two copies of the contract.	
( )	21. Read the contract to the child.	
( )	22. Elicit the child's verbal affirmation and give your own affirmation.	
( )	23. Sign the contract and have the child sign it.	
( )	24. Congratulate the child (and yourself).	

FIGURE 4.3, *continued*

Token Economy

When most of us think of learning, we recall our participation in formal educational systems, which involved acquiring knowledge by listening to teachers, having discussions, taking tests, and the like. This symbolic or verbal learning is essential to our development, but it is not the only kind of learning in which we participate. Human nature permits us to learn directly from experiences in our environment. It is through learning that we develop habitual ways of working our environment for our reinforcers, that is, to obtain and sustain pleasure and to avoid discomfort and pain.

Although they differ in some ways, all learning environments are similar in that they are worked for reinforcers. Reinforcers may be defined as stimuli that induce changes in the person. These are positive reinforcers if they induce a pleasant state and nega-

Date ___*February 3, 1988*___

Contract

This is an agreement between ___*Bob Wellrock*___ and ___*Mr. Bare*___. The contract
　　　　　　　　　　　　　　　　　　　Child's name　　　　　　　Teacher's name

begins on ___*2/8/88*___ and ends on ___*2/10/88*___. It will be reviewed on ___*2/9/88*___.
　　　　　　　Date　　　　　　　　　　　Date　　　　　　　　　　　　　　　　　Date

The terms of the agreement are:

Child will ___*spell with 90% accuracy the 20 assigned spelling words for Friday.*___

Teacher will ___*provide a ticket good for admission to the school movie on February 10,*___
___*1988*___

If the child fulfills his or her part of the contract, the child will receive the agreed-on
reward from the teacher. However, if the child fails to fulfill his part of the contract, the rewards will be withheld.

Child's signature _____

Teacher's signature _____

FIGURE 4.4
Sample contract.

tive reinforcers if they induce an aversive or painful state. Generally we work the environment to acquire positive reinforcers and to avoid or escape negative reinforcers.
Learning occurs by discovering behaviors that produce rewards and then repetitively
working the environment to continue to obtain the reward. In general, the strength of a
reinforcer is judged by the magnitude of the change it produces in the individual. The
stronger or more desirable the reinforcers, the more quickly and easily the individual
learns.

Learning environments generally provide feedback process cues that predict the
presentation of delayed reinforcers. The immediacy of feedback, whether it is reinforcement per se or a process cue predictive of later reinforcement, is an important
determinant of the rate of learning. In general, learning occurs more easily and more
rapidly when feedback is immediate.

Learning environments vary in the consistency of feedback that they provide for the
learner; the more consistent the feedback, the more quickly and easily the individual
learns. Learning environments also vary in the degree to which individuals are allowed
to set their own work rate. In other words, some environments allow individuals more
freedom to work at a self-selected rate than others. Individuals learn more easily and
quickly when they are free to set their own pace in working the environment for the
desired reinforcer (Ayllon & McKittrick, 1982).

Date _____ *April 5, 1988* _____

Contract

This is an agreement between ___*Russell Palmer*___ and ___*Mr. Davis*___. The contract
　　　　　　　　　　　　　　　　Child's name　　　　　　　　Teacher's name

begins on ___*4/8/88*___ and ends on ___*4/13/88*___. It will be reviewed on ___*4/11/88*___.
　　　　　　　Date　　　　　　　　　　Date　　　　　　　　　　　　　　　Date

The terms of the agreement are:

Child will ___*not engage in any fights during the school day for the period of the contract.*___

Teacher will ___*take the child to a Golden Gloves boxing match at the local arena.*___

If the child fulfills his or her part of the contract, the child will receive the agreed-on reward from the teacher. However, if the child fails to fulfill his part of the contract, the rewards will be withheld.

Child's signature _____

Teacher's signature _____

FIGURE 4.5
Sample contract.

Many children are not able to function appropriately if they must wait an extended time for their reinforcer. In addition, there are some children who have not developed to the level at which social rewards alone are satisfactory reinforcers. In these cases the use of a token economy has proved to be an effective behavior change intervention.

The tokens are usually valueless to the children when originally introduced to them. Their value becomes apparent as the children learn that tokens can be exchanged for a variety of reinforcers, such as being first in the lunch line, getting 10 minutes of free time, listening to phonograph records, watching television, purchasing a favored toy, and so on. This versatility makes the token system superior to many interventions.

It is an accepted fact that the child who is first in line for lunch today may not wish to be first in line next week. A properly administered token economy adjusts to this human tendency by providing a variety of rewards, that is, a reward menu.

When the teacher "sells" admission to a movie, use of Play-doh, or the like, the tokens rapidly take on value for the children. When the teacher states the price and asks a child to count out the needed quantity of tokens, they are engaged in a token economy.

Date _____ *March 7, 1988* _____

Contract

This is an agreement between _____ *Tom Hawk* _____ and _____ *Mr. George* _____ . The contract

Child's name   Teacher's name

begins on ____ *3/10/88* ____ and ends on ____ *3/30/88* ____ . It will be reviewed on ____ *3/28/88* ____ .

Date   Date   Date

The terms of the agreement are:

Child will ____ *participate in a teacher-prescribed physical education program for 30 minutes*

a day during the period of the contract. _____

Teacher will ____ *provide one out-of-town basketball trip and admission to the game.* _____

If the child fulfills his or her part of the contract, the child will receive the agreed-on reward from the teacher. However, if the child fails to fulfill his part of the contract, the rewards will be withheld.

Child's signature _____

Teacher's signature _____

FIGURE 4.6
Sample contract.

In this manner the tokens become potent reinforcers. They can be awarded over a period of time for acceptable academic and nonacademic work. The system allows the teacher to structure the learning environment for positive reinforcement and to provide immediate feedback to the children via tokens. Hence, a moderately well run token exchange can promote direct learning regardless of the content of the activity.

We are all exposed to and use tokens daily. The most common form of token exchange is the use of currency to purchase various items and services. It is generally agreed (especially in today's economy) that money itself has no value; only the objects for which it is exchanged have real value. In the classroom the token takes on the same meaning as currency has in the marketplace.

The classroom token economy suffers the same problems as the marketplace economy, that is, loss, theft, and counterfeiting. Some of these problems can be prevented by not using poker chips and other readily available objects for tokens.

For instance, what would you do if Joel came to your classroom every morning with his pockets filled with poker chips? Not only is Joel selling the chips to his classmates, but they are constantly dropping them on the floor—a very distracting practice.

Contract Your Way

Out of a

If I can squeeze through

_____

_____

_____

by _____
   (date)

then I will have a clean start to_____

_____

_____

| _____ | _____ | _____ |
| Squeezer | Squeezee | Date |

FIGURE 4.7
Informal contract between student and teacher.
(From Kaplan, P., and Hoffman, A. It's absolutely groovy. Denver: Love Publishing Co., 1981.)

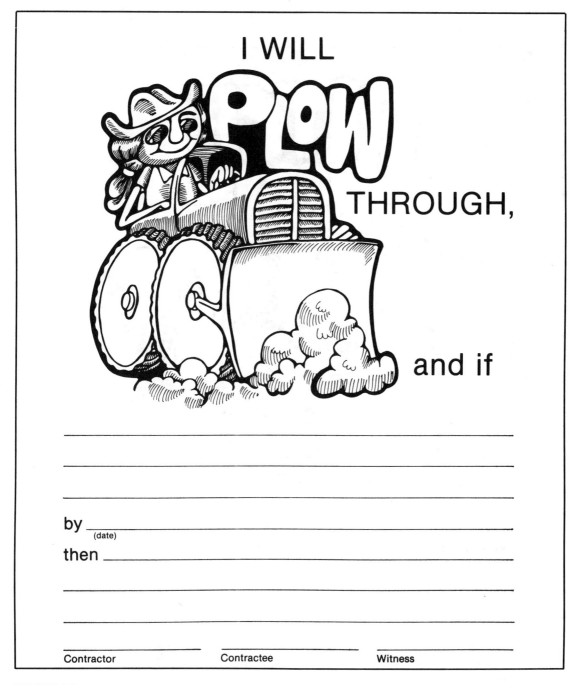

FIGURE 4.8
Informal contract between student and teacher.
(From Kaplan, P., and Hoffman, A. It's absolutely groovy. Denver: Love Publishing Co., 1981.)

_____ and _____
will

and help each other to

_____

_____ by _____
(date)

When we are done, we will be able to _____

_____

_____

_____   _____
Friend #1   Friend #2

_____   _____   _____
Witness   Contractor   Date

FIGURE 4.9
Informal contract between students.
(From Kaplan, P., and Hoffman, A. It's absolutely groovy. *Denver: Love Publishing Co., 1981.)*

I hereby agree to help

_____

OUT OF A PICKLE

by

_____

_____

on or before _____
When this pickle of a problem is
solved, we will be able to

_____

_____

_____

_____   _____
Pickle #1   Pickle #2

_____   _____
Pickler   Date

I hereby

AGREE

to

_____

_____

_____

To do this, I will need _____

_____

_____

When I deliver the finished
product, I will receive _____

_____

_____

_____

_____   _____
Builder   Supplier

FIGURE 4.10
Informal contracts.
(From Kaplan, P., and Hoffman, A. It's absolutely groovy. *Denver: Love Publishing Co., 1981.)*

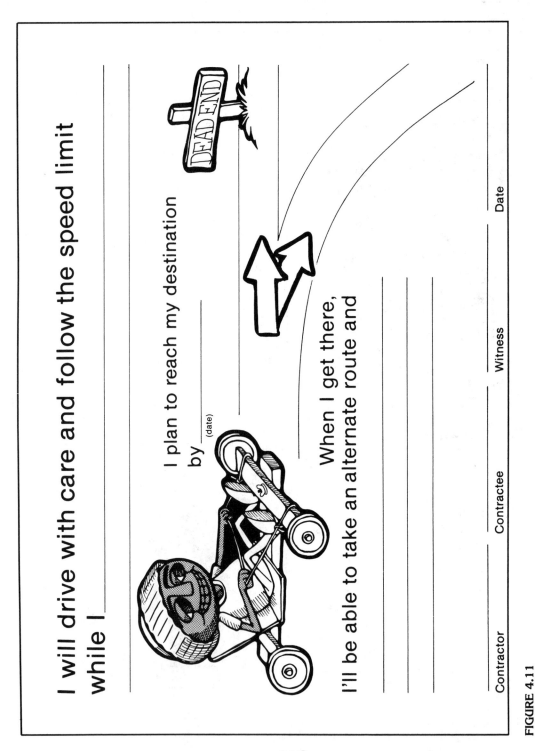

I will drive with care and follow the speed limit while I _____

I plan to reach my destination by _____
(date)

When I get there, I'll be able to take an alternate route and _____

Contractor	Contractee	Witness

Date _____

FIGURE 4.11
Informal contract.
(From Kaplan, P., and Hoffman, A. It's absolutely groovy. Denver: Love Publishing Co., 1981.)

116

Items that could be used instead of poker chips include:

Check marks	Conservation stamps
Points	Trading stamps
Stars	Animal stickers
Smiling faces	Fairy tale character stickers
Point cards	Teacher-made tokens
Point tally forms	Play money

These tokens have several advantages over tokens made of rigid, hard materials such as metal, plastic, and wood. They are made of soft, flexible materials, that is, paper, vinyl, or simple pen and pencil markings. They are less distracting to have in the classroom atmosphere because they neither rattle nor make noise if dropped on a hard surface. These characteristics eliminate much potential and actual distraction and confusion in the classroom. The tokens are easily glued to a paper, desk top, record card, or chart. They can be permanently affixed to various surfaces to minimize the incidence of misplacement, loss, or theft. However, they must be sufficiently distinctive to prohibit unauthorized duplication.

The basic rules applied when establishing a token economy system for the classroom are:

1. Select a target behavior. This topic is thoroughly discussed in Chapter 2 and does not warrant further elaboration here.
2. Conceptualize and present the target behavior to the child or group. It is a well-known fact that an emphasis on "what you can do" is more palatable to children than an emphasis on "what you cannot do." Many unsuccessful behavior modification practitioners have determined their own failure by introducing a program by saying. "Now you boys and girls are going to stop that noise and fooling around in here. I have this new ... [and so on]." The children are immediately challenged; they prepare to defeat the teacher and defend their personal integrity.
3. Post the rules and review them frequently.
4. Select an appropriate token.
5. Establish reinforcers for which tokens can be exchanged.
6. Develop a reward menu and post it in the classroom. The children should be permitted to thoroughly discuss and consider the items on the menu. They should be encouraged to make their selections from among the items available. The children should not be permitted to debate the cost (number of tokens) of the various rewards after prices have been established.
7. Implement the token economy. Introduce the token economy on a limited basis initially. A complex sophisticated system as an initial exposure confuses and frustrates the children. *Start small and build on firm understanding.* Explain the system to the children with great clarity and precision. Be patient and answer all the children's questions. It is better to delay implementation than create confusion and frustration.

8. Provide immediate reinforcement for acceptable behavior. The children will lose interest in the program if the process for obtaining the tokens is more effort than the reward is desirable. Many systems fail because the teacher neglects to dispense tokens at the appropriate time. Rewarding the children immediately reduces frustration and overconcern with the system. When the children are sure they will receive the tokens at the proper time, they can ignore the delivery system and concentrate on their work or behavior.

9. Gradually change from a continuous to a variable schedule of reinforcement. As discussed in Chapter 2, quick, unpredictable, or premature changes in a reinforcement schedule can destroy the program.

10. Provide time for the children to exchange tokens for rewards. If the token economy is a legitimate class program, time during the school day should be made available for the exchange. Time should not be taken from the children's recess, lunch, or free time.

11. Revise the reward menu frequently. Children, like adults, become bored with the same old fare day after day.

The token economy has worked very effectively in the classroom. Two reasons for its success are its lack of emphasis on competition with others and the fact that the reward menu provides sufficient variety to prevent boredom.

Table 4.3 is an example of a reward menu for classroom use.

The menu need not be lengthy or elaborate but should contain at least 10 items and activities. The children should exchange their tokens daily; they should not be allowed to take them home. If they are deferring their reinforcers and saving tokens for long-range ones, their tokens should be collected and recorded each day.

The number of tokens earned may be recorded on a point card or tally form. The teacher can affix the card or form to each child's desk and then either record or circle the points earned by the child. The points are totaled at the end of each day. The child may either delay the reward or accept it immediately.

TABLE 4.3
Reward menu

Reward	Time	Cost (Points)
Getting free time	10 minutes	20
Watching television	30 minutes	45
Reading comic books	5 minutes	15
Listening to records	10 minutes	20
Cutting and pasting	5 minutes	10
Purchasing modeling clay	—	55
Purchasing crayons	—	45
Purchasing coloring books	—	50
Finger painting	12 minutes	25
Playing with toys	10 minutes	25
Borrowing a book	48 hours	35
Borrowing a game	48 hours	50

Examples of the point card and tally form to be used for specific behaviors are presented in Figures 4.12 and 4.13.

The teacher, with little difficulty, may plan and implement a multipurpose token economy in the classroom. In this situation the children earn tokens for a variety of appropriate behaviors as well as academic effort and academic success.

Tokens or points can be presented to the child for any or all of the following behaviors:

☐ Being present at the work station on time.
☐ Having appropriate work tools available for use.
☐ Attending to the instructor's directions.
☐ Exhibiting appropriate social behavior during the work period (raising hand for attention, remaining at the work station, not talking without permission).
☐ Engaging in the assigned work task during the work period (that is, showing effort).
☐ Correctly or satisfactorily completing the assigned work task.
☐ Returning or storing work tools to their appropriate place.

Tokens are presented for various appropriate behaviors and withheld for inappropriate behaviors.

A point card for a multipurpose token economy is presented in Figure 4.14. Copies of each of the forms for recording points in a token economy are provided in the back of the text.

Point Card*

Child's name _____ Date _____

1	2	3	4	5	6	7	8	9	10
11	12	13	14	15	16	17	18	19	20
21	22	23	24	25	26	27	28	29	30
31	32	33	34	35	36	37	38	39	40
41	42	43	44	45	46	47	48	49	50
51	52	53	54	55	56	57	58	59	60
61	62	63	64	65	66	67	68	69	70
71	72	73	74	75	76	77	78	79	80
81	82	83	84	85	86	87	88	89	90
91	92	93	94	95	96	97	98	99	100

*Teacher circles the cumulative total.

FIGURE 4.12
Point card for specific behavior.

Point Tally Form

Child _____ Date _____

Monday												
Tuesday												
Wednesday												
Thursday												
Friday												

TOTAL

Monday	
Tuesday	
Wednesday	
Thursday	
Friday	
Week	

FIGURE 4.13
Tally form for specific behavior.

120

Point Card for Multipurpose Token Economy

Child _____ Day _____ Date _____

Work period	Readiness	Social behavior	Work effort	Work success	Teacher comments
9:00-9:15			*	*	
9:15-10:00					
10:00-10:30					
10:30-10:45			*	*	
10:45-11:30					
11:30-12:00					
12:00-1:00			*	*	
1:00-1:30					
1:30-2:45					
2:45-3:00			*	*	

*Points for work effort and work success are not available during these periods due to the nature of the activity: opening exercises, recess, lunch, and closing exercises.

FIGURE 4.14
Point card with spaces for behavior notation and comments.

EXAMPLES   ■ Mr. Newman, a junior high school math teacher, was having difficulty with Charlie, who had developed the habit of counting and computing aloud while doing math assignments. At first this behavior was not a serious problem, but then it began to distract many of the other students.

Mr. Newman decided to implement a token economy system to modify Charlie's behavior. He discussed the system with the class, established a set of rules, and developed a reward menu before implementing this intervention.

The reward menu is presented in Table 4.4.

The token economy was used with the entire class and effectively modified the behaviors of Charlie and his peers.

Tokens were initially presented on a fixed interval schedule; as the group progressed, however, a variable interval schedule was introduced. Throughout the program Mr. Newman conscientiously paired social rewards with the tokens. ■

■ Two physical education teachers were having problems with student participation in PE class. They were being bombarded with complaints such as headaches, back pains, sore toes, and sore ears. After discussing the token economy system between themselves and with their students, they decided to initiate a program to increase participation. A student delegation aided the teachers in developing the reward menu shown in Table 4.5. ■

■ Mrs. Thomas has been attempting to get Mary, her 16-year-old daughter, to share in the housekeeping. Mrs. Thomas has had very little success.

One day Mary asked if she and three of her friends could go into the city for dinner and the theater. The big evening was to be in 4 weeks. Mrs. Thomas said "yes" if Mary would pay for the trip by helping with the housekeeping. Mrs. Thomas made a list of tasks Mary was responsible for around the house. It included cleaning her room, washing and drying clothes, helping with the cooking, ironing, washing windows, cleaning the bathroom, and so on. Each task was assigned a specific point value. The points could be exchanged for money.

When the time for the trip arrived, Mary had sufficient money for the evening. In addition, she had an improved attitude about helping to take care of the house. ■

TABLE 4.4
Mr. Newman's reward menu

Reward	Time (Minutes)	Cost (Points)
Checkers	10	15
Cards	10	15
Puzzles	15	20
Magazines	18	25
Chess	12	30
Model car kits	10	20
Comic books	5	10
Bingo	15	25
Quiet conversation	10	30

TABLE 4.5
Physical education class reward menu

Reward	Time (Minutes)	Cost (Points)
Getting free time	15	50
Using trampoline	10	40
Shooting baskets	5	30
Acting as activity leader	—	25
Talking with friend	10	40
Playing badminton	10	30
Using trapeze	15	50
Sitting out an activity	—	100

In these three examples the token economy system proved to be effective in increasing participation. In two of the cases the teachers changed the reward menu frequently in cooperation with their students throughout the duration of the program.

Reinforcement Area

A special area may be set aside in the classroom to serve as a reinforcement area. This area should be selected before a behavior change program is implemented and should contain those items needed to provide reinforcers. Among the items may be:

A table and chairs

A rug

Reading material (books, comics, magazines)

Art materials (clay, paint, paper, crayons)

Games (bingo, checkers, chess, cards)

Listening equipment (record player, tape deck)

Viewing equipment (television, slide or filmstrip projector)

For additional examples see the section on reinforcers in Chapter 3.

Obviously, the furnishings, materials, and equipment in a reinforcement area must be selected in response to the age, physical size, developmental levels, and interests of the students using the area. Figure 4.15 is an illustration of a classroom with a reinforcement area.

Modeling

One of the most common forms of human learning is accomplished through the processes of observation and imitation. All parents and teachers can relate a variety of acceptable and unacceptable behaviors exhibited by their children and students that are imitations of their own (the adults') personal acceptable and unacceptable behaviors. This form of learning at various times and by various theorists and practitioners has been called modeling, observational learning, identification, copying, vicarious learning, social facilitation, contagion, role playing, and so on (Bandura, 1969; Striefel, 1981). In this text the term *modeling* is used to describe learning by observation and imitation.

As a behavior change method, modeling is the provision of an individual or group behavior to be imitated by a child. This is one of the oldest and most frequently applied methods of changing behavior.

Mothers and fathers, husbands and wives, and teachers and principals have been suggesting models to their sons, daughters, spouses, and students for generations.

☐   "Be a good boy like your brother John."

FIGURE 4.15
Classroom with reinforcement area.

□ "Why can't you be like George, an excellent father, a great lover, and a good provider?"
□ "Mary, can't you be a good student like Eileen?"
□ "Why can't you behave like the other boys and girls?"

Several state and national organizations exist for the purpose of providing children with an acceptable social model. These organizations provide children with either the direct services of a live model or an abstract model inherent in their program and printed materials. Among these organizations are Big Brother and Big Sister, Boy Scouts and Girl Scouts, 4-H, and Little League.

According to Bandura (1969), Bandura and Walters (1963), and Clarizio and Yelon (1967), exposure to a model has three effects:

1. *Modeling effect or observational learning.* Children may acquire behavior from a model that was not previously a part of their behavioral repertoire. In this situation

the model performs a behavior that is imitated by the child in substantially identical form. Examples of the modeling effect are teaching a nonverbal child to verbalize in imitation of a model and teaching a child signing skills as a method of communication.

2. *Inhibitory and disinhibitory effects.* Modeling is not confined exclusively to the learning of new behaviors as in the modeling effect above. Modeling includes imitating a model for the purpose of disinhibiting or inhibiting a behavior. For example, a child may observe and imitate a peer who is positively reinforced for exhibiting a behavior. Or the child may observe and *not* imitate a peer who is punished or ignored for exhibiting a behavior. In these situations the child may be said to be experiencing the other child's behavior and its consequences vicariously.

3. *Eliciting or response facilitation effect.* In this situation the model's behavior is employed to facilitate the occurrence of a previously learned but dormant behavior from the child. For example, a child may know that it is appropriate to say "Thank you" when given a cookie at snack time. However, this child may not say "Thank you" as a matter of common practice. Appropriate social responsiveness may be facilitated if all the children who receive cookies previous to this child during snack time say "Thank you."

Before implementing a modeling intervention, the teacher or parent should consider the following factors:

1. Is the child able developmentally and cognitively to imitate the model? Practitioners must be cognizant of the fact that some children are simply not ready to use modeling.
2. Will the child be rewarded for imitating the model? Some children are simply not intrinsically rewarded by performing behaviors that others consider acceptable.
3. Is the model "good"? Caution must be taken when a model is being selected for a child. Remember, what the model does in science class may be quite different from what this individual does in English, shop, on the playground, at home, or behind the barn.
4. Is the model acceptable to the child? A model who is too good, too bright, too fast, or just plain obnoxious will be rejected by the child.

Modeling techniques can be effectively applied by teachers in an effort to change behavior only when consideration is given to the above factors.

EXAMPLES　■　Ms. Simpson is a resource teacher of educable mentally handicapped children. Dave and Carl work with Ms. Simpson in the resource room for 1 hour each day. Until recently Dave would usually attempt his assigned tasks, whereas Carl would seldom attempt his assigned work.

It was determined by Ms. Simpson that both boys were reinforced by her attention. Therefore she decided to use her attention as a reward they received for completing their work. Dave was reinforced by Ms. Simpson's attention. She praised him each time he did his class work, attended to the appropriate stimulus, or completed an assigned task; she ignored Carl's inappropriate behavior.

After several sessions during which Dave's behavior was rewarded, Carl began to imitate Dave to receive Ms. Simpson's attention. She immediately reinforced Carl whenever he exhibited the appropriate behavior.

The result of this intervention was a dramatic change in Carl's behavior. He is now completing his work to gain approval from Ms. Simpson. ■

■   Mr. Cohen is an instructor of three boys and one girl in a class for behaviorally disordered children. The students' names are John, James, Charles, and Shirley. Of the four students, Charles is the most troublesome. Charles constantly moves about the room, exhibiting feelings of indignation at assignments and disrupting the activities of Mr. Cohen and his classmates. This behavior occurs throughout the school day. Originally when the behavior occurred, the other children remained busy at their seats. On these occasions, Mr. Cohen would chase after Charles or provide him with attention for the unacceptable behavior he was exhibiting. The acceptable behaviors manifested by Shirley, John, and James were ignored. Lately Shirley, John, and James have begun to move about the room and exhibit behaviors that disturb Mr. Cohen. They are imitating the behavior of Charles.

One can conclude that Shirley, John, and James are modeling Charles' behavior for the purpose of receiving attention from their teacher. ■

In both of these examples the procedure of modeling is effective; in fact, it is effective in developing both appropriate and inappropriate behaviors. The consequence of behavior is again the key factor. Teachers like Mr. Cohen, in the previous example, should be aware that they are models.

In too many classrooms appropriate behavior is taken for granted. Modeling is a potentially effective preventive technique.

SUMMARY

In this chapter the practitioner of behavior modification is provided with an overview of the five most common techniques used to increase appropriate behavior: (1) positive reinforcement, (2) shaping, (3) contingency contracting, (4) the token economy, and (5) modeling.

Positive reinforcement is defined as the process of rewarding an appropriate target behavior to increase the probability that the behavior will be repeated. Also known as positive attention, approval, social reinforcement, and rewarding, this technique requires two things: (1) during the initial stage, the target behavior must be reinforced each time it occurs and (2) when the target behavior is established at a satisfactory rate, it should be reinforced intermittently.

Shaping is the reinforcement of successive approximations of the desired behaviors that have not been previously manifested in the individual's behavioral repertoire. The steps in behavior shaping are (1) selecting a target behavior, (2) collecting baseline data, (3) selecting a reinforcer, (4) reinforcing successive approximations of the desired behavior, (5) reinforcing the approximations immediately and continuously, and (6) changing to a variable reinforcement schedule.

Contingency contracting involves the completion of behavior X before reinforcement Y is given or allowed. This process is actively used in day-to-day living. Contracts may be verbal or written. Verbal contracts are commonly used in schools, but written contracts are more appealing to the reluctant learner. When developing a contract, the practitioner should know the developmental level of the child or children with whom the contract is being negotiated. Contracting is more effective when the child is allowed to share in its development.

A token economy is a system of exchange. Children earn tokens that are exchanged for specific rewards. The tokens themselves are valueless; their value lies in the rewards for which they can be exchanged. There are a number of objects that can be used as tokens, such as check marks, points, smiling faces, stars, and other similar items. An important component of a token economy is the reward menu, which should be developed with the child or group.

Modeling, one of the oldest and most frequently applied methods of behavior change, has been effective in developing appropriate behaviors in children. Modeling is the provision of an individual or group behavior to be imitated or not imitated by the child.

EXERCISES

Quiz

1. The five most common techniques used to increase behavior are _____,

_____, _____, _____,

and _____.

2. The process of providing an example of behavior for imitation is known as _____

_____.

3. Contracts may be either _____ or _____.

4. Another term for reinforcing successive approximations of appropriate behavior

is _____.

5. A schedule of reinforcers is referred to as a reward _____.

6. A method of increasing behaviors that provides an exchange system of reinforcers is the

_____.

7. Mr. O'Shea tells his son, Tim, that when he cleans his bedroom, he can go outside to play.

This is an example of a _____.

8. Mr. Johnson has been rewarding Jim for his good attending behavior. He also rewards Martha, whose previously poor attending behavior has started to improve as a result

of observing Jim being rewarded by Mr. Johnson. He is using an intervention called

_____.

9. Mr. Walker is constantly out-of-sorts and shouting at his wife. His son, Joshua, was reprimanded by the principal yesterday for screaming at his teacher. Joshua is using his father as a _____.

10. When Mary's mother says, "Mary, when you eat your spinach, you can have ice cream," she is making a _____ with Mary.

Projects
1. Select a target behavior to change and describe how you would implement each step of shaping the behavior.
2. Write two examples of modeling as a technique for increasing behaviors.
3. Develop and implement a contract for (a) an individual child in a class and (b) an entire class.
4. Develop a reward menu for your class.
5. Develop a token economy system.

REFERENCES

Ayllon, T., & McKittrick, S. M. (1982). *How to set up a token economy.* Austin, TX: Pro-Ed.

Bandura, A. (1969). *Principles of behavior modification.* New York: Holt, Rinehart & Winston.

Bandura, A., & Walters, R. H. (1963). *Social learning and personality development.* New York: Holt, Rinehart & Winston.

Becker, W. C. (1979). Introduction. In L. Homme, Csanyi, A. P., Gonzales, A. M., & Rechs, J. R. (Eds.), *How to use contingency contracting in the classroom.* Champaign, IL: Research Press.

Clarizio, H. F., & Yelon, S. L. (1967). Learning theory approaches to classroom management: Rationale and intervention techniques. *Journal of Special Education, 1,* 267–274.

Hall, R. V., & Hall, M. C. (1982). *How to negotiate behavioral contracts.* Austin, TX: Pro-Ed.

Homme, L., Csanyi, A. P., Gonzales, M. A., & Rechs, J. R. (1979). *How to use contingency contracting in the classroom.* Champaign, IL: Research Press.

Kaplan, P. G., & Hoffman, A. G. (1981). *It's absolutely groovy.* Denver: Love Publishing Co.

Neisworth, J. T., Deno, S. L., & Jenkins, J. R. (1969). *Student motivation and classroom management: A behavioristic approach.* Newark, DE: Behavior Technics.

Panyan, M. C. (1980). *How to use shaping.* Austin, TX: Pro-Ed.

Premack, D. (1965). Reinforcement theory. In D. LeVine (Ed.), *Nebraska symposium on motivation.* Lincoln: University of Nebraska Press.

Schloss, P. J. (1986). Sequential prompt instruction for mildly handicapped learners. *Teaching Exceptional Children, 18*(3), 181–184.

Shea, T. M., & Bauer, A. M. (1987). *Teaching children and youth with behavior disorders, Second edition.* Englewood Cliffs, NJ: Prentice-Hall.

Shea, T. M., Whiteside, W. R., Beetner, E. G., & Lindsey, D. L. (1974). *Contingency contracting in the classroom.* Edwardsville: Southern Illinois University.

Striefel, S. (1981). *How to teach through modeling and imitation.* Austin, TX: Pro-Ed.

CHAPTER FIVE

Methods of Decreasing Behavior

Mrs. Hamilton dreaded coming to school today. It is raining, and her fourth-grade students will have to remain inside during recess. When the students do not get to go outside for recess, they seem to go crazy. As the recess period approaches, they become increasingly disruptive.

On this day, when the recess period arrives, Mrs. Hamilton tells the students that they are to engage in silent reading. They can choose any book from the classroom library. With little enthusiasm each student selects a book. Within 5 minutes the disruptive behavior begins. Charlie pinches George; Mary reports that Mike is pulling her hair; Fred and Martin are using their desks as drums; Gloria is blowing kisses at Larry; Sharon, Pat, and Carol are giggling; Walter is asleep; Mrs. Hamilton is angry.

Maybe if Mrs. Hamilton knew something about methods of decreasing disruptive behavior, her rainy day recesses could be filled with sunshine.

Mr. Bell hates teaching, schools, students, other teachers, and most of all, his principal, whom he refers to as "the superintendent's flunky." Mr. Bell never wanted to be a teacher. But after failing premed, prelaw, and biology, his college advisor counseled him into education. After completing college, Mr. Bell planned to teach a year or two and begin another career. That was 15 years ago.

At Washington High School where he teaches physical science he is viewed as the most negative person on the faculty. His colleagues tend to avoid him, especially in the faculty lounge, because of his constant complaining. He complains about the following: the school not being clean; teachers trying to act as young as their students; how dumb the students are; the limited exposure the faculty has to the world; a lack of materials with which to work; crime on the streets; drugs; sex; athletic program expenses; overpaid administrators; the do-nothing union; school board members being afraid of the superintendent; and so on.

Maybe if the faculty and principal knew something about methods of decreasing unacceptable behavior, the teacher's lounge would provide a positive and relaxing environment.

During the course of a single school day a teacher may observe a number of behaviors that may either be decreased in frequency or eliminated. Examples of behaviors he or she may observe are:

☐ Rusty's incessant talking
☐ Richard's constant bullying
☐ Mary's endless complaining
☐ Barbara's inability to keep her hands off things and people
☐ Martin's thumb sucking

In this chapter six methods of decreasing and eliminating behavior are discussed and exemplified. These are (1) extinction, (2) time-out, (3) satiation, (4) punishment, (5) reinforcement of incompatible behaviors, and (6) desensitization.

Extinction

The discontinuation or withholding of the reinforcer of a behavior that has previously been reinforcing it is called *extinction*. This process is also known as systematic ignoring (Hall & Hall, 1980). (This process is also discussed in Chapter 2.)

EXAMPLE
■ Timmy was constantly attempting to obtain Mr. Calm's attention in class by jumping up and down in his seat, frantically waving his hand, and whispering in a loud voice, "Mr. Calm, Mr. Calm, me, me, I know."

Mr. Calm knew he would have to change his name to Mr. Storm if this behavior did not stop or at least decrease in frequency. In an effort to retain his composure and aid Timmy, he commenced to study the situation.

Baseline observation data indicated that Timmy exhibited the target behavior an average of 8 times per day, or 40 times during the 1-week baseline data-collecting phase. During this phase Mr. Calm also collected data on his personal overt reactions to the unacceptable behavior. He discovered that 90% of the time he responded to the behavior by either permitting Timmy to answer the question, telling the child to be quiet and sit still, or signaling his disapproval nonverbally. Regardless of his specific reaction, Mr. Calm realized that he was *attending* to Timmy's attention-getting behavior.

Mr. Calm devised an intervention whereby he *would not* reinforce the behavior with his attention and would thus extinguish it. He would only respond to Timmy when he was exhibiting acceptable behavior in response to questions directed to the class.

As indicated in Figure 5.1, the behavior was extinguished within 2 weeks, although there were brief periods of regression thereafter.

Timmy's behavior (attempts to obtain attention) increased during the days immediately following the implementation of the intervention. This increase in the target behavior appeared to be an attempt by the child to defend his method for obtaining attention against the loss of effectiveness. This phenomenon is discussed in detail in Chapter 2, and the reader is referred to that section for further clarification. ■

As demonstrated in the case of Timmy, extinction techniques, when properly applied, result in a gradual decrease in the target behavior and its eventual elimination.

Extinction is only as effective as the teacher or parent is consistent and persistent in implementation of the intervention. The most effective approach to extinguishing behavior that has been previously reinforced is ignoring that behavior. This is easier said than done. Most of us are conditioned to the point that we find it difficult to ignore inappropriate behavior. But to ignore a behavior means exactly that—to totally and consistently ignore the target behavior. We are aware that there are some behaviors so serious that they cannot be ignored. However, if the individual is not inflicting pain to himself or others, then extinction may be the intervention of choice.

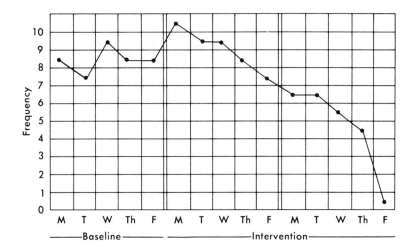

FIGURE 5.1
Frequency of Timmy's attention-getting behavior before and during the intervention.

Some guidelines for those wishing to apply extinction are:

1. When the target behavior is exhibited, remain impassive; give no indication that you are aware of the behavior.
2. Continue whatever activity you are presently doing.
3. If the behavior persists, turn your back and walk away.

A note of caution: In some cases, during the initial stage when a behavior is ignored, it will increase in frequency for a period of time before it begins to decrease. This is called an "extinction burst" and appears to be a natural occurrence when an individual's habitual coping behavior is not receiving the anticipated environmental response.

Time-Out

In general, time-out is the removal of a child from an apparently reinforcing setting to a presumably nonreinforcing setting for a specified and limited period of time. Time-out is "time away from positive reinforcement" (Powell & Powell, 1982). Such removal can effectively decrease a target behavior (Hall & Hall, 1980).

Harris (1985) noted five types of time-out: (1) isolation, (2) exclusion, (3) contingent observation, (4) removal of reinforcing stimulus conditions, and (5) ignoring. Systematic ignoring or extinction is discussed in the previous section. According to Lewellen (1980), there are three types of time-out: (1) observational, (2) exclusion, and (3) seclusion. These three are of the most interest to teachers and parents.

Observational time-out is a procedure in which the student is withdrawn from a reinforcing situation by doing one of the following: (1) placing him or her on the outer perimeter of the activity, where the child can see and hear the activity, but not participate in it, (2) requesting the child to place his or her head on the desk (called "head-down"), (3) removing activity materials, or (4) eliminating or reducing response maintenance stimuli, for example, room illumination.

Exclusion is a procedure in which the student leaves a reinforcing situation to a presumed nonreinforcing situation while remaining in the classroom. The student is not allowed to observe the group. An example is placing a screen between the student and the group.

Seclusion is a procedure that makes use of a "time-out room." In this situation the student leaves the classroom and goes to an isolated room.

EXAMPLE   ■   Benji is a hyperactive child in first grade. The boy was having great difficulty remaining in his seat and refraining from impulsive grabbing of persons and objects near him. He was also appropriating and ingesting his classmates' lunches. Benji's teacher realized that these behaviors were interfering with his classroom progress and that of his classmates. She attempted several procedures to help Benji control the behavior. Among these were verbal reprimands, ignoring the inappropriate behavior and reinforcing appropriate behavior, and peer pressure. Observation data revealed that none of these interventions was effective, although her efforts were sufficient.

A behavior management consultant observed Benji and recommended time-out as a potentially effective intervention. Together, the teacher and the consultant decided that *each time Benji left his seat, he was to be sent to time-out for 2 minutes.*

This intervention necessitated defining and specifying several factors:

1. Out-of-seat behavior was defined as any time Benji's posterior was not in contact with his chair.
2. When the unacceptable behavior did occur, the teacher's aide was to escort Benji to the time-out area. Benji was to remain in time-out for 2 minutes; during this time he had to be quiet and seated.
3. After the time-out period Benji would return to the group. There would be no discussion or reprimand.
4. Benji's desk and chair were relocated in the classroom to ensure that he would not participate in unacceptable behavior such as grabbing people and lunches without leaving his seat.
5. A time-out area with a chair was arranged in the corner of the classroom. The time-out area was constructed by rearranging two 5-drawer filing cabinets. A chair was provided outside the area for the aide, who was to monitor Benji whenever he was in time-out.

The intervention was imposed, and although the behavior did not decrease immediately, significant progress was observed during the first months, as indicated in Figure 5.2 and 5.3.

Benji's out-of-seat behavior was brought under control within a period of several months. However, it remains an occasional problem; therefore time-out procedures remain in effect.   ■

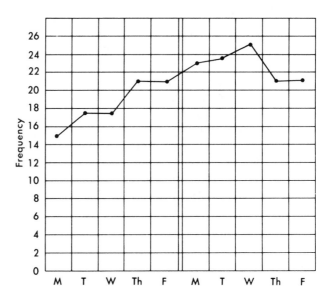

FIGURE 5.2
Frequency of Benji's out-of-seat behavior before and during the first week of intervention.

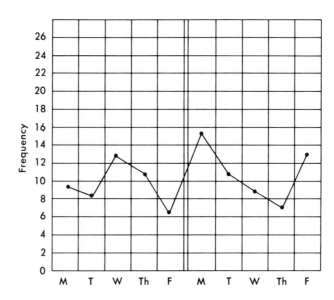

FIGURE 5.3
Frequency of Benji's out-of-seat behavior during the fourth and fifth weeks of intervention.

The time-out intervention includes the reinforcement of acceptable behavior. A child who is performing or approximating the desired behavior in the classroom should be reinforced for these efforts.

The effectiveness of time-out as an intervention is contingent on several factors (Cuenin & Harris, 1986):

- ☐ Characteristics of the individual child
- ☐ Teacher's consistent application of the intervention
- ☐ Child's understanding of the rules of time-out
- ☐ Characteristics of the time-out area
- ☐ Duration of time-out
- ☐ Evaluation of the effectiveness of the intervention

Characteristics of the Child

The practitioner must know the characteristics of the individual child before implementing a time-out intervention. For the acting-out, aggressive, group-oriented child, time-out may be very effective. Such children wish to be with the group and attended to by the teacher. Consequently time-out is not rewarding. However, for a withdrawn, passive, solitary child who is prone to daydreaming, time-out may be rewarding and would be contraindicated. These children may engage in their own little world while in the time-out area.

EXAMPLE   ■ Cheryl, a 6-year-old girl, is in Mr. Roy's class for behaviorally handicapped children. Cheryl is quiet, shy, and withdrawn; she frequently engages in daydreaming.

Mr. Roy read about a new technique for behavior problems in a popular magazine. This technique was time-out. He decided to impose the intervention on Cheryl in an effort to force her to participate in class discussions and activities. He planned to put her in time-out each time she was inattentive in class.

Cheryl appeared to enjoy the opportunity to go to time-out for 3 minutes. Her rate of inattentiveness increased dramatically immediately after the intervention was implemented. She evidently appreciated the opportunity to legitimately participate in her dream world. ■

This example is a stark illustration of an abuse of time-out by its use with a child whose behavior was reinforced by the intervention.

EXAMPLE   ■ Richard, a 11-year-old boy in Ms. Jones' physical education class, was constantly arguing and fighting with his teacher and classmates about the rules of a game or how an activity should be conducted. This behavior occurred particularly when he was losing. Observation indicated that Richard truly enjoyed the activities and the company of his peers and Ms. Jones. However, the behavior was obtrusive and had to be eliminated for the sake of the group.

Ms. Jones selected time-out as a potentially effective intervention. Before the technique was imposed, it was decided that each time Richard started to argue or fight during PE he was to be sent to time-out. The time-out area was out of view but not out of hearing of class activities. Under these conditions Richard's disruptions were eliminated very rapidly. ■

Time-out in this situation was effective because Richard preferred to be with his classmates and teacher rather than in the less stimulating time-out area.

Teacher's Consistency of Application

If time-out is to be applied as an intervention with a particular child, it must be used with consistency over a predetermined period of time. Frequently teachers are inconsistent in their application of time-out. As a result, the child becomes confused, and the target behavior is reinforced. This situation is analogous to the confusion that results when a child is forced on Monday, Wednesday, and Friday to eat green vegetables under pain of death at the hands of Father, but on Tuesday and Thursday Father is not so insistent, and on the weekend at Grandma's house, the child does not have to eat green vegetables at all.

Child's Understanding of the Rules

Children should know specifically what behaviors are not acceptable in their classrooms. In addition, they should know the consequences of exhibiting the forbidden behaviors. If time-out is to be used as an intervention, the rules for time-out should be communicated to the children; they should be posted and reviewed frequently. The rules assist the teacher in trying to remain consistent and fair in the application of the intervention.

Time-out should never be used whimsically with children; that is, one day a child is sent to time-out for talking in class, the next day for chewing gum, the next day for not completing a homework assignment, and so on. Such misuse will confuse the child and reduce the effectiveness of the intervention.

When time-out is imposed on the behavior of very young children the teacher is often confronted with an additional problem. Frequently it is impossible to communicate verbally to such children the rules governing time-out and its imposition. In this situation it is necessary to initiate the program and demonstrate the intervention through implementation.

Whether the reason is communicated verbally or by demonstration, children should understand why they are being placed in time-out.

Time-out is not a technique that includes lecturing, reprimanding, or scolding before, during, or after the intervention. These techniques, although frequently used in everyday classroom exchanges, can provide unwanted reinforcement to the child. Time must be taken to explain why time-out is warranted, but the explanation should be brief and explicit. Going to time-out should not be a matter for debate between child and teacher. As the program continues, these explanations need only be reminders of the rules and consequences of exhibiting certain behaviors.

EXAMPLE

■ Mrs. Smith selected time-out as an intervention to decrease Elmo's talking in class. Each time Elmo talked out of turn in class, Ms. Smith would grab him by the arm and drag him to the time-out area. There she would proceed to babble at him (rather incoherently) for about 10 minutes. She would always conclude with the statement, "Now, be quiet for two minutes." She would then proceed to stare at Elmo for two minutes. At the end of that time she would say, "Now, get back to your seat."

Ms. Smith's intervention is an example of the improper use of time-out. The results were as expected:

1. Elmo continued to talk out in class because, although he was not particularly interested in Ms. Smith's lectures, he was pleased with his classmates' reactions to her behavior.
2. Ms. Smith's classroom group certainly enjoyed the circus.
3. Ms. Smith suffered from nervous tension. ■

Characteristics of the Time-Out Area

Care must be taken in the selection of the time-out area. Teachers should avoid selecting an area that may appear nonreinforcing but is in effect reinforcing to children. For instance, placing a child in the corridor for time-out may be extremely reinforcing. In the hallway the child has an opportunity to communicate with everyone who passes. In addition, the child is provided with a legitimate opportunity to get out of the classroom and assignments.

Another commonly used but generally ineffective area for time-out is the principal's office. The office has been demonstrated to be one of the most stimulating and reinforcing areas in the school for the majority of children. In the office the child has an opportunity to observe peaked parents, out-of-sorts mailmen, and anxious administrators in their natural human state. In addition, the child has opportunities to pick up the latest school news and gossip for dissemination among peers and teachers.

Many administrators do not understand the concept of time-out, and on occasion the child is given various clerical tasks to perform in the office, such as stapling, folding, carrying messages, and making announcements. The child who is in time-out just happens to be available when a body is needed to do something; the reason for the child's presence in the office is not considered when the task is assigned. An investigation of the use of the office for time-out would probably reveal that it is a far more attractive alternative for the child than sitting in the classroom reading, writing, or doing math problems.

The time-out area should be as nonreinforcing as possible and devoid of extraneous visual and aural stimulation. In most classroom settings it is not necessary to construct a time-out room, although this practice is followed in many special classes for severely disturbed children. A chair in an out-of-the-way corner of the classroom is adequate. In some settings room dividers, screens, filing cabinets, or the backs of bookcases can be arranged to construct the walls of the time-out area. It is necessary to ensure that the area is supervised, safe, properly lighted, and ventilated. A chair may be placed in the time-out area. However, many children, especially young children, prefer to sit on the floor, and this practice should be permitted.

The area selected should be (1) away from high traffic, (2) away from doors and windows, (3) out of the other children's view, and (4) within view of the observer.

It is recommended that a chair be placed outside the area for the observer-supervisor. A paraprofessional can serve as observer-supervisor if properly instructed. However, in cases where an aide is not available for this duty, the area must be in a location that permits the teacher to observe it from his or her teaching station. Figure 5.4 is a diagram of a time-out area in a classroom.

Duration of Time-Out

Time-out loses its effectiveness as an intervention if a child is left in the setting for too lengthy or too brief a period of time (Harris, 1985). Time-out should be limited to approximately 2 minutes after the child has quieted. Four or 5 minutes in time-out should be maximum except under extraordinary circumstances. Never should a child remain in time-out for more than 10 minutes. It is strongly recommended that the

FIGURE 5.4

Classroom with time-out area. A, Time-out area; B, bookcase; C, child's chair; D, supervisor's chair; E, library; F, science or game area; G, teacher's station; H, students' desks; I, discussion center.

teacher use an inexpensive, bell-type egg timer to ensure that the time limit of time-out is not violated. The timer alerts both teacher and child to the exact moment the time-out period expires. In addition, it reassures the child that the teacher is being fair in the application of the intervention.

Evaluation of Effectiveness

Records of time-out incidents should be recorded and analyzed by the teacher or parent. Teachers should prepare a log such as the one in Figure 5.5. A copy of this log is provided in the back of the text.

The log should include (1) the time the child was sent or escorted to time-out, (2) the time the child returned to the activity, (3) any incidents during time-out, (4) the activity taking place just before the child was timed-out, and (5) the activity to which the child returned after time-out.

The log should be posted on the exterior wall of the time-out area. The teacher or parent evaluates the overall effectiveness of the technique by studying the child's time-out record. In addition, the records, if closely analyzed, provide clues as to why time-out is an effective or ineffective intervention in a particular case.

EXAMPLE ■ Mr. Sherman was recently called to a day school for severly disturbed boys to consult on the case of Hector, a 14-year-old student. When Hector enrolled in the school 2 years ago, he was exposed to time-out as a behavior control intervention. During the following 2 years, time-out was effective in modifying much of Hector's behavior.

The boy had progressed to a point of being sent to time-out on an average of only once each day. However, he had never progressed beyond this point. His daily disruption prohibited his integration into a regular classroom.

Fortunately, at the day school precise time-out records were maintained for all children and were available for study. An analysis of Hector's log indicated that he was in time-out each day immediately after the teacher announced that it was time for math. Although math time varied, it was discovered that Hector's disruptive time varied with it.

Mr. Sherman suggested that for Hector, time-out was more reinforcing than math; that is, it was the lesser of two evils. In an effort to test this hypothesis, Hector's math period was eliminated; Hector no longer went to time-out.

Hector's skill in math has progressed acceptably under the guidance of a tutor. The tutor assists him individually during regular math periods. ■

It is highly recommended that the child return to the task that was interrupted by the time-out. Of course, the feasibility of the child's returning to the interrupted task will vary with the structure of the class schedule and activities. If the child is returned to and held responsible for the task being engaged in before time-out, the child learns that time-out cannot be used as a means of avoiding assignments he or she finds difficult or simply dislikes. This recommendation assumes that the assigned task is appropriate to the child's learning level and competency.

The following examples will further clarify the process of time-out.

Time-out Log

Child _____

Supervisor _____

Date _____

Time		Behavior before time-out	Behavior during time-out	Behavior after time-out
Enters	Leaves			

FIGURE 5.5
Data log to be posted at time-out area.

EXAMPLES   ■   Ms. Drake was confronted with the problem of Donald striking other children in the stomach. She was so distressed by this behavior that she was about to reciprocate in kind. Ms. Drake had tried every intervention she knew to change the behavior (and a few she didn't know she knew), but they only increased it.

First, a set of "classroom rules of behavior" was presented to the children. Next, a time-out as a technique to decrease inappropriate behavior was described. After absorbing the available knowledge about time-out and becoming somewhat comfortable with the concept, Ms. Drake implemented it in her classroom.

First, a set of "classroom rules of behavior" was presented to the children. Next, a time-out area was designed, and the concept of time-out was introduced and explained to the group.

The new rules included "Do not strike other children." Persons exhibiting this behavior would be in time-out for 3 minutes in an area located in a corner of the classroom. The area was screened off, devoid of visual stimuli, and unfurnished with the exception of a chair. A child in time-out could neither see nor be seen by classmates (Figure 5.4). After the rules were communicated and apparently understood by all members of the class, time-out was implemented.

When Donald struck another child, he was quietly escorted to the time-out area for 3 minutes. After sitting quietly in the area for that period of time, Donald was asked why he was sent to time-out. If his response indicated that he understood the reason, he was instructed to return to his regular seat. However, if his response indicated that he did not understand the reason for being sent to time-out, it was briefly explained to him. He was then instructed to return to his seat. After several repetitions of the time-out routine, both Donald and Ms. Drake became aware of the potency of the intervention.

Donald's baseline and intervention data are presented in Figure 5.6.   ■

■   Mr. Seltz had used every method possible to decrease Shauna's unacceptable burping behavior in the classroom. Finally time-out was used as a technique to eliminate this behav-

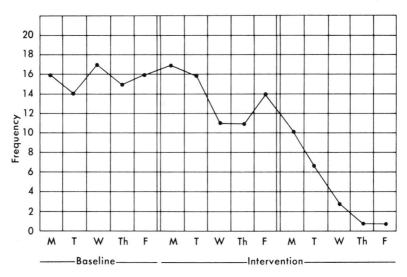

FIGURE 5.6
Frequency of Donald's striking behavior before and during the intervention.

ior. Shauna was told that each time she burped in class she was to go to the time-out area for 2 minutes. Mr. Seltz reinforced Shauna with attention and praise whenever she performed appropriately in the class. The baseline and intervention data for the behavior are presented in Figure 5.7. The data clearly indicate that Shauna preferred to cease burping rather than be placed in time-out. ■

As indicated in the examples, time-out can work effectively if it is properly applied. When implementing a program, the new practitioner of behavior modification should adhere closely to the suggestions in this section.

Satiation

Satiation is the decreasing or elimination of an unacceptable behavior as a result of continued and increased reinforcement of the behavior. Satiation is a more common occurrence than is generally realized. Because it is so common, we are frequently unaware of its effect on our behavior.

Many of us engage in certain sports and recreational activities (golf, baseball, camping, cards, and the like) with such frequency and regularity that we become satiated; that is, we discontinue the activity.

Some of us smoke, often in excess. Mr. Don, a book editor, was a 2- or 3-pack-a-day smoker. He honestly and sincerely wished to stop smoking. His self-selected intervention was to smoke continuously until he was satiated. He made himself ill and as a result stopped smoking (the hard way but perhaps for him the only way).

Bob loved (not just liked, but loved) chocolate ice cream. He would snitch it from the freezer any time of the day or night. His wife, Louise, scolded and deprived him in

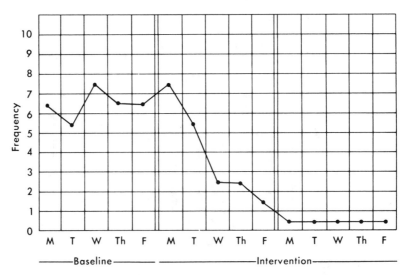

FIGURE 5.7
Frequency of Shauna's burping behavior before and during the intervention.

an effort to decrease his intake. One day, with great ceremony, Louise presented Bob with 2 gallons of chocolate ice cream. He was given ice cream at every opportunity, day and night, until he became satiated. Bob now prefers gelatin.

All of us have remembrances from our college days of the class hero who wished to gain immortality in the books on world records. This individual is the one who today hates bananas, pizza, blueberry pie, goldfish, raw eggs, frankfurters, and a score of other questionable edibles.

Perhaps everyone reaches the point of satiation in relation to some behavior. Grandma used to call this phenomenon "getting too much of a good thing."

The continued and increased reinforcement of a behavior can result in a decrease in that behavior. The central factor that influences the effectiveness of satiation as an intervention is the reinforcement schedule.

As discussed in Chapter 2, a variable reinforcement schedule is more resistant to satiation than a continuous or fixed reinforcement schedule. Consequently the key to successful application of satiation as an intervention is *continuous or fixed reinforcement schedule.*

The following example will clarify the application of a satiation intervention in the classroom.

EXAMPLE

■ Charles, a student in Ms. Barker's classroom, borrowed paper without permission from his teacher's and classmates' desks. Ms. Barker wanted to decrease this behavior. She tried techniques such as reprimanding, parent counseling, and having Charles counseled by the school psychologist. Nothing appeared to work. The school psychologist suggested trying a satiation procedure. Ms. Barker was impressed and willing to try any technique that might prove successful. She decided to implement the satiation program.

She placed a ream of paper on her desk at the beginning of the school day. After the children had arrived and morning exercises were completed, Ms. Barker gave Charles three sheets of paper. Four minutes later she returned to Charles's desk and gave him three more sheets of paper; 4 minutes later Charles received three more sheets of paper and so on throughout the day. This process continued day after day until Charles's possession of paper lost its value to him. Charles began to tell Ms. Barker that he did not need or want any paper; he had more than he could use to complete his assignments for the next 6 months. Figure 5.8 presents the baseline and intervention data for Charles's stealing behavior.

Charles's behavior was placed on a fixed reinforcement schedule. The behavior rapidly decreased because of satiation. ■

The process of satiation can be a very helpful tool in decreasing certain inappropriate classroom behaviors, such as pencil sharpening, putting paper in a wastebasket, getting drinks of water, and constantly requesting the time.

Punishment

Briefly discussed in Chapter 2, punishment is perhaps the most misunderstood and emotionally explosive of the behavior modification techniques. It is an intervention used to decrease or eliminate an inappropriate behavior.

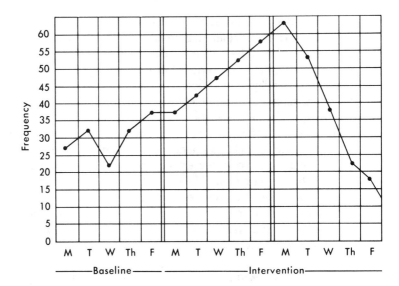

FIGURE 5.8
Frequency of Charles's stealing behavior before and during the intervention.

There are two distinct forms of punishment that the teacher or parent may consider for application with students. As commonly understood and applied by parents and teachers, punishment is the *addition* of an aversive stimulus (something unpleasant) as a consequence of a behavior. Punishment of this form can be either physical or psychological. Examples are a spanking (physical punishment) or a scolding or reprimand, extra work, after school detention, or an undesirable additional task (psychological punishment).

The other form of punishment is the *subtraction* of something the child perceives as desirable. Examples are the taking away of television privileges, late bedtime hours, freedom to leave the house, or tokens and points.

The subtraction of previously earned tokens or points in the token economy intervention presented in Chapter 4 is called *response-cost.* In this situation students are informed that not only can they earn points for privileges and goods, but if they exhibit specific unacceptable behaviors, they can lose points. A specific number of points are subtracted from the total for each transgression. In a word, the child is punished for exhibiting specific inappropriate behaviors.

Punishment by deprivation or response-cost is generally considered less harmful to the child and a more effective intervention than the addition of physical or psychological aversive stimuli.

The short-term effectiveness of punishment for decreasing behaviors is difficult if not impossible to dispute (Wood, 1978). Punishment is *effective* for obtaining short-term goals. However, other interventions such as extinction and ignoring the behavior are probably more effective for attaining permanent long-range changes.

Clarizio and Yelon (1967) and Wood and Lakin (1978) presented several reasons for avoiding the use of punishment:

1. It does not eliminate but merely suppresses the behavior.
2. It does not provide a model for the desired acceptable behavior.
3. Aggression on the part of the practitioner presents an undesirable model.
4. The emotional results of punishment may be fear, tension, stress, or withdrawal.
5. The child's resulting frustration may result in further deviation.

In addition, physical punishment may result in physical harm to the child, although such harm may be unplanned.

Punishment in the perception of the punished child is frequently associated with the punisher rather than with the unacceptable behavior. As a result, the punished child's reactions may be avoidance and dislike of the punisher rather than a change in behavior. Teachers who acknowledge that they are in effect behavioral models for their students will avoid assuming the role of punisher.

It may be helpful at this point to clarify some of the punishments that are frequently applied in school and homes. The following is a list of commonly used punishments:

☐ Denying participation in scheduled activities (games, field trips).
☐ Denying snacks (milk, cookies, candy).
☐ Physical punishment (paddlings, spankings, slaps).
☐ Verbal punishment (scoldings, reprimands, sarcasm, derogation, curses).
☐ Having the child stand apart from the others (in the corner, hallway).
☐ Having the child wear a sign ("I am a bad boy").

As members of the teaching profession, we seem to be very efficient in developing and applying harsh physical and psychological punishment. However, a variety of other methods of behavior management are available for the teacher's use. Punishment, especially harsh physical and psychological punishment, should be a last resort if it is used at all. "All reasonable positive alternatives should have been considered, if not actually tried before decision is made to use an aversive procedure" (Wood, 1978, p. 120).

If punishment is to be used, the teacher or parent should adhere to the following guidelines:

1. Specify and communicate the punishable behavior to the children by means of classroom rules for behavior.
2. Post the rules where the children can see them; review them with the group frequently.
3. Provide models of acceptable behavior.
4. Apply the punishment immediately.
5. Apply the punishment consistently, not whimsically.
6. Be fair in using the punishment (what is good for Peter is good for Paul).

7. Impose the punishment impersonally. Do not punish when you are angry or otherwise out of self-control.

The following are examples of the misuse of punishment.

EXAMPLE ■ Paul, an 11-year-old boy in Ms. Woods's classroom, was constantly punching other boys during recess. Ms. Woods told Paul he would receive two swats with the paddle each time he hit another child.

Paul went to morning recess and within 10 minutes had punched three children and the playground supervisor. Paul was returned to the classroom. Nothing was said or done about his behavior.

At about 2:30 PM Mr. Brinks, the assistant principal, arrived at the classroom door. Paul was called into the hallway. Mr. Brinks struck him eight times with the paddle (two swats for each person). Ms. Woods observed the punishment as a witness.

After accomplishing this task, Mr. Brinks returned to his office without comment; Ms. Woods returned to the classroom without comment; Paul returned to his seat, crying and confused. ■

The absurdity of this example is that it happened at all and continues to happen.

EXAMPLES ■ In the Meyers' kitchen is a cookie jar for petty cash. On the first day of each month Mr. Meyer places $50 in bills and coins in the cookie jar. The rules for removing money from the jar are (1) anyone can take up to $5 at any time for legitimate reasons and (2) the purpose for which the money is used, the date, and the borrower's signature are written on a slip of paper and put in the cookie jar.

At the end of each month Mr. Meyer totals the amounts of the slips. The total is seldom $50 because their teenage son, Herman, takes $15 to $20 without putting a slip in the jar.

The Meyers have discussed this behavior with Herman several times without effect. It was decided that the next time the behavior occurred Herman would no longer be allowed to take money from the petty cash fund. Herman considers his parents' action cruel and unusual punishment. However, he is complying with their wishes. ■

■ Mr. Sayers is a master at applying sarcasm and degradation. He is quick and devastating with his tongue, much to the discomfort of his students. His favorite epithets are "stupid," "dumbbell," "idiot," "meathead," and "dink."

One day Rosemary was fooling around in English class. This behavior greatly disturbed Mr. Sayers. He grabbed 17-year-old Rosemary by the arm, shook her, and called her a "dink." The girl was very embarrassed and began to cry. Encouraged by her reaction, Mr. Sayers added a few more names to the list and caused the other students to laugh.

This is an example of a teacher losing self-control and perhaps causing psychological damage to a student. Mr. Sayers was unaware, or so he claimed, of the contemporary meaning of "dink." However, Rosemary and her peers were very aware of its meaning. ■

We are irrevocably opposed to the use of corporal punishment, whether it is paddling, slapping, spanking, or using a cattle prod or electric wand. We are opposed to psychological punishment, which at minimum can erode the already fragile self-concept of the developing child. If punishment must be implemented, two forms are preferred: loss of privileges and reprimands (Shea & Bauer, 1987).

Unlike the vast majority of interventions discussed in this text, loss of privileges is a negative behavior management intervention, though its results may be positive. Loss of privileges is also known as deprivation of privileges or response-cost. When the loss of privileges is applied, a portion of the child's present or future positive reinforcers are taken away following the exhibition of the target behavior.

This intervention is most effective when the privilege the child loses is a natural or logical consequence of the inappropriate behavior. For example, if a child refuses to work on assignments during class time, then the privilege of free time is lost. Likewise, if a child is late for the school bus, then he misses it. It is not always possible to impose natural consequences; thus, the teacher on occasion must impose an artificial consequence. In an artificial consequence, the relationship between the privileges lost and the behavior exhibited is arbitrary. It exists only because the teacher decides it will exist. Such artificial relationships must be carefully explained to the child.

When using loss of privileges the teacher has several guidelines to follow. These are:

1. Be sure the child understands the relationship between the target behavior and the privilege to be lost.
2. Be sure the child knows the punishable behavior and the consequence of exhibiting it.
3. When possible use natural or logical consequences.
4. Apply the loss of privilege interventions fairly.
5. Avoid warning, nagging, or threatening.
6. Do not debate the punishable behaviors, the rules, or the punishment once these have been established.
7. Do not become emotionally involved. Don't feel guilty when the child loses a privilege. If the child knows the rules and the consequences of the behavior, then he or she has chosen to break the rule and suffer the consequences.
8. Be consistent.
9. Reinforce appropriate behavior; do not emphasize inappropriate behaviors only.

Another form of punishment is the reprimand (Houten, 1980). To be reprimanded is to be scolded, "yelled at," "bawled out," or otherwise verbally chastised for exhibiting an inappropriate target behavior. Reprimands are useful when a child is engaging in behavior which necessitates immediate action because it is potentially harmful to self, others, or property.

It is suggested that reprimands be used selectively in response to specific behaviors. A reprimand should include a statement of an appropriate alternative to the inappropriate behavior.

Some guidelines to effectively using reprimands are:

1. Be specific. Tell the child exactly what inappropriate behavior is being reprimanded.
2. Reprimand the behavior, do not derogate the child.
3. Reprimand immediately.

4. Be firm in voice and physical demeanor.
5. If either the child or others may be harmed by the behavior, remove the child.
6. If necessary, back up the reprimand with loss of privileges.
7. Encourage the child to behave appropriately and include a statement of the appropriate behavior in the reprimand.
8. Be calm.
9. When it's over, it's over. Do not keep reminding the child of past inappropriate behavior; avoid embarrassing the child in the presence of peers and others. To this end, use nonverbal reprimands: shake your head "no," point your finger, frown, and so on.
10. Always observe the child's reaction to the reprimand to determine if it is aversive.

Reinforcement of Incompatible Behaviors

At times it is necessary or desirable to decrease a behavior by systematically reinforcing a behavior that is in opposition to or incompatible with it. This intervention is called the process of reinforcing incompatible behaviors.

For instance, a teacher has two students in the classroom who are constantly bickering with each other. After analysis of the situation, it is proposed that the behavior would decrease if one of the students' seats were relocated to the opposite side of the room. The students are separated, and the behavior decreases.

The assumption underlying the intervention in this example is that the distance between the seats is incompatible with the bickering.

The effectiveness of this intervention is heavily dependent on the selection of the two truly incompatible behaviors (sitting apart and bickering).

EXAMPLE   ■   For a major part of the school year Mr. Weber had been trying to decrease Wallace's random walking about the classroom. All efforts appeared to have been in vain. It seemed that the more effort Mr. Weber put forth to modify Wallace's out-of-seat behavior, the more frequent it became. Evidently the attention Wallace received from Mr. Weber for being out of his seat was reinforcing.

As a last resort Mr. Weber decided to attempt the technique of reinforcing incompatible behaviors. To remain in one's seat would be incompatible with walking about the classroom. Mr. Weber decided to positively reinforce Wallace's in-seat behavior and ignore his out-of-seat behavior. Initially Wallace resisted the program. However, after a short time the out-of-seat behavior decreased and was eventually eliminated. Figure 5.9 represents the data collected on Wallace's behavior.

There is no known explanation for the recurrence of Wallace's out-of-seat behavior on the sixteenth and seventeenth days of the intervention. One possible explanation is that since the target behavior had not been exhibited for 2 days, Mr. Weber acted as though the behavior had been eliminated. He may have altered his response to either the behavior he was reinforcing or the behavior he was ignoring.   ■

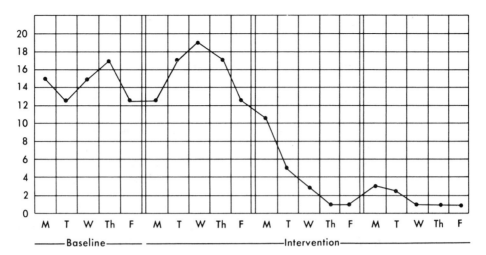

FIGURE 5.9
Frequency of Wallace's out-of-seat behavior before and during the intervention.

The classroom teacher could probably think of a number of other situations wherein reinforcing an incompatible behavior might decrease a target behavior.

Desensitization

Desensitization, the process of systematically lessening a specific, learned fear or phobic reaction in an individual became a popular therapeutic technique in the second half of the 1970s. It was developed by Wolpe during the 1950s and 1960s.

> The desensitization method consists of presenting to the imagination of the deeply relaxed patient the feeblest item in a list of anxiety-evoking stimuli repeatedly, until no more anxiety is evoked. The next item of the list is presented, and so on, until eventually, even the strongest of the anxiety-evoking stimuli fails to evoke any stir of anxiety in the patient. It has consistently been found that at every stage a stimulus that evokes no anxiety when imagined in a state of relaxation will also evoke no anxiety when encountered in reality.*

As indicated by Wolpe, the process of desensitization has been demonstrated to be an effective technique when applied to individuals with fears and anxieties related to public speaking, school attendance, participation in large groups, water, animals, heights, flying, test taking, and the like.

*From "The Systematic Desensitization Treatment of Neuroses" by J. Wolpe, 1961, *Journal of Nervous and Mental Diseases, 132,* pp. 189–203. Copyright 1961 by The Williams & Wilkins Co.

The process of systematic desensitization, according to Wolpe, involves three phases or steps:

1. Training the subject in deep muscle relaxation
2. Constructing an anxiety-evoking hierarchy of stimuli
3. Counterposing relaxation and the anxiety-evoking stimuli

The importance of these three phases can not be overemphasized; they are interdependent.

The practitioner is *not* encouraged to apply systematic desensitization on the basis of the information provided in this text alone. Teachers and parents should study other sources and obtain the services of a behavior therapy consultant before implementing a desensitization intervention.

The following reports of research are presented to clarify the procedures and effects of systematic desensitization under various conditions with a variety of problems.

Kravetz and Forness (1971) reported an experiment with a 6½-year-old boy who was unable to verbalize in the classroom. Psychiatric and medical reports did not reveal any known reason for his not talking in the classroom. The child's school progress was poor; however, test results indicated that he had above-average potential. A desensitization intervention of 12 sessions (2 per week) was implemented to reduce the child's fear of speaking in class.

The anxiety-evoking stimulus hierarchy used in this study is presented here:

1. Reading alone to investigator;
2. Reading alone to roommate;
3. Reading to two classroom aides (repeated);
4. Reading to teacher and classroom aides (repeated);
5. Reading to teacher, classroom aides, and small group of classroom peers (repeated);
6. Reading to entire class;
7. Asking question or making comment at weekly ward meeting when all patients, teachers, and staff were present.*

The reader should note that steps 3, 4, and 5 were repeated during the behavior change process.

This desensitization program, combined with positive reinforcement, was successful in helping the boy overcome his fear of verbalizing in the classroom.

Deffenbacher and Kemper (1974) applied systematic desensitization in a program to reduce test-taking anxiety in 28 junior high school students. The group was composed of 12 girls and 16 boys. All of the students had been referred by either a counselor, their parents, or a teacher. The test-taking anxiety-evoking stimulus hierarchy used with these students included:

---

*From "The Special Classroom as a Desensitization Setting" by R. Kravetz and S. Forness, 1971, *Exceptional Children, 37*, pp. 389–391. Copyright 1971 by The Council for Exceptional Children.

☐ You are attending a regular class session.

☐ You hear about someone who has a test.

☐ You are studying at home. You are reading a normal assignment.

☐ You are in class. The teacher announces a major exam in 2 weeks.

☐ You are at home studying. You are beginning to review and study for a test that is a week away.

☐ You are at home studying, and you are studying for the important test. It is now Tuesday and 3 days before the test on Friday.

☐ You are at home studying and preparing for the upcoming exam. It is now Wednesday, 2 days before the test on Friday.

☐ It is Thursday night, the night before the exam on Friday. You are talking with another student about the exam tomorrow.

☐ It is the night before the exam, and you are home studying for it.

☐ It is the day of the exam, and you have 1 hour left to study.

☐ It is the day of the exam. You have been studying. You are now walking on your way to the test.

☐ You are standing outside the test room talking with other students about the upcoming test.

☐ You are sitting in the testing room waiting for the test to be passed out.

☐ You are leaving the exam room, you are talking with other students about the test. Many of their answers do not agree with yours.

☐ You are sitting in the classroom waiting for the graded test to be passed back by the teacher.

☐ It's right before the test, and you hear a student ask a possible test question which you cannot answer.

☐ You are taking the important test. While trying to think of an answer, you notice everyone around you writing rapidly.

☐ While taking the test you come to a question you are unable to answer. You draw a blank.

☐ You are in the important exam. The teacher announces 30 minutes remaining but you have an hour's work left.

☐ You are in the important exam. The teacher announces 15 minutes remaining but you have an hour's work left.*

The desensitization treatment consisted of eight sessions (one per week) in groups of two to five students. The intervention effectively reduced test-taking anxiety.

There have been several applications of desensitization techniques in cases of school phobia. A study especially worthy of notation is by Garvey and Hegrenes (1966).

They reported a study concerning Jimmy, a 10-year-old with school phobia. During treatment the therapist eliminated the child's fear of school by having him approach the school accompanied by the therapist and by proceeding with the following anxiety-evoking stimulus hierarchy:

---

*From "Systematic Desensitization of Test Anxiety in Junior High Students" by J. Deffenbacher and C. Kemper, 1974, *The School Counselor, 21,* pp. 216–222. Copyright 1974 by the American Personnel and Guidance Association. Reprinted with permission.

1. Sitting in the car in front of the school;
2. Getting out of the car and approaching the curb;
3. Going to the sidewalk;
4. Going to the bottom of the steps of the school;
5. Going to the top of the steps;
6. Going to the door;
7. Entering the school;
8. Approaching the classroom in a certain distance each day down the hall;
9. Entering the classroom;
10. Being present in the classroom with the teacher;
11. Being present in the classroom with the teacher and one or two classmates;
12. Being present in the classroom with a full class.*

After 20 consecutive daily treatments Jimmy resumed a normal school routine. No return of the phobia was noted during a 2-year follow-up study.

We have found desensitization to be a potent intervention that can be applied in a modified form by the teacher in the classroom. However, if desensitization is to be applied in the classroom, the following conditions must exist;

1. The teacher must have a positive interpersonal relationship with the child. The child must trust the teacher and be free to express fears in the teacher's presence.
2. The teacher must construct an anxiety-evoking stimulus hierarchy.
3. The teacher must be willing (and have adequate time) to accompany the child in the progression from the least to the most anxiety-evoking stimulus in the hierarchy.

Under normal classroom conditions the desensitization process is time consuming. The teacher must be consistent and patient in the application of this intervention. It may be necessary to repeat some of the specific anxiety-evoking situations until their effect on the child has been eliminated.

EXAMPLES   ■ David, a 5-year-old boy in Ms. Philly's class for children with behavior problems, was afraid of dogs. Whenever the boy saw a dog, he would crawl under the nearest object or person and scream until the animal disappeared from view.

This behavior made it impossible for David to go out on the playground during recess with his peers, to walk to and from school, or to play outdoors in his neighborhood.

Desensitization was suggested as a possible intervention. Ms. Philly thought it was an excellent idea but suggested that implementation be deferred until she knew David better. A stimulus hierarchy was constructed, but the intervention was held in abeyance until 3 months after the beginning of the school year.

The following anxiety-evoking stimulus hierarchy was used to reduce David's fear of dogs:

1. Pictures of dogs were hung on the walls of the classroom. The pictures were initially

---

*From "Desensitization Techniques in the Treatment of School Phobia" by W. P. Garvey and J. R. Hegrenes, 1966, *America Journal of Orthopsychiatry, 36,* pp. 147–152. Copyright 1966 by the American Orthopsychiatric Association.

placed as far away from David's desk as possible. As desensitization continued, they were moved nearer to David.

2. Pictures of dogs were observed by David in motion pictures and filmstrips.
3. Pictures of dogs were affixed to David's desk and notebook covers.
4. David observed dogs playing in the school yard from his classroom window.
5. David observed dogs playing in the school yard from the door of the school.
6. David observed dogs playing in the school yard as he stood at a distance that was systematically decreased.
7. David permitted dogs to walk past him in the school yard.

At *no time* during the desensitization process was David encouraged to touch or pet a dog. This precaution was taken simply because *some* dogs do bite *some* children.

During the desensitization process, Ms. Philly removed David from an anxiety-evoking situation whenever he manifested the slightest discomfort. The lessening of David's fear permitted him to tolerate dogs and to increase his interactions with his peers in the school yard and neighborhood. ■

■ Keith, an 8-year-old third-grade student, was enrolled in summer camp. Keith had a fear of water. Swimming lessons were a part of the camp program. Although swimming was not mandatory, it was encouraged. At the first suggestion of swimming or going to the pool, Keith would have a temper tantrum of considerable magnitude.

It was decided that Keith should overcome this irrational fear. The staff concluded that systematic desensitization would be an effective intervention.

The following stimulus hierarchy was constructed and applied during desensitization:

1. Swimming was announced to the group and discussed with Keith's peers. Keith did not attend swimming lessons but watched his peers, who were very happy and excited, get on the bus and depart for swimming.
2. Keith rode the bus to the pool and waited outside the building.
3. Keith rode the bus to the pool and waited outside the locker room.
4. Keith entered the locker room, put on his trunks, and remained in the locker room.
5. Keith, in trunks, observed the lesson from the pool observation room.
6. Keith observed the lesson from the poolside (approximately 10 feet from the water).
7. Keith observed the lesson from the edge of the pool.
8. Keith observed the lesson while sitting on the edge of the pool with his feet in the water.
9. Keith stood in the pool with his hands on the edge of the pool.
10. Keith walked in the shallow end of the pool with his hands on the edge of the pool.

Throughout this procedure Keith was accompanied by his counselor, who provided positive reinforcement. As a result of this process and within 3 weeks, Keith began his swimming lessons. After 3 years it was noted that the fear had not returned. Keith is an excellent swimmer.

SUMMARY

In this chapter some techniques to decrease behaviors are discussed.

Extinction is the discontinuation or withholding of the reinforcer of a behavior that has previously reinforced that particular behavior. The technique is based on the principle that if the reinforcer is taken away, the probability of recurrence of the behavior is decreased.

The second technique recommended, time-out, is a frequently misunderstood behavioral intervention. Time-out is the removal of a child from an apparently reinforcing setting to a presumably nonreinforcing setting for a specified and limited period of time. Six factors related to the effectiveness of time-out are (1) the characteristics of the individual child, (2) the consistency of application by the teacher, (3) the child's understanding of the rules, (4) the characteristics of the time-out area, (5) the duration of time-out, and (6) the evaluation of the effectiveness of the intervention.

Satiation is the decreasing or elimination of an inappropriate behavior as a result of continued and increased reinforcement of that behavior. This intervention is effective for decreasing behaviors such as "borrowing" materials, stealing, and dominating time.

Punishment, the most familiar of the interventions discussed, is the addition of an aversive stimulus or the subtraction of a desired reinforcer or privilege as a consequence of behavior. There are a number of serious concerns associated with the use of punishment. The major problem with the use of punishment to modify behavior is that punishment does not eliminate inappropriate behavior; it only suppresses the behavior. Punishment should be used very infrequently, if ever, in the school. Reprimand and loss of privileges were discussed as useful forms of punishment.

The reinforcement of incompatible behaviors involves systematically reinforcing a behavior that is in opposition to or incompatible with the target behavior. The effectiveness of this technique depends greatly on the pairing of incompatible behaviors.

Desensitization is the process of systematically lessening a specific fear in an individual.

EXERCISES

Quiz

1. The six most common methods of decreasing behavior are:

   a. _____   d. _____

   b. _____   e. _____

   c. _____   f. _____

2. _____ is the process of discontinuing or withholding the reinforcer of a behavior that has previously reinforced that particular behavior.

3. Time-out is the removal of a child from an apparently _____ setting to a

   presumably _____ setting for a specified and limited period of time.

4. List at least three of the factors that a behavior modifier should consider when designing a time-out intervention.

a. _____

b. _____

c. _____

5. When selecting a time-out area within the classroom, which four factors should a teacher or parent consider?

   a. _____

   b. _____

   c. _____

   d. _____

6. _____ is the decreasing or elimination of an unacceptable behavior as a result of continued and increased reinforcement of the behavior.

7. _____ should only be used to decrease or eliminate behaviors as a last resort.

8. Reinforcing incompatible behaviors is accomplished by _____

   _____

   _____

9. _____ is the process of lessening an individual's particular fear.

10. Three of the logical reasons presented by Clarizio and Yelon (1967) for avoiding the use of punishment are:

    a. _____

    _____

    b. _____

    _____

    c. _____

    _____

Projects

1. Joanie, a girl in Ms. Jewel's classroom, is constantly asking, "What time is it?" She requests the time about 15 times per day. The teacher considers this to be an attention-getting behavior and wishes to eliminate it. She usually responds to Joanie's request by telling her the time. Using this example, design four interventions for eliminating the behavior using the processes of:
   a. Extinction   c. Satiation
   b. Time-Out   d. Reinforcement of incompatible behaviors
2. Write a brief essay (250 words or more) emphasizing the pros and cons of the use of corporal punishment in the school.

REFERENCES

Clarizio, H. F., & Yelon, S. L. (1967). Learning theory approaches to classroom management: Rationale and intervention techniques. *Journal of Special Education, 1,* 267–274.

Cuenin, L. H., & Harris, K. R. (1986). Planning, implementing, and evaluating time-out interventions with exceptional students. *Teaching Exceptional Children, 18*(4), 272–276.

Deffenbacher, J., & Kemper, C. (1974). Systematic desensitization of test anxiety in junior high students. *The school counselor, 21,* 216–222.

Garvey, W. P., & Hegrenes, J. R. (1966). Desensitization techniques in the treatment of school phobia. *American Journal of Orthopsychiatry, 36,* 147–152.

Hall, R. V., & Hall, M. C. (1980a). *How to use planned ignoring.* Austin, TX: Pro-Ed.

Hall, R. V., & Hall, M. C. (1980b). *How to use timeout.* Austin, TX: Pro-Ed

Harris, K. R. (1985). Definitional, parametric, and procedural considerations in time-out interventions and research. *Exceptional Children, 51*(4), 279–288.

Houten, R. V. (1980). *How to use reprimands.* Austin, TX: Pro-Ed.

Kravetz, R., & Forness, S. (1971). The special classroom as a desensitization setting. *Exceptional Children, 37,* 389–391.

Lewellen, A. (1980). *The use of quiet rooms and other time-out procedures in the public school:* *A position paper.* Mattoon, IL: Eastern Illinois Area of Special Education.

Powell, T. H., & Powell, I. Q. (1982). Guidelines for implementing time-out procedures. *The Pointer, 26,* 18–21.

Shea, T. M., & Bauer, A. M. (1987). *Teaching children and youth with behavior disorders.* Englewood Cliffs, NJ: Prentice-Hall.

Wolpe, J. (1961). The systematic desensitization treatment of neuroses. *Journal of Nervous and Mental Diseases, 132,* 189–203.

Wolpe, J. (1974). *The practice of behavior therapy (2nd ed.).* New York: Pergamon Press.

Wood, F. H. (1978). *Punishment and special education: Some concluding comments.* In F. H. Wood & D. C. Lakin (Eds.), *Punishment and aversive stimulation in special education: Legal, theoretical and practical issues in their use with emotionally disturbed children and youth* (pp. 119–122). Minneapolis: University of Minnesota.

Wood, F. H., & Lakin, K. C. (1978). The legal status and use of corporal punishment and other aversive procedures in schools. In F. H. Wood & K. C. Lakin (Eds.). *Punishment and aversive stimulation in special education: Legal, theoretical and practical issues in their use with emotionally disturbed children and youth* (pp. 3–27). Minneapolis: University of Minnesota.

CHAPTER SIX

Psychodynamic Behavior Management

Jack, a handsome 13-year-old seventh grader, is enrolled in Mr. Bird's junior high resource room for students with adjustment difficulties.

Jack functions well in the academic areas. He performs above grade level in all subjects. However, his social behavior is creating difficulties for Jack, his classmates, and his teachers. Jack's unacceptable social behaviors have caused him to be ignored by some students, overtly rejected by others, and used as a scapegoat by a few.

Essentially Jack believes he is unacceptable to (unwanted by) his peers. He appears to believe that others are making fun of him or rejecting him when they are being overtly friendly. When Jack feels he is being rejected, he immediately attempts to escape his discomfort. He escapes by putting his head in his lifttop desk and closing the top, placing an open book over his face, placing his backpack over his head, walking the hallways sideways with his face to the wall, and so on.

Mr. Bird recognizes that eventually this behavior will affect all facets of Jack's functioning including academics. Mr. Bird realizes that he is not a trained psychotherapist. However, he wishes to assist Jack in a practical manner with his unacceptable overt social behavior in the classroom and school.

Mrs. Lietner, a sixth-grade teacher, is watching 12-year-old Wendell and his classmate, Tommy, shooting baskets in the schoolyard. They are playing "21," and Tommy is winning 16 to 10.

Suddenly and for no observable reason, Wendell throws the basketball in Tommy's face with great force. When Tommy recovers, he begins to chase Wendell. Wendell runs around the playground for a few minutes and then begins to climb over the fence with Tommy in hot pursuit. As Wendell climbs the fence, his shirt catches on a wire and tears. He immediately runs to Mrs. Lietner and reports that Tommy tore his shirt.

Mrs. Lietner calls both boys to her side. Each is asked to review the incident. They are encouraged to verbally reconstruct the game, Wendell's throwing of the basketball into Tommy's face, the chase, fence climbing, and the torn shirt. During the discussion it becomes apparent to Mrs. Lietner that Wendell fails to see any connection between his behavior, Tommy's behavior, and the torn shirt.

The teacher recognizes that this incident is similar to many others in which Wendell has been involved throughout the year. He appears either unable or unwilling to perceive the relationship between his actions and their consequences.

Mrs. Lietner recognizes her need for a behavior management intervention to assist Wendell.

Several behavior management interventions derived from the psychodynamic model are presented in this chapter. Four categories of interventions are discussed. These are counseling techniques, the expressive arts, behavior influence techniques, and self-control curriculum. The counselng techniques discussed are the life-space interview and reality therapy. The expressive arts include free play, puppetry, role playing and psychodrama, creative movement and dance, music, the written word, the spoken word, bibliotherapy, and art therapy. The behavior influence techniques reviewed are planned ignoring, signal interference, proximity control, interest boosting, tension reduction through humor, hurdle helping, program restructuring, support from routine, direct appeal, removing seductive objects, antiseptic bouncing, and physical restraint. Also presented in this chapter is a discussion of the psychoeducational model.

Several important psychodynamic interventions employed by professionals in the mental health disciplines are not presented in this text because of their complexity and special training requirements. These include individual and group psychotherapy, directive and nondirective counseling, psychoanalysis, and family therapy.

Before studying the remainder of this chapter, the reader is urged to review the theoretical framework underlying the psychodynamic model presented in Chapter 1.

Psychoeducational Model

A broad perspective for the education and management of children is the *psychoeducational model.* Originally the psychoeducational model was closely associated with the teaching strategies classified as psychoanalytic-psychodynamic (Berkowitz and Rothman, 1960, 1967; Peter, 1965; Morse, 1985).

According to Long and others, however, (1980), the psychoeducational approach is a general term that is representative of a theory, method, or viewpoint on the education of troubled children. As a generic term it includes a variety of psychological and educational approaches to helping such children and youth (Nichols, 1984). It is this model with which the many interventions detailed in this chapter appear to be most compatible.

The psychoeducational model as interpreted by Long, Morse, and Newman follows:

> To give this concept some substance, the following operating principles are considered basic to the psychoeducational approach. We believe:
>
> 1. Cognitive and affective processes are in continuous interaction.
> 2. Accepting the existence of mental illness, our task is to describe the pupil in terms of functioning skills that highlight areas of strength and pinpoint areas of weakness for remediation.
> 3. The psychoeducational process involves creating a special environment so that initially each pupil can function successfully at his present level.
> 4. Given this specialized environment, each pupil is taught that he has the capacity and resources to function appropriately and successfully.
> 5. Understanding how each pupil perceives, feels, thinks, and behaves in this setting facilitates educational conditions for optimal behavioral change.

6. There are no special times during the school day. Everything that happens to, with, for, and against the pupil is important and can have therapeutic value.

7. Emotionally troubled pupils have learned a vulnerability to many normal developmental tasks and relationships such as competition, sharing, testing, closeness, etc. As teachers, we are responsible for awareness of these areas and for modifying our behavior in appropriate fashion.

8. Emotionally disturbed pupils behave in immature ways during periods of stress. They will lie, fight, run away, regress, and deny the most obvious realities. We can anticipate immature behavior from children in conflict; our hope for change is to expect mature behavior from adults.

9. Pupils in conflict can create their feelings and behaviors in others; aggressive pupils can create counter-aggressive behaviors in others; hyperactive children can create hyperactivity in others; withdrawn pupils can get other children and adults to ignore them; passive-aggressive pupils are effective in getting others to carry their feelings for days. If a child succeeds in getting the adult to act out his feelings and behavior, he succeeds in perpetuating his self-fulfilling prophecy of life, which in turn reinforces his defenses against change.

10. Emotionally troubled children have learned to associate adult intervention with adult rejection. One staff goal is to reinterpret adult intervention as an act of protection rather than hostility. The pupil must be told over and over again that adults are here to protect him from real dangers, contagion, psychological depreciation, etc.

11. We are here to listen to what the pupil says, to focus on what he is feeling.

12. We are to expect and accept a normal amount of hostility and disappointment from pupils and colleagues.

13. Pupils' home and community life is an important source of health that must be considered by any remedial process. However, if all attempts fail, the school becomes an island of support for the pupil.

14. We must demonstrate that fairness is treating children differently. Although group rules are necessary for organizational purposes, individualized expectations are necessary for growth and change.

15. Crises are excellent times for teachers to teach and for pupils to learn.

16. Behavioral limits can be a form of love, i.e., physical restraint can be a therapeutic act of caring for and protecting pupils.

17. Teaching pupils social and academic skills enhances their capacity to cope with a stressful environment.

18. Pupils learn through a process of unconscious identification with significant adults in their lives. This means the teacher's personal appearance, attitudes, and behavior are important factors in teaching which must be evaluated continuously.*

It is within the context of the psychoeducational model, presented above, and the psychodynamic model, presented in Chapter 1, that the counseling, behavior influencing, and expressive art interventions discussed in this chapter take on their significance. The reader is urged to study both models with great care.

---

*From *Conflict in the classroom,* 3rd ed., by Nicholas J. Long, William C. Morse, and Ruth G. Newman. © 1976 by Wadsworth Publishing Company, Inc. Reprinted by permission of the publisher.

Counseling Techniques

Life-Space Interview

Redl (1959) recommended the life-space interview as an integral part of milieu therapy. Milieu therapy is discussed in Chapter 7 as an environmental intervention.

The life-space interview is a here-and-now intervention built around a child's direct life experience. It is applied by a teacher perceived to be significant in the child's life-space. The interviewer has a definite role and power influence in the child's daily life. The life-space interview technique is imposed to structure an incident in the child's life to enable the child to solve the problems confronting him or her. The interviewer's role is facilitator.

According to Redl, the life-space interview technique may be applied for either of two purposes: clinical exploitation of life events or emotional first aid on the spot.

In the first situation, *clinical exploitation of life events,* the interviewer uses an actual incident to explore with the child habitual behavioral characteristics. This is an effort to use the incident to attain a long-range therapeutic goal previously established for the child by a clinical or individualized educational program team.

When the life-space interview technique is employed for the exploitation of life events, the interviewer assists the child in increasing conscious awareness of distorted perceptions of existing realities, pathological behavioral characteristics, hidden social and moral values and standards, or reactions to the behaviors and pressures of the group. The interviewer uses the technique to discuss with the child more personally productive and socially acceptable means of solving problems. This particular application of the life-space interview requires training and experience.

EXAMPLE ■ Jack, who was introduced to the reader at the beginning of this chapter, is an excellent example of the application of the life-space interview of the clinical exploitation of life events. Jack's bizarre methods of escaping from what he perceived to be rejections were habitual behavioral characteristics. The unacceptable behavior was repeated several times each day.

The staff discussed and agreed that life-space interviewing was an appropriate intervention in Jack's case. Each time Jack engaged in the behavior, he was immediately removed from the setting in which the behavior occurred by a supportive teacher.

The incident was reconstructed and discussed, and a plan for a more acceptable response by Jack to a peer's smile, wave, and so on, was agreed on by Jack and the supportive teacher. Jack returned to the setting in which the behavior was manifested and continued his daily schedule.

Over time and after many life-space interviews, Jack increased his capacity to differentiate between social acceptance and rejection. ■

The life-space interview technique also provides a child *emotional first aid on the spot* at times of unusual stress. The purpose of the life-space interview technique in on-the-spot first aid is to assist the child over a rough spot in the road in order to continue an activity. The interview is imposed to (1) reduce the child's frustration level, (2) support the child in emotionally charged situations, (3) restore strained child-teacher and child-child communications, (4) reinforce existing behavioral and social limits and realities, or (5) assist the child in efforts to find solutions to everyday problems of living and emotionally charged incidents, such as fights and arguments.

EXAMPLE
■ John and Thomas, both 11-year-old fifth-grade students, were on a camping trip with their teacher and classmates. The boys were in the process of erecting their two-man tent before the evening meal.

During the process of erecting the tent, John shouted at Thomas: "Come on, stupid. Get the stakes in right. Boy, am I sick of you. You're slow. Hurry up. I'm hungry. We can't eat until you get this dumb tent up."

Thomas proceeded to tell John: "Do it yourself, big mouth. I don't care if I ever eat. Besides I'm not sleeping in there with you anyway."

Both boys were extremely frustrated after a long day of backpacking. They began fighting.

Mr. Wise recognized that *emotional first aid on the spot* by means of a life-space interview was needed. He stopped the fight and allowed the boys to calm down before beginning the interview. During the interview each boy reconstructed the incident as he perceived it, listened to Mr. Wise's perception of the incident, and agreed to try again with a specific plan of action. The tent was erected quickly, and the evening meal was eaten. ■

As in any counseling situation, the application of the life-space interview is dependent on a variety of variables: the purpose and goal, the specific environment, the training and experience of the teacher, and especially the child and the particular problem or difficulty.

The application of the life-space interview technique in the school is a decision involving all members of the team responsible for the child. When the technique is adopted for use, it should be used with consistency by all personnel under the supervision of trained and experienced professionals.

Morse (1971) has outlined a series of steps that occur during the life-space interview. This is not a rigid series of steps; on occasion during an interview, some steps are omitted and others reordered.

Generally the interview begins as a result of a specific incident in the individual's (or group's) actual life-space. The interviewer encourages those involved in the incident to state their personal perceptions of the occurrence. At this time the interviewer must determine if this is an isolated happening or a significant part of a recurring theme.

The interviewer *listens* to those involved in the incident as they reconstruct it, accepting their feelings and perceptions without moralizing or attacking. Although individual perceptions of the incident are accepted, the interviewer may suggest alternative perceptions for consideration.

The interview process then moves into a resolution phase. This phase should be nonjudgmental in tone. Many conflicts and confrontations are resolved at this point, and the interview is terminated.

However, if the problems are not resolved, the interviewer may offer his or her view of the happening as it is related to the situation in which the individual or individuals find themselves. Finally, those involved and the interviewer develop an acceptable plan to deal with the present problem and similar problems in the future.

Several guidelines for interviewer behavior have been offered by Brenner (1969):

1. *Be polite.* If you do not have control of your emotions, do not begin the interview.
2. Sit, kneel, or stand to *establish eye contact.* Talk with, never at, the individual being interviewed.
3. When you are unsure of the history of the incident, investigate. *Do not conduct an interview on the basis of second- or third-hand information or rumors.*
4. *Ask appropriate questions* to obtain a knowledgeable grasp of the incident. However, do not probe areas of unconscious motivation; limit the use of "why" questions.
5. *Listen to the individual* and attempt to comprehend his or her perception of the incident.
6. Encourage the individual to ask questions. Respond to the child's questions appropriately.
7. When the individual is suffering from apparent shame and/or guilt as a result of the incident, *attempt to reduce and minimize these feelings.*
8. *Facilitate the individual's efforts to communicate* what he or she wishes to say. If the individual is having difficulty in this area, provide help.
9. *Work carefully and patiently* to develop a mutually acceptable plan of action for immediate or future implementation.

Reilly, Imber, and Cremins (1978) and DeMagistris and Imber (1980) researched the effectiveness of the life-space interview in educational settings. In the former study, researchers found that in the resource room, the interview decreased inappropriate behavior. In the second study, conducted in a self-contained special class with eight disturbed boys, researchers found academic performance improved and inappropriate behavior decreased. Caution should be exercised in generalizing the findings of these studies due to sample limitations. A comprehensive discussion of the purpose, application, and effectiveness of the life-space interview is found in a special issue of *The Pointer* (Long & Fagen, 1980).

Reality Therapy

In his 1965 and 1969 publications, Glasser offers a unique perspective on mental health and the treatment of mental illness. His thesis is a departure from traditional Freudian and neo-Freudian theoretical frameworks that mental health is a state of contentment and mental ill health is a state of discontent. From the reality therapy point of view, mental health is the ability to function competently in the environment, whereas mental illness is incompetence.

An individual in need of psychiatric assistance is unable to fulfill essential psychological needs. The objective of reality therapy is to lead the individual toward competent functioning in the environment. This technique is designed to help the individual grapple successfully with the tangible and intangible aspects of the real world and as a result be able to fulfill personal needs.

According to Glasser (1965), human beings have two basic psychological needs: (1) to love and be loved and (2) to feel worthwhile to self and others.

To feel worthwhile to self and others, an individual must maintain satisfactory standards of behavior. The individual who fails to maintain acceptable standards suffers pain or discomfort. This discomfort is *mental illness*, that is, lack of responsible involvement with significant others in the environment. A mentally ill person desiring to return to the state of mental health, that is, responsible and competent functioning, must have someone whom he or she genuinely cares about, and the person must believe that the feeling is mutual.

In reality therapy the process of therapy and the process of teaching are identical. The therapist or teacher's primary objective is to teach the mentally ill person responsible behavior. Responsibility is the ability to fulfill one's personal needs in a manner that does not deprive other individuals of their ability to fulfill their personal needs.

According to Glasser's thesis, learning to be a responsible person is not a natural developmental process. Individuals are taught to be responsible through involvement with responsible and significant others. This involvement with others includes love and discipline. The majority of individuals learn to be responsible from loving and disciplining parents or guardians and others, such as teachers.

In summary, reality therapy is the process of teaching an irresponsible individual to face existing reality, to function responsibly, and, as a result, to fulfill personal needs.

For the mentally ill individual, the therapeutic process includes:

☐ Involvement with an acceptable person who is perceived by the mentally ill person as caring about him or her. The quality of the involvement must be sufficient to permit the ill individual to face existing reality and begin to view personal behavior as irresponsible.

☐ A therapist who is accepting of the individual and maintains involvement with the individual while rejecting irresponsible behavior.

☐ The learning of responsible means of fulfilling personal needs in reality. This learning process is a cooperative activity that may include direct instructions, discussions, conversations, and planning sessions relative to any element of the individual's present life-style.

Reality therapy processes assume that the therapist is an acceptable and accepting person. The therapist, who may be a teacher, is also assumed to be appropriately trained and experienced in reality therapy techniques.

In an educational program reality therapy's goal is to guide individuals toward more responsible behavior. This goal is attained by means of the reality therapy interview.

Guidelines for teachers engaged in the interview are:

1. Be personal. Demonstrate that you are a person who cares about the individual and who is interested in his or her welfare.

2. Focus the therapeutic process on present behavior, not on past behavior. Accept the individual's expressed feelings, but do not probe into unconscious motivation. Ask "what," "how," and "who" questions. Limit the asking of "why" questions.
3. Do not preach, moralize, or make value judgments about the individual's behavior.
4. Help the individual formulate a practical plan to increase responsible behavior. Planning is a cooperative effort.
5. Encourage the individual to overtly make a commitment to the mutually agreed-on plan.
6. Do not accept excuses for irresponsible behavior. When a plan fails or cannot be implemented, develop another.
7. Do not punish the individual for irresponsible behavior. Allow the individual to realize the logical consequences of irresponsible behavior unless the consequences are unreasonably harmful.
8. Provide emotional support and security throughout the therapeutic process.

Because it is primarily verbal in nature, reality therapy is perhaps most appropriately used with upper elementary school children and adolescents who are capable of carrying on meaningful verbal transactions with others.

EXAMPLE   ■   Kyle, a tenth-grade student at Greenwood High School, had superior academic potential. However, he was failing several subjects. It became evident that Kyle's future relative to graduation and college was being affected by his behavior.

Mr. Germaine, Kyle's favorite teacher, decided he must help the young man. He did not want Kyle to jeopardize his future. Mr. Germaine decided to use the reality therapy approach with Kyle. After all, he and Kyle were friends; he cared about the young man; and he knew Kyle could improve with help.

In their first session it was found that Kyle would not work in any subject areas if he did not like the teacher. If the teacher was too demanding, unfriendly, and so on, Kyle just gave up—he refused to study.

Kyle recognized that his behavior was only harmful to himself. He and Mr. Germaine developed a plan of action. During the next few months they met regularly to monitor Kyle's progress. Kyle learned to accept responsibility for his behavior. His grades improved dramatically.   ■

Glasser (1969) suggested reality therapy for application with classroom groups. In an effort to reduce the emphasis in schools on competition and achievement, he proposed reality therapy meetings to teach decision making, social responsibility, and cooperation. These purposes are accomplished through social-problem-solving, open-ended, and educational-diagnostic meetings. The social-problem-solving meeting is focused on individual and group problems in classroom and school. Open-ended meetings are discussions of any thought-provoking questions related to the members of the group or the group itself. Educational-diagnostic meetings focus on the content of the educational program in which the group is involved.

Few studies of the effect of reality therapy have been conducted. In general, studies lack experimental rigor and yield mixed results. Cook [(1972) in Shearn & Randolph, 1978] reported no significant changes in positive or negative behaviors or sociometrically underchosen adolescents exposed to reality therapy. Hawes [(1970) in Shearn & Randolph, 1978] reported significant gains in the self-concept of black children in reality therapy. However, Glick [(1968) in Shearn and Randolph, 1978] reported no significant changes in self-concept and self-responsibility of emotionally disturbed boys in residential school. However, significant changes in self-esteem were reported.

Sheaf [(1972) in Shearn & Randolph, 1978] noted no significant changes in the reading achievement of delinquents involved in reality therapy. Shearn and Randolph (1978), using a four-group experimental design, studied the effects of reality therapy on the task-oriented behaviors and self-concept of fourth grade students; results were not significant. In a follow-up study of adolescents who had successfully left a facility using reality therapy and contingency management procedures, most of the students were found to be moderately successful young adults; only 1 of the 18 subjects returned to the facility and only 4 were unemployed 2 to 4 years after leaving the program, despite substantial deficits in academic skills (Leone, 1984).

Expressive Arts

The expressive arts refers to interventions that encourage and permit children to express personal feelings and emotions in creative activities with minimal constraints.

All human beings have feelings and emotions that must be expressed in some manner if mental health is to be maintained. A child's feelings and emotions, positive and negative, can be expressed verbally and physically. Frequently children (and adults) unconsciously express their feelings and emotions in socially unacceptable ways. This can result in conflicts with others and may have a negative impact on the individual's self-concept.

The expressive arts, applied in an appropriate environment and under competent guidance, can be an acceptable and legitimate means for expressing positive and negative feelings and emotions. Adults frequently reduce personal stresses and frustrations in verbal exchanges with trusted friends and relatives or by means of avocations, hobbies, games, projects, trips, sports, vacations, and so on. For children, who are generally less capable in verbal communications and less in control of their personal life-style, the expressive arts are an opportunity to reduce stresses and frustrations without danger of conflict with others.

The expressive arts can provide many benefits for children. Not only are they beneficial in the affective domain, but they provide a variety of cognitive and psychomotor learning benefits.

If the arts are to be used as a behavior management technique, the child must be provided with opportunities to find a personally satisfying medium of expression. The individual must be provided with consistent, repeated opportunities to express feelings and emotions through the chosen medium.

Cheney and Morse (1972) summarized the value of the expressive arts for children as follows:

This group of interventions supports and develops the child's expressive abilities. Such techniques serve to mobilize the child's internal resources in a number of ways: they facilitate involvement through activity rather than retreat and withdrawal; they provide acceptable channels for cathartic release; they serve as means of both externalizing the child's conflicts and communicating his feelings about them to others (though both the signal and response may be nonverbal, and nonconscious and not discussed); many of the expressive media seem to embody inherent "therapeutic" qualities. For children with verbal inhibitions the whole "language" may be nonverbal. (p. 352).

Axline (1947) presented eight basic principles for therapeutic play. These principles appear to be applicable to the expressive arts interventions discussed in this section:

1. The therapist must develop a warm, friendly relationship with the child, in which good rapport is established as soon as possible.
2. The therapist accepts the child exactly as he is.
3. The therapist establishes a feeling of permissiveness in the relationship so that the child feels free to express his feelings completely.
4. The therapist is alert to recognize the *feelings* the child is expressing and reflects these feelings back to him in such a manner that he gains insight into this behavior.
5. The therapist maintains a deep respect for the child's ability to solve his own problems if given an opportunity to do so. The responsibility to make choices and to institute change is the child's.
6. The therapist does not attempt to direct the child's actions or conversation in any manner. The child leads the way; the therapist follows.
7. The therapist does not attempt to hurry the therapy along. It is a gradual process and is recognized as such by the therapist.
8. The therapist establishes only those limitations that are necessary to anchor the therapy to the world of reality and to make the child aware of this responsibility in the relationship. (pp. 75 and 76)

Although the eight principles were proposed for play therapists, they are applicable for teachers with one possible exception. This exception is related to Principle 4, which states, "reflects those feelings back to him." Skill in the art of interpreting and reflecting feelings back to an individual in nondirective therapy requires training and experience. Most teachers lack training in nondirective therapy.

Although some limitations and structure in the therapeutic application of expressive arts relative to time, place, media, and behavior are desirable, the child's activities should not be prescribed. The child is encouraged to express self as he or she desires, not as the teacher wishes.

Ginott (1959) offered the following rationale for setting limits on the child's behavior during play therapy sessions.

1. Limits can direct catharsis into symbolic channels.
2. Limits enable the therapist to maintain attitudes of acceptance, empathy, and regard for the child.

3. Limits assure physical safety.
4. Limits strengthen the child's ego control.
5. Limits exist for reasons of law, professional and personal ethics, and social acceptability.

Minimal limits include (1) time, (2) use and location of materials and equipment, (3) prevention of the destruction of facilities, equipment, and materials, and (4) restrictions to ensure the safety of the child and the teacher.

Free Play

Play therapy as described by Axline (1947), Baruch (1952), Moustakas (1953), and Solomon (1951) is difficult, if not impossible, to initiate in the classroom because of (1) restrictions inherent with the classroom setting, (2) the traditional role of the teacher, and (3) the teacher's lack of training in play therapy.

However, free-play sessions can be provided for individuals or groups. If a free-play program is instituted, sessions should be scheduled with regularity. Play materials and equipment, located in the designated free-play area, should be "primitive" or basic materials that the child or group can use to create an environment in which to express feelings and emotions. Complicated toys and games, although entertaining, may restrict the child's creative activities. These complex items require the child to be passive rather than active during the sessions.

In a free-play session the child is invited to play with any of the materials in the play area and is encouraged to select materials of interest. Activity is only restricted by the limits previously discussed. The teacher's role is that of observer and activity facilitator.

EXAMPLE

■ Elmer, a 6-year-old severely emotionally disturbed child, is assigned full-time to Mr. Parker's special class. Elmer is severely withdrawn. He is unable to interact verbally and nonverbally with Mr. Parker and his classmates. He spends his days quietly sitting at his desk unless physically moved from activity to activity and location to location.

Mr. Parker believes that a daily 30-minute free-play period might decrease Elmer's withdrawal. Mr. Parker believes that if Elmer will begin playing with the objects in the free play area of the classroom, he will, in time, begin relating to his classmates and teacher.

During the first several sessions of free play, Mr. Parker, with great enthusiasm, demonstrates to Elmer the use of the various play objects and manually guides Elmer through simple activities. Elmer is introduced to the sandbox, watertable, doll house, tools, dishes, toy animals, trucks and cars, toy soldiers, and so on.

After several weeks of free play, Mr. Parker observes that Elmer is quietly and carefully manipulating some of the toys without encouragement. He is particularly interested in the dolls, doll house, hammer, and toy guns.

As the months progress, Elmer begins playing and talking with the toys with vigor. Before the end of the school year, Elmer is silently playing with one of his classmates and occasionally talking to Mr. Parker. ■

Puppetry

Puppets may help children express feelings and emotions. Many children who cannot or will not communicate with others directly will do so through a puppet.

Many language development and affective education programs have successfully implemented puppetry into their programs. Perhaps the child feels safe and secure in the world of puppets, which can be manipulated and managed to express personal needs and moods.

Our experience in clinical, classroom, and camp settings has been that sophisticated puppets and puppet stages are unnecessary. Simple hand puppets, which often are created and constructed by the children and may be personal possessions, are effective (D'Alonzo, 1974). The puppet stage may be a tabletop and a cardboard box decorated by the children.

Children enjoy not only playing spontaneously with the puppets but also creating and producing puppet shows. Children who are not involved directly in the puppet show can profit from this activity. They respond and converse with the puppet being manipulated by a teacher or peer.

EXAMPLE   ■   Mary Lou, a shy, pretty kindergarten student, either refused or was unable to communicate verbally with her classmates and teacher during the first 3 months of the school year. Mary Lou was not a disruptive child, she was always smiling and cheerful, followed directions, and completed all tasks not requiring verbalization. Her mother reported that she was very verbal at home. In addition, Mary Lou's mother said that her daughter enjoyed kindergarten.

Mrs. Hotz, the kindergarten teacher, believed that puppet play might help Mary Lou overcome her shyness. Mary Lou and her teacher worked together to make and decorate personal puppets. When the puppets were complete, Mrs. Holtz and Mary Lou held semi-private play sessions for 15 minutes each day. After several days Mary Lou's puppet began talking to Mrs. Holtz's puppet. As other children joined the puppetry group, Mary Lou's puppet cautiously talked to other puppets. Before the Easter break arrived, Mary Lou was very talkative in school. Her puppet was seldom used.   ■

Role Playing and Psychodrama

Role playing and psychodrama are potentially valuable therapeutic interventions for use with children. Psychodrama was originally developed for therapeutic purposes by Moreno (1946). These techniques are based on the assumption that individuals may gain greater understanding of their behavior if they act out various aspects of their lives (Newcomer, 1980).

According to Raths and others (1966), role playing can assist an individual in the clarification of feelings and emotions as they relate to existing reality in three ways:

1. It can focus on real occurrences. An incident may be reenacted and the participants told to attend to the feelings aroused, or an incident may be reenacted with

the participants changing roles and attending to the feelings aroused by these new roles. An individual may be directed to deliver a soliloquy to re-create an emotionally loaded event (Moreno, 1946). Emphasis here is on expressing feelings that were hidden or held back when the event first occurred.

2. It can focus on significant others. The individual may portray a significant person in his or her life about whom a great amount of conflict is felt.

3. It can focus on processes and feelings occurring in new situations. Directions for this type of role playing may be very specific, with the participants provided with special characters and actions, or directions may be vague, allowing the participants to form their own characters.

Role playing and psychodrama techniques have been incorporated into several affective education programs concerned specifically with the learning of values and standards.

EXAMPLE   ■   Thomas, a 15-year-old tenth grader, was extremely overweight. He was the class scapegoat. His classmates were constantly making fun of his size. They called him "porky," "fatso," "pig," "slob," "tubby," and so on. Each day someone came up with a new name to call him.

Thomas was a sensitive person, and whenever he was called a name, he withdrew. Frequently the teacher saw tears in his eyes.

Mrs. Minup was very concerned about Thomas's mental well-being and his classmates' lack of consideration and compassion for Thomas and other children who were different. She believed that role playing might be a method of helping the whole class, including Thomas, gain insight into their behavior.

Without including obesity, Mrs. Minup conducted a series of role-playing activities with the class. The students role played their reactions and feelings to roles concerned with height, complexion, race, religion, and so on.

As the students began to empathize with the feelings of the characters they were role-playing, Thomas became more accepted and less a target of their hurtful behavior.   ■

Drama, as a therapeutic technique, can be used with students for several purposes in the education setting (Newcomer, 1980; Necco, Wilson and Scheidmantel, 1982; Creekmore and Madan, 1981). Among these are:

☐   To assist in finding solutions, making decisions, and assuming responsibility for personal social-emotional problems.

☐   To assist in affective education, increase feelings and emotions, and improve communication skills.

☐   To assist in solving problems associated with normal child and adolescent development.

☐   To facilitate group cohesiveness.

☐   To facilitate experimentation with adult roles.

☐   To aid in the the conceptualization of abstracts in subject matter such as language, science, etc.

☐ To offer entertainment and recreation opportunities.

☐ To offer the teacher opportunities to observe students in various situations.

Newcomer (1980) cautions teachers to apply drama therapy with care. Student preparation includes a clear understanding of the purpose, objectives, and benefits of drama. Rules and regulations should be explained. Participation is always voluntary and devoid of personal criticism.

Creative Movement and Dance

As a therapeutic intervention, creative movement and dance and other physical activities have the capacity to assist children in expressing their feelings and emotions in an acceptable manner (Chace, 1958). This can be accomplished in a variety of ways, such as by imitating nature or animals or by expressing the feelings of others or expressing personal feelings under varying circumstances. During creative movement sessions the child can express past, present, and even future feelings and emotions. These activities encourage the child to externalize personal feelings and begin to deal with them.

Movement activities can be conducted with or without music (Hibben & Scheer, 1982). On occasion, voices, hand clapping, feet stamping, recorded environmental sounds, and rhythm instruments are used to facilitate sessions.

EXAMPLE ■ At Camp R&R it was noticed by the staff that the preteen group known as the "cool persons" was the most "uptight" of all the groups. Children in this group appeared afraid to "let go," to have a good time, or to relax. They appeared concerned about making mistakes in front of their peers.

Ms. Taphorn, a dance enthusiast, suggested that a daily early morning session of creative movement might relax the group and develop cohesiveness. During the sessions, in which Ms. Taphorn and the staff participated, the group became trees, grass, wind, rain, sun, and flowers. They acted out sadness, happiness, joy, sorrow, excitement, fear, and so on.

Within a few days, the "cool persons" were acting as "happy cool persons." The campers began to relax and enjoy each other's company. ■

Physical activities have been used to provide both aerobic activity and therapeutic restructuring of the environment (Lane, Bonic, & Wallgren-Bonic, 1983). Group "walk-talks" have demonstrated the production of healthy levels of fatigue and improve peer relationships among adolescents (Lane et al., 1983). Daily jogging programs have decreased disruptive behaviors among behavior disordered children (Allen, 1980; Hoenig, Shea, & Bauer, 1986).

Music

It is an accepted fact in contemporary society that people are affected by music. We are exposed to mood-modifying music in restaurants, factories, supermarkets, department stores, banks, and so on. Presumably this music has some effect on our behavior and moods (Roter, 1981).

Music is applied as a therapeutic intervention for children in several ways (Purvis & Samet, 1976; Lament, 1978):

1. Children enjoy listening to recordings.
2. Music is an effective tool for reducing excitement and activity levels after high-interest, strenuous activities.
3. Young people enjoy producing music. Although every child cannot successfully learn to play a piano or guitar, most children can learn to enjoy singing and participating in a rhythm band.

Through music children can express feelings and emotions in an acceptable way.

EXAMPLE ■ Mr. Binckly used music for two purposes in his class for behavior-disordered acting-out elementary school boys. Music was used (1) to calm the group after vigorous outdoor activity and (2) to allow the group to express pent-up energy and aggression.

After outdoor activities the class devoted 5 minutes to sitting quietly and listening to calming music. Mr. Binckly found this an excellent way to help the group make the transition from recess and physical education to academics.

In addition, Mr. Binckly used music to channel the students' energy after a test or long period of seatwork. On such occasions the group would sing a few songs. No effort was made to perfect the technique. ■

Music as therapy has several advantages for children. It encourages personal freedom and interpretation, and provides "a unique personal experience that has its own meaning for each individual" (Thursby, 1977, p. 77). Music responds to the needs of individuals within a broad range of ages, intellectual abilities, social and educational experiences, and emotional characteristics. Music encourages self-subordination through cooperation and encourages self-discipline and self-directed behavior (David and Newcomer, 1980).

In a discussion of the advantages of music as an integral component of the Developmental Therapy curriculum for severely emotionally disturbed children, Wood (1976) suggested that for such children: "Communication must be established as a basis for trust if there is to be subsequent growth; and of all the ways to communicate, perhaps music is the most universal ... Whatever form the disturbance takes, and whatever the age of the child, there is a way to reach each child through music in order to begin the gradual movements toward healthier responses" (p. vii).

Michel (1976) suggested that music therapy techniques may be of assistance even though a trained music therapist is not available. Music can be used by the teacher as part of a child's education program, as an adjunct to daily programming, and to teach specific subject matter (Duerksen, 1981). As part of a child's education, music may be used for the following purposes (Lament, 1978; Hibben & Scheer, 1982; Ferolo, Rotatori, Macklin, & Fox, 1983; Ferolo, Rotatori, & Fox, 1984; Thursby, 1977; David & Newcomer, 1980):

□ To facilitate cognitive development, through increasing abstract thinking, increasing attending, and providing practice for conceptual skills.

□ To facilitate affective development and social skills and encourage social interaction.

□ To increase psychomotor skills, coordination, body image, position in space, movement skills, and auditory and visual discrimination.

□ To assist in the development of self-concept, to develop self-reliance, and to provide an opportunity to be successful.

□ To provide creative experiences and increase expressive skills, and to provide an expressive outlet for "blowing off steam."

There are several adjunctive uses of music in the educational setting (Duerksen, 1981; David & Newcomer, 1980). Music may be used to manage the behaviors of individuals and groups, to produce a relaxing atmosphere, or to serve as a distraction for children and youth with behavior disorders. Musical activities may serve to motivate students: They can be used as reinforcement for improved behavior, completed work, or other target behaviors. Because it is nonverbal, music may serve both as a form of communication and an aesthetic outlet for some children and youth with behavior disorders.

Music may also be used to teach subject matter (Duerksen, 1981; Thursby, 1977). For instance, it can provide musical background and context for academic subject areas. In nonacademic areas music can also be used to inspire creative writing, art, and story telling.

In whatever its applications, it is important to remember that the goals of music therapy are not to teach specific musical skills and knowledge but to assist the student in reaching nonmusical developmental goals (Duerksen, 1981).

Written Word

Few studies have been conducted on the therapeutic benefit of writing as an intervention for children, although writing has been repeatedly demonstrated to be a useful therapeutic intervention for adults. It seems logical that children can express personal feelings and emotions through written communications. By writing and at times sharing with others that which is written, it is possible to externalize personal conflicts and frustrations (Levinson, 1982; Dehouske, 1982).

"The written word is a modality for self-expression, self-exploration, and problem solving. Through story writing, students reveal their perceptions, attitudes, coping skills and problem-solving strategies. Story-writing tasks can be structured to encourage students to explore the decision-making process and identify behavioral alternatives and consequences" (Dehouske, 1982, p. 11).

Writing for therapeutic benefit is not concerned with any particular format. Concern is focused entirely on content. The written forms may include poetry, stories, essays, articles, books, journal entries, and so on.

EXAMPLE ■ For a teenager, Michael had several serious problems on his mind. He was not only concerned about himself and his future, but he was concerned about his parents, who were separated and considering divorce.

Michael had great difficulty talking about his problems to anyone, including parents, teachers, and friends. The school counselor suggested that Michael might keep a journal in which he could write about his concerns and his feelings. The counselor told Michael not to be concerned about spelling, grammar, hand-writing, and so on—just write what he wished. The counselor offered to discuss these writings with Michael if and when Michael wished.

Michael wrote a daily journal. He did not discuss the content with the counselor but did report that it helped to write about his problems and reread his daily entries. ■

Spoken Words

Although many children are not developmentally or emotionally prepared to enter formal verbal psychotherapy, they frequently enjoy and profit from communicating verbally. Communications may take the form of group story-telling sessions or informal conversations and discussions with teachers. In each of these the child is encouraged to express feelings and emotions.

EXAMPLE ■ Mr. Blackside believed a special camp was a setting in which emotionally disturbed campers could express their feelings.

It was suggested that the campers' aggressions, in part, could be channeled into evening campfire discussions and story-telling sessions. During these sessions the campers were encouraged to review the day's activities. They were encouraged to discuss their arguments, fights, and hurt feelings. ■

Newcomer (1980) suggests the therapeutic benefit of the spoken word is greatest if creative, original materials are emphasized. The teacher helps the children create stories and cast themselves as characters in the story. The story may be acted out by the children with emphasis on the affective content.

Bibliotherapy

Bibliotherapy is an indirect intervention which uses the interaction between the reader and literature for therapeutic purposes. This intervention can be applied with children and youth to encourage them to fulfill their needs, relieve pressures, and improve mental and emotional well-being (Russell and Russell, 1979).

For bibliotherapy to be effective, the child must be able to read, motivated to read, and be exposed to appropriate materials. Literature is selected by the teacher and child which focuses on the child's needs, is at the appropriate level, is realistic, and accurately represents the characters in the story (Cianciolo, 1965).

Hoagland (1972) indicates that bibliotherapy works as a three-phase process. First, the children identify themselves in the literature—they must perceive themselves as a part of the story or as a character. Second, children become emotionally involved in the story and the problem it presents. Finally, they arrive at a greater understanding of themselves and their problems by identifying with the characters or situations in the story.

Learning activities used to facilitate bibliotherapy include:

1. Writing a summary of the book for discussion.
2. Dramatizing, role playing, or presenting skits or puppet shows on the message in the literature.
3. Making art works which represent characters and situations in the literature.

Art Therapy

Art productions, from the young child's scribbling to the young adult's realistic drawings and paintings, are expressions of self. Art as a therapeutic treatment medium is a growth-oriented experience which benefits children in many ways: communication, socialization, creativity, self-expression, self-exploration, and manipulation of the environment (Williams and Wood, 1977).

Children should be afforded opportunities to express their feelings and emotions through the two-dimensional arts. These productions may be finger paintings, pencil drawings, water colors, oil, tempera, and so on. Teachers should remember that their personal perceptions of the form and content of a child's art production are secondary. The important element is the child's perceptions and feelings.

Two excellent volumes on art as a therapeutic intervention for use by teachers are by Kellogg and O'Dell (1967) and Kramer (1971). In their text Kellogg and O'Dell review the development of artistic skills. Their work is useful to teachers wishing to place a child's art skill into the normal developmental sequence. In Kramer's text an extensive overview and in-depth discussion of art, art therapy, and several therapeutic techniques are provided.

The three-dimensional arts are more limited than the two-dimensional arts for classroom use because of the nature of the materials and equipment. They are, nevertheless, valuable therapeutic tools.

In three-dimensional art forms the child can externalize feelings and emotions through the manipulation of clay, plaster, sand, wood, plastic, and a variety of other materials. Arts and crafts projects are included in this group of therapeutic interventions.

Photography may be of interest to students who are dissatisfied with their creative visual expressions (Minner, 1981).

EXAMPLE ■ Mrs. Fingerling believed that children would express their feelings and emotions through the two- and three-dimensional art forms if encouraged to do so. She established an art center in the classroom. The center included the materials and equipment needed for painting with various media, drawing, sculpting, molding, and so on. She scheduled 45 minutes of art activities 3 days each week. The period was scheduled at the end of the day so those children wishing to continue their work could remain for an extra few minutes. To introduce the program, Mrs. Fingerling systematically demonstrated the use of various media. Each child was encouraged to choose his or her medium. They were encouraged to experiment and produce objects meaningful to them. ■

Behavior Influence Techniques

Psychodynamic theorists and practitioners recognize that many of the counseling and expressive arts techniques do not immediately change unacceptable behaviors to acceptable behaviors. Techniques of behavior management are needed that can be implemented to interfere with on-going unacceptable behaviors in the classroom, resource room, school, or playground.

Teachers have a responsibility to interfere with behaviors which:

☐ Present a real danger.
☐ Are psychologically harmful to the child and others.
☐ Lead to excessive excitement, loss of control, or chaos.
☐ Prohibit the continuation of the program.
☐ Lead to destruction of property.
☐ Encourage the spread of negativisim in the group.
☐ Provide opportunities to clarify individual and group values, standards, and social rules.
☐ Lead to conflict with others outside the group.
☐ Compromise the practitioner's mental health and ability to function.

Redl and Wineman (1957) suggested 12 behavior management interventions, compatible with psychodynamic framework, for the management of surface behaviors. The work of Redl and Wineman has been expanded on by Long and Newman (1961, 1965) and Shea and others (1974). The behavior influence techniques are planned ignoring, signal interference, proximity control, interest boosting, tension reduction through humor, hurdle helping, program restructuring, support from routine, direct appeal, removal of seductive objects, antiseptic bouncing, and physical restraint.

Planned Ignoring

At one time or another most children engage in unacceptable behavior in an effort to gain the attention of their classmates, teacher, and parents. These unacceptable behaviors are legion in number and may include pencil tapping, body movements, hand waving, whistling, snorting, desk top dropping, book dropping, and so on. Such behavior, although relatively benign, is annoying to others.

Planned ignoring may be used to eliminate many of these behaviors. The teacher using this technique simply ignores the disruptive behavior. No response is made when the behavior occurs. It is generally true that when attention-seeking behaviors are ignored, they become nonfunctional and decrease in frequency.

Signal Interference

There are a variety of nonverbal techniques that a teacher may use to interfere with unacceptable behaviors. Nonverbal techniques or signals, such as eye contact, a frown, finger snapping, toe tapping, book snapping, light flicking, and so on, can alert a child or group to their unacceptable behavior. Often nonverbal behavior influence techniques help the disruptive child "save face" with his or her peers, and thus the disruption is not escalated. They also save the shy child from unnecessary embarrassment.

Conversely, nonverbal signals can be used to reinforce acceptable behaviors in the classroom.

Proximity Control

Very frequently the proximity of an authority figure (teacher, parent, police officer) results in the discontinuation of unacceptable behaviors. Even college professors find it useful to walk about the classroom in an effort to reduce the level of conversation and side comments.

Proximity can have a positive effect on children experiencing anxiety and frustration. The physical presence of a teacher or parent available to assist has a calming effect on troubled children.

Interest Boosting

All persons become bored with routine and difficult tasks. Interest tends to wane with time. The teacher who observes a child losing interest or becoming bored with a task should make an effort to boost the child's interest. This may be accomplished by offering to help, noting how much work has been accomplished, noting how well done the completed part of the task is, discussing the task, and so on. Interest boosting may help the child reorganize a task and mobilize his or her energies to complete it.

Tension Reduction Through Humor

Humor has been used to reduce tension, frustration, and anxiety for as long as human beings have been laughing. Children, quite naturally, become tense when engaged in significant tasks. The prudent teacher will apply humor in an effort to help children relax and place their tasks in perspective when they become frustrated. A joke or a humorous comment will frequently reduce tension. Caution must be used to be sure the humor is not harmful to any individual.

Hurdle Helping

Hurdle helping is a technique applied to assist a student who is experiencing difficulty with a specific task. Hurdle helping may simply be an encouraging word from the teacher, an offer to assist with a specific task, or the making available of additional materials and equipment. Help is provided before the child becomes disruptive or simply gives up on the assignment.

Program Restructuring

Occasionally teachers, especially new teachers, are so committed to a lesson, task, or schedule that they will continue regardless of student response. Prudent teachers are sufficiently observant to recognize when a lesson or activity is going poorly; they are flexible. Before the class becomes disruptive or loses all interest, the teacher either restructures the lesson or postpones it until a more appropriate time.

Support from Routine

All persons, including children, like to know their daily schedule. We appreciate being able to plan our day and knowing where, when, why, and with whom we will be at various times. It appears to be especially important to behavior-disordered children that they be provided with a schedule and a routine.

The teacher is wise to announce and post the day's schedule in the classroom. Changes in the schedule should be announced in advance, if possible. The children should be reminded of future special events.

Direct Appeal

Many times during an unacceptable behavior incident, the teacher can quickly and effectively resolve the problem through direct appeal to the students' sense of fairness. The direct appeal is derived from the following:

1. The teacher's personal positive relationship with the individual or group.
2. The consequences that will result if the unacceptable behavior continues.
3. The effect of the behavior on the student's peers.
4. The teacher's authority over the student and group.

Many teachers neglect this approach to influencing behavior in favor of more indirect interventions. They neglect to simply and forcefully state, "Stop this behavior because . . ."

Removal of Seductive Objects

Frequently misbehavior occurs because the student has available some object of attention that is distracting him or her from the task at hand. Young children bring small toys, games, and other objects to the classroom that distract them. Older children are distracted by books, magazines, pocketknives, combs, keys, and so on. When the teacher finds that these objects are keeping the child from the assigned task, the objects should be confiscated until after class or school. The confiscation should be kind and firm. Discussion is not necessary. It is more effective if children are trained to routinely store such objects in an appropriate place before school and until it is time to use them.

Antiseptic Bouncing

When a student becomes agitated and frustrated with an activity and before he or she is physically or verbally disruptive, it is prudent to remove the student from the work setting. This removal is called antiseptic bouncing. It is viewed as a positive behavior influence technique and not as a punishment. Antiseptic bouncing, properly applied, provides the student with an opportunity to avoid embarrassment, calm down, reorganize thought, and begin the task anew.

Physical Restraint

Perhaps no children are more concerned with their physical and emotional well-being —and perhaps their continued existence—than children who have lost control of self in a tantrum. These children feel totally and absolutely helpless. They simply cannot control their physical and verbal behaviors. On such an occasion physical restraint is necessary. The child is held until calm. The teacher communicates physically and verbally to the child in a calm voice or whisper. The teacher communicates to the child "You are safe; I will protect you; I will not let you harm yourself."

After the child regains control, the teacher may wish to discuss the incident with the child. They may plan ways the child can avoid similar problems in the future.

The behavior influence techniques discussed in this section are effective in the control of directly observable behaviors. They should be a part of the behavior management method of all teachers. The techniques are most effective when used with consistency.

Self-Control Curriculum

A significant occurrence in the field of education in recent years is the renewed emphasis on self-control curriculum and affective education. This approach emphasizes helping children focus on increasing their awareness and understanding of personal emotions, values, and attitudes through educational activities (Edwards & O'Toole, 1985; Epanchin & Monson, 1982; McGinnis, Sauerbry, & Nichols, 1985). Through affective education, children become increasingly aware of the relationship between self and others and improve their interpersonal problem-solving skills.

Goldstein, Spafkin, Gershaw, and Klein (1983) list fifty social skills in six categories needed by children and youth to enhance their social functioning. These skills are listed in Table 6.1.

TABLE 6.1
Social skills by skill groups

Group I. Beginning Social Skills	25. Negotiating
1. Listening	26. Using self-control
2. Starting a conversation	27. Standing up for one's rights
3. Having a conversation	28. Responding to teasing
4. Asking a question	29. Avoiding trouble with others
5. Saying "thank you"	30. Keeping out of fights
6. Introducing oneself	
7. Introducing other people	*Group V. Skills for Dealing with Stress*
8. Giving a compliment	31. Making a complaint
	32. Answering a complaint
Group II. Advanced Social Skills	33. Showing sportsmanship after the game
9. Asking for help	34. Dealing with embarrassment
10. Joining in	35. Dealing with being left out
11. Giving instructions	36. Standing up for a friend
12. Following instructions	37. Responding to persuasion
13. Apologizing	38. Responding to failure
14. Convincing others	39. Dealing with contradictory messages
	40. Dealing with an accusation
Group III. Skills for Dealing with Feelings	41. Getting ready for a difficult conversation
15. Knowing one's feelings	42. Dealing with group pressure
16. Expressing one's feelings	
17. Understanding the feelings of others	*Group VI. Planning Skills*
18. Dealing with someone else's anger	43. Deciding on something to do
19. Expressing affection	44. Deciding what caused a problem
20. Dealing with fear	45. Setting a goal
21. Rewarding oneself	46. Deciding on one's abilities
	47. Gathering information
Group IV. Skill Alternatives to Aggression	48. Arranging problems by importance
22. Asking permission	49. Making a decision
23. Sharing something	50. Concentrating on a task
24. Helping others	

(From "Structures Learning: A Psychoeducational Approach for Teaching Social Competencies" by A. P. Goldstein, R. P. Spafkin, N. J. Gershaw, and P. Klein, 1983, Behavioral Disorders, 8(3), pp. 161–162. Copyright 1983 by Behavioral Disorders. Reprinted by permission.)

The social skills curriculum most compatible with the psychoeducational framework discussed previously in this chapter is the "Psychoeducational Curriculum for the Prevention of Behavioral and Learning Problems" (commonly referred to as the "Self-Control Curriculum") by Fagen, Long, and Stevens (1975).

This curriculum is based on the assumption that a common denominator for disruptive behaviors of children with behavior and learning problems is a lack of self-control. To function effectively children must develop the capacity to control their behavior, even when frustrated. Self-control is defined as "one's capacity to direct and regulate personal action (behavior) flexibly and realistically in a given situation" (Fagen & Long, 1976). An important objective of the curriculum is the reduction of students' anxiety over losing self-control by increasing the skills and confidence they have in the ability to regulate their impulsive behavior.

Skillful self-control depends on the integration of eight skill clusters. These skill clusters, in turn, are composed of several specific skills. The clusters and skills are presented in Table 6.2.

TABLE 6.2
The self-control curriculum: Overview of curriculum areas and units

Area	Curriculum Unit
Selection	1. Focusing and concentration 2. Mastering figure-ground discrimination 3. Mastering distractions and interference 4. Processing complex patterns
Storage	1. Developing visual memory 2. Developing auditory memory
Sequencing and ordering	1. Developing time orientation 2. Developing auditory-visual sequencing 3. Developing sequential planning
Anticipating consequences	1. Identifying feelings 2. Evaluating consequences
Appreciating feelings	1. Identifying feelings 2. Developing positive feelings 3. Managing feelings 4. Reinterpreting feeling events
Managing frustration	1. Accepting feelings of frustration 2. Building coping resources 3. Tolerating frustration
Inhibition and delay	1. Controlling action 2. Developing part-goals
Relaxation	1. Developing body relaxation 2. Developing thought relaxation 3. Developing movement relaxation

(From Teaching Children Self-Control: Preventing Emotional and Learning Problems in the Elementary School *(p. 77) by S. A. Fagen, N. J. Long, and D. J. Stevens, 1975, Columbus, OH: Merrill Publishing Co. Copyright 1975, by Merrill Publishing Co. Reprinted by permission.)*

In the curriculum, the learning of each specific skill is accomplished through a variety of learning activities. Through growth in the eight skill clusters, the authors predict growth in the student's capacity to direct and regulate personal action in given situations. Activities which make up the curriculum include games, role playing, lessons, and discussion. Activities are implemented in small, developmental steps and include positive feedback. Short, regular training sessions are advised.

There are a variety of social skills and affective education curricula available in the literature. The practitioner must give careful consideration to the appropriateness of a particular program for the children for whom it is to be applied. Schumaker, Pederson, Hazel, and Meyen (1983) suggest five questions for practitioners to address when selecting a social skills curriculum:

1. Does the curriculum promote social competence?
2. Does the curriculum accommodate the learning characteristics of the students for whom it is to be applied?
3. Does the curriculum target the social skills deficits of the students for whom it is to be applied?
4. Does the curriculum provide training in situations as well as in skills?
5. Does the curriculum include instructional methodologies found to be effective with the population of students for whom it is to be applied?

SUMMARY

In this chapter we have discussed a variety of behavior management interventions derived from psychodynamic theory. Attention is given to the psychoeducational model; a broad perspective applied to the management and education of children. Two counseling techniques, life-space interviewing and reality therapy interviewing for use by teacher, with minimal training, are discussed in detail.

The expressive arts are presented as indirect behavior management interventions. The expressive arts include free play, puppetry, role playing and psychodrama, creative movement and dance, music, the spoken and written word, bibliotherapy, art therapy, and others. The expressive arts are recommended as therapeutic interventions which encourage children to express their positive and negative feelings and emotions in an acceptable manner.

Several behavior influence techniques are discussed as interventions teachers may wish to apply when a student's surface behavior interferes with daily function. (These interventions *must* be applied in circumstances which endanger the student, teacher, peers, and property.) The chapter concludes with a discussion of social skills curriculum which may be applied to instruct students in socially appropriate behaviors.

In the next chapter, attention is focused on interventions derived from environmental and biophysical theories.

EXERCISES

Quiz

1. The four categories of psychodynamic behavior management interventions discussed in this chapter are:

   a. _____   c. _____

   b. _____   d. _____

2. The life-space interview may be applied for either of two purposes. They are:

   a. _____   b. _____

3. According to Glasser, the two basic psychological needs of all human beings are:

   a. _____   b. _____

4. Five expressive arts that may be applied as behavior management interventions are:

   a. _____   d. _____

   b. _____   e. _____

   c. _____

5. Six of the behavior influence techniques discussed in the chapter are:

   a. _____   d. _____

   b. _____   e. _____

   c. _____   f. _____

6. The six major areas for self-control in the Fagen, Long, and Stevens curriculum are:

   a. _____   d. _____

   b. _____   e. _____

   c. _____   f. _____

Projects

1. Write a brief essay (300 words) on the advantages and disadvantages of the psychodynamic behavior management interventions.
2. Conduct a life-space interview with a classmate. Invite your other classmates to evaluate your performance.
3. Conduct a reality therapy interview with a classmate. Invite your other classmates to evaluate your performance.
4. Conduct a library research study of one of the expressive arts as a behavior management intervention. Report your finding in a formal presentation to your classmates.
5. Discuss the advantages and disadvantages of the behavior influence techniques for the teacher.
6. Research the literature on self-control curriculum and report your findings to your class.

REFERENCES

Allen J. I. (1980). Jogging can modify disruptive behaviors. *Teaching Exceptional Children, 12*(2), 66–70.

Axline, V. M. (1947). *Play therapy.* Boston: Houghton Mifflin Co.

Baruch, D. W. (1952). *One little boy.* New York: Dell Publishing Co.

Berkowitz, P. H., & Rothman, E. P. (1960). *The disturbed child: Recognition and psychoeducational therapy in the classroom.* New York: New York University Press.

Berkowitz, P. H., & Rothman, E. P. (Eds.). (1967). *Public education for disturbed children in New York City.* Springfield, IL: Charles C. Thomas.

Brenner, M. B. (1969). Life space interviewing in the school setting. In H. Dupont (Ed.), *Educating emotionally disturbed children.* New York: Holt, Rinehart & Winston.

Chace, M. (1958). Dance in growth or treatment settings. *Music Therapy, 1,* 119–121.

Cheney, C., & Morse, W. C. (1972). Psychodynamic interventions in emotional disturbance. In W. C. Rhodes & M. L. Tracy (Eds.), *A study of child variance: Vol. 2. Interventions.* Ann Arbor: The University of Michigan Press.

Cianciolo, P. J. (1965). Children's literature can affect coping behavior. *Personnel and Guidance Journal. 43*(9), 897–903.

Cook, J. H. (1972). *The effects of small group counseling on the classroom behavior of sociometrically underchosen adolescents.* Unpublished doctoral dissertation, University of Georgia. (Discussed in Shearn & Randolph, 1978.)

Creekmore, N. N., & Madan, A. J. (1981). The use of sociodrama as a therapeutic technique with behavior disordered children. *Behavior Disorders, 7*(1), 28–33.

D'Alonzo, B. (1974). Puppets fill the classroom with imagination. *Teaching Exceptional Children, 6*(3), 141–144.

David D., & Newcomer, P. L. (1980). Art and music therapy. In P. L. Newcomer (Ed.), *Understanding and teaching emotionally disturbed children* (pp. 391–408). Boston: Allyn & Bacon.

Dehouske, E. J. (1982). Story writing as a problem solving vehicle. *Teaching Exceptional Children, 15*(1), 11–17.

DeMagistris, R. J., & Imber, S. C. (1980). The effects of life space interviewing on the academic and social performance of behavior disordered children. *Behavior Disorders, 6*(1), 12–25.

Duerksen, G. L. (1981). Music for exceptional students. *Focus on Exceptional Children, 14*(4), 1–11.

Edwards, L. L, & O'Toole, B. (1985). Application of self-control curriculum with behavior disordered students. *Focus on Exceptional Children, 17*(8), 1–8.

Epanchin, B. C., & Monson, L. B. (1982). Affective education. In J. L. Paul & B. C. Epanchin (Eds.), *Emotional disturbance in children: Theories and methods for teachers.* Columbus, OH: Merrill Publishing Co.

Fagen, S. A. & Long, N. J. (1976). Teaching children self-control: A new responsibility for teachers. *Focus on Exceptional Children, 7*(8), 1–10.

Fagen, S. A., Long, N. J., & Stevens, D. J. (1975). *Teaching children self-control: Preventing emotional and learning problems in the elementary school.* Columbus, OH: Merrill.

Ferolo, M. A., Rotatori, A. F., & Fox, R. (1984). Increasing visual attention by music therapy programming for sensory stimulation with profoundly retarded children. *ICEC Quarterly, 33*(2), 17–21.

Ferolo, M. A., Rotatori, A., Macklin, F., & Fox, R. (1983). The successful use of behavior modification in music therapy with severely/profoundly retarded people. *ICEC Quarterly, 32*(2), 30–34.

Ginott, H. G., (1959). The theory and practice of therapeutic interventions in child treatment. *Journal of Counsulting Psychology, 23,* 160–166.

Glasser, W. (1965). *Reality therapy: A new approach to psychiatry.* New York: Harper & Row.

Glasser, W. (1969). *Schools without failure.* New York: Harper & Row.

Glick, B. H. (1968). *The investigation of changes in self-concept, social self-esteem, and academic self-responsibility of emotionally disturbed boys who participate in open-ended classroom meetings.* Unpublished doctoral dissertation, Syracuse University. (Discussed in Shearn & Randolph, 1978.)

Goldstein, A. P., Spafkin, R. P., Gershaw N. J., & Klein, P. (1983). Structures learning: A psychoeducational approach for teaching social competencies. *Behavioral Disorders, 8*(3), 161–170.

Hawes, R. M. (1970). *Reality therapy in the classroom.* Unpublished doctoral dissertation, University of the Pacific. (Discussed in Shearn & Randolph, 1978.)

Hibben, J. & Scheer, R. (1982). Music and movement for special needs children. *Teaching Exceptional Children, 14*(5), 171–176.

Hoagland, J. (1972). Bibliotherapy: Aiding children in personality development. *Elementary English, 15,* 390-394.

Hoenig, G. K., Shea, T. M., & Bauer, A. M. (1986). Jogging and children with behavior disorders: Effects on self-doubting and aggressive behaviors. *ICEC Quarterly, 36*(4), 16–21.

Kellogg, R., & O'Dell, S. (1967). *The psychology of children's art.* New York: CRM-Random House Publication.

Kramer, E. (1971). *Art as therapy with children.* New York: Schocken Books.

Lament, M. M. (1978). Reaching the exceptional student through music in the elementary classroom. *Teaching Exceptional Children, 11*(1), 32–35.

Lane, B., Bonic, J., & Wallgren-Bonic, N. (1983). The group walk-talk: A therapeutic challenge for secondary students with social-emotional problems. *Teaching Exceptional Children, 16*(1), 12–17.

Leone, P. (1984). A descriptive follow-up of behaviorally disordered adolescents. *Behavior Disorders, 9*(3), 207-214.

Levinson, C. (1982). Remediating a passive aggressive emotionally disturbed pre-adolescent boy through writing: A comprehensive psychodynamic structured approach. *The Pointer, 26*(2), 23–27

Long, N. J., & Fagen, S. A. (Eds.) (1980). *The Pointer, 25*(2).

Long, N. J., Morse, W. C., & Newman, R. G. (1980). Milieu therapy. In N. J. Long, W. C. Morse, & R. G. Newman (Eds.). *Conflict in the classroom: The education of emotionally disturbed children* (4th ed). Belmont, CA: Wadsworth Publishing Co.

Long N. J., & Newman, R. G. (1965). Managing surface behavior of children in school. In N. J. Long, W. C. Morse, & R. G. Newman (Eds.), *Conflict in the classroom: The education of emotionally disturbed children.* Belmont, CA: Wadsworth Publishing Co.

Long, N. J., & Newman, R. G. (1961). A differential approach to the management of surface behavior of children in school. *Bulletin of the School of Education, 37,* Indiana University.

McGinnis, E., Sauerbry, L., & Nichols, P. (1985). Skill-streaming: Teaching social skills to children with behavior disorders. *Teaching Exceptional Children, 17*(3), 160–167.

Michel, D. E. (1976). *Music therapy: An introduction to therapy and special education through music.* Springfield, IL: C.C. Thomas.

Minner, S. (1981). Using photography as an adjunctive and creative approach. *Teaching Exceptional Children, 13*(4), 145–147.

Moreno, J. L. (1946). *Psychodrama,* Beacon, NY: Beacon House.

Morse, W. C. (1971). Worksheet on life space interviewing for teachers. In N. J. Long, W. C. Morse, & R. G. Newman (Eds.), *Conflict in the classroom: The education of emotionally disturbed children* (2nd ed.). Belmont, CA: Wadsworth Publishing Co.

Morse, W. C. (1985). *The education and treatment of socioemotionally impaired children and youth.* Syracuse, NY: Syracuse University Press.

Morse, W. C., & Wineman, D. (1957). Group interviewing in a camp for disturbed boys. *Journal of Social Issues, 13*(1), 23–31.

Moustakas, C. E. (1953). *Children in play therapy.* New York: McGraw-Hill Book Co.

Necco, E., Wilson C., & Scheidmantel, J. (1982). Affective learning through drama. *Teaching Exceptional Children, 15*(1), 22–24.

Newcomer, P.L. (1980). *Understanding and teaching emotionally disturbed children.* Boston: Allyn & Bacon.

Nichols, P. (1984). Down the up staircase: The teacher as therapist. In J. Grosenick, S. Huntze, E. McGinnis, & C. Smith (Eds.). *Social/affective interventions in behavioral disorders.* Des Moines: State of Iowa Department of Public Instruction.

Peter, L. J. (1965). *Perscriptive teaching.* New York: McGraw Hill Book Co.

Purvis, J., & Samet, S. (1976). *Music in develop-*

mental therapy. Baltimore: University Park Press.

Raths, L. E., Harmin, M., & Simon, S. B. (1978). *Values and teaching.* Columbus, OH: Merrill Publishing Co.

Redl, F. (1959). The concept of the life space interview. *American Journal of Orthopsychiatry, 29,* 1–18.

Redl, F., & Wineman, D. (1957). *The aggressive child.* New York: The Free Press.

Reilly, M. J., Imber, S. C., & Cremins, J. (1978). *The effects of life space interviews on social behaviors of junior high school special needs students.* Paper presented at the 56th International Council for Exceptional Children, Kansas City.

Roter, J. (1981). Music a therapeutic intervention for emotionally disturbed youth. In F. H. Wood (Ed.), *Perspective for a new decade: Education's responsiblity for seriously disturbed and behaviorally disordered children and youth* (pp. 154–162). Reston, VA: Council for Exceptional Children.

Russell, A. E., & Russell, W. A. (1979). Using bibliotherapy with emotionally disturbed children. *Teaching Exceptional Children, 11,* 168–169.

Scheaf, W. A. (1972). *The effects of paired learning and Glasser-type discussions on two determinants of academic achievement and on reading achievement of male delinquents.* Unpublished doctoral dissertation, Case Western Reserve University. (Discussed in Shearn & Randolph, 1978.)

Schumaker, J. B., Pederson, C. S., Hazel, J. S., & Meyen, E. L. (1983). Social skills curricula for mildly handicapped adolescents: A review. *Focus on Exceptional Children, 16*(4), 1–16.

Shea, T. M., Whiteside, W. R., Beetner, E. G., & Lindsey, D. L. (1974). *Microteaching module: Behavioral interventions.* Edwardsville: Southern Illinois University.

Shearn, D. F., & Randolph, D. L. (1978). Effects of reality therapy methods applied in the classroom. *Psychology in the Schools, 15,* 79–83.

Solomon, J. C. (1951). Therapeutic use of play. In H. H. Anderson & G. L. Anderson (Eds.), *An introduction to projective techniques.* Englewood Cliffs, NJ: Prentice Hall.

Thursby, D. D. (1977). Everyone's a star. *Teaching Exceptional Children, 9*(3), 77–78.

Williams, G. H. & Wood, M. M. (1977). *Developmental art therapy.* Baltimore: University Park Press.

Wood, M. M. (1976). Foreword. In J. Purvis & S. Samet (Eds.), *Music in developmental therapy* (pp. vii–viii). Baltimore: University Park Press.

CHAPTER SEVEN

Environmental and Biophysical Behavior Management

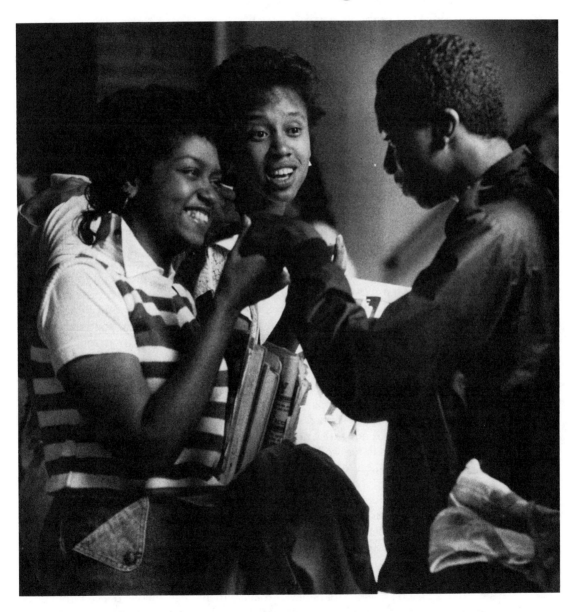

Jack and his gang were loitering near the front door of Hooverville High School planning their Monday morning activities. By general consensus their target for the day was to be Marcie Meek. Jack conducted a discussion during which the group of five boys decided how to make life miserable for Marcie. They agreed to whistle and catcall at her in the corridors. They were going to tell everyone they met that Marcie was "easy." Finally, every time she was called on during class, they would grumble and sigh.

Jack and the gang were of considerable concern to the whole school population, especially to Mr. Whiteburn, Assistant Principal for Discipline. It appeared that Jack and his friends selected a different student or teacher each day as a target for their hostility. Each of the boys had been referred to Mr. Whiteburn several times during the year for disciplining. He had punished them, individually and as a group, many times without success. He had even called their parents.

Although the group's behavior was disruptive, it was not severe enough to result in expulsion or suspension.

Mr. Whiteburn knows that the group's behavior must be redirected from negative to positive goals before the boys become involved in a serious incident. He must seek out a means to help the gang plan and carry out appropriate activities.

Six-year-old John was being observed by the first-grade teacher, Mrs. Prime. As she observed John, he climbed over the worktable, ran to the toy box, and threw several blocks, trucks, and dolls on the floor. Next John ran around the room touching each child and the four walls.

After this he returned to his seat at the worktable, grabbed his crayon, and scribbled on his work sheet for about 10 seconds. While he was scribbling, John was wiggling in his chair and tapping his feet.

Suddenly John fell to his hands and knees and began crawling to the toy box. He climbed into the box and threw the remaining toys on the floor. Having accomplished this, John returned to the worktable. John's hyperactive behavior continued throughout Mrs. Prime's 1-hour observation session.

That afternoon, in discussion with John's mother and preschool teacher, Mrs. Prime learned that John's behavior during the observation session was typical of his behavior at home and in preschool. Both the preschool teacher and his mother reported using a variety of behavior modification interventions without success. John appeared unable to control his activity; he appeared driven.

Mrs. Prime knew she must have some assistance if John were to attend her first grade. He simply could not succeed in class unless his behavior was controlled.

In this chapter a variety of behavior management interventions derived from environmental (i.e., sociological and ecological) and biophysical theories are reviewed and exemplified. The environmental behavior management interventions include child-centered, environment-centered, child-environment-centered and interface-centered strategies. Other environmental interventions include strategies related to group composition and processes, the classroom setting, and class meetings. The section concludes with a review of milieu therapy and the levels system.

The second section of this chapter is devoted to a discussion of biophysical strategies such as prenatal and postnatal care, nutrition, medication, diets, and so on. This section concludes with discussion of the educator's role in biophysical interventions.

It should be noted that, for the most part, environmental interventions focus attention on the manipulation of groups and the environment rather than on individual students.

Several environmental and biophysical interventions employed by professionals in the mental health disciplines are not presented in this chapter because of their complexity and the special training requirements necessary for implementation. The reader is urged to review the theoretical frameworks underlying the environmental and biophysical models presented in Chapter 1 before studying this chapter.

It should be noted that the educator has limited direct involvement in the diagnosis, prescribing, implementation, and evaluation of biophysical interventions.

Environmental Interventions

In varying degrees, the interventions discussed in this section focus attention on the child's environment as the locus of the behavior problem. There are four groups of environmental interventions; these are distinguished from one another by the degree of emphasis placed on the individual's environment as the determiner of his or her behavior.

According to Rhodes and Gibbens (1972) and Wagner (1972), these groups are:

1. Excitor or child-centered interventions, which focus almost exclusively on the child.
2. Respondent or environment-centered interventions, which focus almost exclusively on the responding environment.
3. Excitor-respondent or child-environment-centered interventions which focus on both the child and environment with near equal emphasis.
4. Exchange or interface-centered interventions, which focus on the exchange patterns between the child and the environment.

The distinctions among these classifications are blurred; the degree of emphasis focused on the child, the environment, and the relationship between these two variables is not clear-cut. Wagner, however, made an attempt to place the environmental interventions on a continuum ranging from primary emphasis on the child to primary emphasis on the environment.

Child-Centered Interventions

Among the child-centered interventions, which are primarily concerned with accommodating the child to the environment, are the following.

Remedial Programs Aimed at Psychomotor, Cognitive, and Affective Learning. These interventions include programs in gross and fine motor coordination, perceptual training, academic education, and affective education, among others. The activities normally conducted in special education rooms or by itinerant teachers are excellent examples of child-centered interventions as applied in the school.

Natural Community Interventions. Although few if any opportunities exist for this type of intervention in this century, the general goal of these interventions is the placement of an individual in a natural community setting where behavior is changed by naturally occurring processes inherent in community living (Byrne, 1869; cited in Wagner, 1972).

The natural community intervention was one of the objectives of the community mental health movement that began in the 1960s and continues to the present in the United States. During this period many mentally ill and mentally retarded persons were returned to live in the community with the hope that a natural environment would have a therapeutic effect on their behavior.

School Community Interventions. Primarily aimed at the child, these interventions involve the manipulation of the school environment for the child's therapeutic benefit (Stickney, 1968).

Artificial Community Interventions. Aimed at the child, these interventions involve the development and systematic manipulation of an artificial community (commune, collective, or residential center) to modify the child's behavior (Makarenko, 1951). There are many examples of artificial community interventions in contemporary society. These include halfway houses, community living centers, residential schools, and so on.

Artificial Group Interventions. These interventions involve attempts to change the child in the home community by means of an artificial group. This approach is used frequently in delinquency rehabilitation programs. Groups are organized to maintain and change the individual in the community. The group provides the individual with social and psychological support as well as guidance and direction. Contemporary examples of artificial group interventions include the Guardian Angels and similar positively oriented street gangs as well as the Scouts, Big Sister, Big Brother, and so on.

Environment-Centered Interventions

Among the environment-centered interventions, which are primarily focused on changing the child's environment, are the following.

Architectural Interventions.   These interventions are primarily concerned with the designing of physical environments to modify behavior. The architect's focus is on designing a physical setting that has the capacity to modify the disturbed child's behavior (Bayes, 1967). This intervention is discussed in greater detail under Classroom Environment later in this chapter.

Family Environment Interventions.   Aimed at the child's family unit, these interventions are accomplished primarily by training and education in child rearing, behavior management, and family living. Family counseling and therapy are often included in this intervention (Vogel and Bell, 1960). Many examples of family environment interventions are presented in Chapter 8.

School Environment Interventions.   Aimed at modifying the school environment and thus increasing the child's probability of success and acceptance, these interventions are accomplished through in-service teacher training, consultation, and the like (Newman, 1967).

Child-Environment-Centered Interventions

Child-environment-centered interventions, which focus on both the child and the environment, include the following.

Natural Group in Urban Environment Interventions.   These interventions involve the manipulation and redirection of existing natural groups, such as street gangs. The gang is redirected from primarily destructive or deviant effects on the community to constructive effects (Leissner, 1965). The natural group in the urban environment intervention is similar to the artificial group intervention noted earlier.

Child-School-Environment Interventions.   In these interventions the focus is on the remediation of the child's behavior and learning and on the environment's responsiveness to the child (Lewis, 1967; Weinstein, 1968). Child-school-environment interventions are best exemplified by the Re-Ed Schools and similar schools that focus attention on all facets of the child, his or her behavior, the family, the school, residential care unit, and the community.

Interface-Centered Interventions

These interventions are aimed at modifying the reciprocal relationship between the child and the environment, including persons in the environment. The focus is on assessing and changing the quality of individual-environment transactions (Rhodes, 1967). Emphasis is on specific problem areas.

Examples of these interventions include (1) training students in behavior modification techniques which they apply in school with teachers and peers and (2) evaluating and modifying a specific problem interface in which a student is functioning ineffectively.

Group Composition

Several behavior management interventions are closely associated with classroom and activity groups. Some specific management techniques employed as a part of these environmental interventions are discussed in Chapter 6 as counseling techniques (under that heading) and throughout this text as behavior modification interventions. However, when the group is a significant part of a child's overall behavior management program, two important topics must be considered in the selection and imposition of these management techniques: group composition and group processes.

Grouping children on the basis of school records and admission data is an important but difficult task (Morse and Wineman, 1957). It is a process that of necessity involves the cooperation of all persons familiar with the children.

Among the variables to be considered during the grouping process are (1) age, (2) sex, (3) interests, (4) handicapping conditions, if any, (5) personality traits, (6) the degree, intensity, and kind of behavior problems, if any, and (7) group experiences and skills. When grouping children, an effort is made to avoid extremes in group composition while at the same time attempting to form a "balanced" group. In the organization of groups the adult members of the group, such as the teacher and aide, are considered group members.

Extremes in group (and subgroup) composition are avoided when:

1. Children of greatly different ages are not placed in the same group.
2. Children without common interests are not placed in the same group.
3. An individual is not placed in a group that lacks a like-sex peer.
4. A child with a severe handicap is not placed in a group of nonhandicapped or mildly handicapped children if the placement prohibits either from participating in important curricular activities. However, if adequately trained personnel (aides or teaching assistants) are available to assist, the curriculum can be modified and this potential limitation circumvented.
5. Children with potentially conflicting personality traits and behavior problems are not placed in the same group.
6. An unskilled child is not placed in a group composed of individuals who are highly skilled and experienced in group processes. This placement is only permissible if the group members, including the adults, are aware of the child's lack of skill and experience in groups and agree to facilitate the child's integration.
7. An individual who is neither ready nor willing to participate in group activities is not placed in a group environment. Reference here is to children with severe behavior and learning problems who lack skills needed for meaningful group participation. Frequently these individuals remain in the group but do not become "functioning" members.

Grouping is a difficult process because the staff must deal with intangible variables that defy precise measurement.

Group Process

The group process itself can be of therapeutic benefit to some children. Loughmiller (1965) used self-governing, problem-solving groups in the camp setting. Also applicable in the school setting, these groups are set up to expose students to a wide range of successful interpersonal experiences and as a result of these experiences encourage participation, responsibility, and cooperation in activities (Rickard et al., 1971).

In this intervention children and teachers are responsible for their daily activities within predetermined limits established by the administration. The members find themselves in a situation where majority rule prevails. Each individual is responsible for his or her personal behavior and for the behavior of the group (Rickard & Lattal, 1969; Shea, 1977).

Some limits on the group's behavior and activities are imposed by an administrator or other nongroup authority figure rather than by the teacher, who is a member of the group. However, the group members may impose, by means of majority rule, additional limits on behavior and activities. The limits imposed by the administrator are few in number and are concerned with dining and work schedules, attendance at assemblies, transportation, health, safety, and the like. These limits must be imposed by the administration if it is to meet its responsibilities to the members of the group.

Any social cosmos requires certain routines (Morse and Wineman, 1957). Without routines, limits, and prescribed ways of behaving, anarchy would result and the group would disintegrate. Thus the group, as a group, decides (1) the limits to be set on social interaction, (2) how extreme behaviors are to be managed if they occur, (3) how activities and schedules of events are to be developed and executed, (4) who is to be responsible for various phases of daily living, and (5) how problems and conflicts are to be resolved.

The problem-solving process becomes a part of the group's daily life. When conflicts or unfamiliar problems occur that prohibit the group from attaining its immediate goals, problem solving is initiated. During the problem-solving process, the group attempts to develop alternative solutions to the circumstances confronting them. The members have two major tasks: (1) identifying and clarifying their problem and (2) discussing (evaluating) and agreeing on one or more solutions to the problem. The agreed-upon solution can be imposed either immediately or in similar situations in the future (Rickard et al., 1971). In addition to the above tasks, the members of the group must deal with the positive and negative social-emotional behaviors that naturally occur during the problem-solving process (Hare, 1962; Hare et al., 1965; Redl, 1942).

Morse and Wineman (1957) recommended the application of life-space interview techniques in the group on a regular and emergency basis. Discussed in Chapter 6 as a counseling technique, the life-space interview may focus on a variety of critical group-process issues:

- Existing social realities that prohibit group desires
- Existing defense or coping mechanisms that the group and its members unconsciously apply for protection against those who are not members of the group
- Techniques for application by the members to admit mistakes, misdeeds, and asocial behaviors
- Ways to use the group as a setting in which emotions and frustrations may be expressed and the limits on such expression
- Ways to strengthen the group's and the individual members' self-concept, especially after conflicts, frustrations, and failures
- Procedures for identifying, clarifying, and agreeing to mutually acceptable solutions to common problems

As a group member, the educator's role is important if group behavior management interventions are to be effectively applied in the classroom and school. The teacher must be a model of "give and take" democratic leadership and must be willing to permit the members of the group to make meaningful decisions, implement programs, and realize the consequences of their actions.

The teacher allows the logical consequences of the group's decisions and actions to occur. At the same time, however, the teacher protects the group from repeated or excessive failure and individual members from physical and psychological harm.

Discussion Groups

Anderson and Marrone (1979) described the use of therapeutic discussion groups in public school classes for emotionally disturbed students. As a result of twelve years of experience with over six thousand children, they concluded " . . . we cannot imagine a program for emotionally handicapped students that would not fit the proven, cost-effective methodology of therapeutic discussion groups in the classroom" (p. 15).

After a period of experimentation during which students were involved in individual therapy, therapeutic discussion groups, or non-therapeutic treatment, it was concluded that the group model benefited the children and teachers in several ways. Teachers benefited by receiving support through teamwork with mental health professionals. In addition, they received training in psychodynamic theory and techniques which enhanced their understanding of student behavior. For students, the group provided structured time for communication and affective education. The goal of the therapeutic discussion groups was to change behavior. Through the group, appropriate student behavior could be reinforced and empathy, concern, and caring encouraged. Group discussion also increased the opportunities for early intervention with children who had potential problems. Group techniques were applied successfully with psychotic, passive aggressive, and depressed children.

When implemented, group sessions of 30 to 60 minutes are conducted weekly with the psychologist or psychiatrist, teacher, aide, and social worker present. The group sits in a circle, and meeting length varies according to the age and needs of the children. Pre- and post-meeting sessions are conducted by the mental health consultant with the teacher to evaluate the session and to discuss concerns, needs, and behaviors of the children. Group sessions become then a standard part of each student's program.

Anderson and Marrone suggest the following group discussion guidelines:

1. Children may speak on any topic. Physical aggression and obscene language are considered inappropriate.
2. Confidentiality is stressed.
3. Discussion may be initiated or facilitated by centering on a specific student interest, need, positive behavior, or similar topic.
4. After several weekly meetings, when the team has an increased understanding of each student's needs, the following therapeutic progression is applied:
    a. Help each student recognize his or her ineffective behavior.
    b. Help the student explore and recognize the feelings behind the ineffective behaviors.
    c. Identify the source of the feelings.
    d. Connect these feelings with the student's actions and their consequences.
    e. Facilitate the student's commitment to change.
    f. Plan alternatives with the student.
    g. Support the student's efforts to change.
    h. Recognize the new behavior and encourage it.

There are several prerequisites for the successful implementation of groups in the public schools. Anderson and Marrone maintain that a belief in the use of therapeutic discussion groups and administrative support are essential. The program must also have a competent mental health consultant (psychiatrist, clinical psychologist, case worker, counselor) who accepts the team concept.

Classroom Environment

The classroom environment has a significant impact on behavior. A classroom should be designed to facilitate the implementation of the behavior management interventions and instructional methods (Hewett, 1968; Valett, 1969; Wagner, 1972).

Some variables to be considered in the planning of the classroom environment include the following.

Comfort. The classroom should be a comfortable environment in which the children feel free to function. It should be a place in which they enjoy working and playing. This may require the placing of couches, bean bag chairs, pillows, area rugs, and the like, in the room. It may require the elimination of distracting sights and sounds.

Organization. The room should be organized to facilitate large- and small-group lessons as well as individual study. This requires the educator to organize the environment to facilitate activities with a minimum of physical movement of furnishings and persons.

Interpersonal Communications. Communications among group members should be maximized by the elimination of unnecessary physical barriers. With the exception of the time devoted to individual study, the student should be within the teacher's field of vision so that assistance can be provided. During individual work periods the student should be able to signal the teacher, either personally or mechanically, if help is needed.

Movement. Learning centers should be arranged about the room to minimize unnecessary movement and to facilitate the daily schedule. Noise levels are considered in the location of the various centers. Centers for potentially distracting activities should not be located near centers for quiet activities and individual study. The teacher's and teaching assistant's work stations should be located in the interior of the classroom to minimize physical movements and maximize supervision and communication.

Privacy. All children need privacy. Each student should be provided with an area of the room that belongs to that student alone. The student's desk and locker are "private property" where treasures and work materials can be stored. One area of the classroom should be provided for students who are frustrated or who have lost control of their behavior. This area should be available to others who wish to be alone for a short period of time. The classroom itself should be private. The number of unexpected visitors should be minimized.

Size and Shape. A standard-size classroom is recommended. It is easier to divide a large room into several working areas than to attempt to organize a small room. A square or rectangular room is preferable to an odd-shaped angular room. A square or rectangular room provides structure and definite boundaries for group activities.

Scale. All furnishings except those of the teacher and teaching assistant should be scaled to the appropriate size for the children using them. Oversized furnishings are difficult for children to manipulate. Undersized chairs and desks are equally frustrating and uncomfortable for larger students.

Interest. A child should find the classroom environment interesting. Areas of the classroom should be designated for exploring and constructing activities. These areas should contain high-interest materials and equipment, including games, pets, science experiments, audiovisual materials, reading materials, puzzles, and the like.

Accessibility. The materials and equipment in a classroom are primarily for student use. Although cabinets are recommended for storage of materials and equipment, they should be readily accessible to the students.

Usability. The materials and equipment should be usable. All materials should be evaluated for ease of operation, safety in the hands of children, and durability.

Class Meetings

Class meetings can be instituted as a part of the normal classroom procedure. Meetings can be called to deal with the common problems of living and learning in a group setting. Over a period of time the members of the class learn, with guidance, to seek solutions to problems through verbal transactions with peers and the teacher. During class meetings, members grow in understanding of themselves and others. They learn to conceptualize problems from another's point of view.

Three kinds of meetings for classroom application have been suggested by Vogel and Smith (1974), Harth and Morris (1976), and Morris (1982).

Open Meeting. This meeting is called to permit an individual to express covert feelings. The individual is given an opportunity to state to the group the frustrations and feelings that the individual believes are the result of another member's actions. This other member, or antagonist, may be a peer or the teacher. Any member of the group may request an open meeting. The session is generally conducted by a peer.

EXAMPLE ■ Billy's ninth-grade class was responsible for planning and conducting the all-school assembly for the Christmas holiday. It was the most important activity of the school year for the class. Each member of the class had a role to play in the program.

Unfortunately for Billy, he was absent from school with the flu on the day his class planned the program. Neither teacher nor fellow students remembered to assign a function to Billy. Consequently he was very frustrated and angry. He was angry with the teacher, the aide, and his peers. He was hurt and sad because he was a forgotten person. After all, it was not his fault that he got the flu and his mother made him stay at home.

Mr. Jetro had always suggested to his students that if they had a concern about the group they should request a class meeting. At the meeting they could express and discuss their concern with the group.

Billy asked Mr. Jetro for a meeting. At the meeting he stated his personal concerns. As a result of his action Billy not only was assigned a role in the assembly but also was apologized to by the program chairperson and teacher for their oversight. ■

Problem-Solving Meeting. This meeting is focused primarily on potential problems. It may be called by any member of the class. Topics include such items as tardiness, disorganization, lack of follow-through on previous commitments, group responsibilities, distractions in the classroom, lack of time to complete assignments, and the like. During the meeting a solution to the problem is sought by the group. The agreed-upon solution is implemented.

EXAMPLE ■ Mr. Kaat always tells his senior honors German classes that if they are honestly overburdened by the class assignments they may request a class meeting to discuss the problem.

On one particular occasion, Mr. Kaat assigned the class a 10-page technical translation and a term paper just 3 days before midyear examinations. The students believed they were severely overburdened and would as a result do inadequate work on translation, term paper, and examinations. They were also concerned about having sufficient time to prepare for their other examinations.

A problem-solving meeting was called at which a more realistic schedule was agreed to by Mr. Kaat and the class. ■

Decision-Making Meeting. This meeting focuses primarily on program and curriculum decisions. It gives the program direction: What is to be done? How is it to be accomplished? Where? When? Who is responsible? Why? The decision-making meeting is an excellent medium for involving all members of a class in the curriculum-planning.

EXAMPLE

■ Mrs. Picoff was faculty advisor for the Blaskit Island High School Future Teachers Society. She was very concerned about the group's future because of lack of interest on the part of the members. The principal had told her that he was considering disbanding the group because they did not plan or complete any projects of benefit to the school or community.

Mrs. Picoff called the officers and members of the group together for a problem-solving meeting. At the meeting she presented the problem confronting the group. As a consequence, the members planned an annual schedule, assigned responsibilities to various members, and established a feedback mechanism to ensure that each person met his or her responsibilities. ■

These class meetings are designed to find practical solutions to real problems. In addition, the class meeting intervention has significant potential as a preventive technique if consistently and appropriately applied.

Milieu Therapy

Milieu therapy is a clinical concept, and although it varies in ease of application, it can be applied in any setting in which children function. In varying degrees this intervention can be applied in residential settings, day school, special classrooms, regular classrooms, and camp settings.

According to Long and others (1980), "Milieu implies the total environment a child lives in, the whole culture that surrounds him, in other words, everything that is done to, with, for, or by an individual in the place where he finds himself."

According to Redl (1959), a specific milieu is not "good" or "bad" for an individual in itself; its effects on the person or group are dependent on their needs in interaction with the milieu. Redl further indicated that no single aspect of the environment is more important than any other aspect. The importance of the various discrete aspects of the environment are dependent on the needs of the individual or group living in that particular setting.

Because it is not possible, a priori, to design with certitude a therapeutic milieu for an individual, milieu therapy is a continuous process throughout the child's placement in a particular setting. The staff must be constantly alert to the impact of the milieu on the individual and adjust it when necessary. Although these adjustments may appear simple when presented in a written statement, such environmental manipulations are difficult tasks requiring personnel who are observant and sensitive to the needs of the individual and the group.

Redl (1959) identified several critical elements in the milieu; these elements are presented here as questions that persons responsible for a particular milieu must ask themselves:

□ *Social structures:* What are the roles and functions of various individuals and groups in the milieu? What is the role of the therapist? Of the teacher? Of the administrator? Of the children? Are staff members parent surrogates? Are they like brothers and sisters? Are they confidants? Are they friends? Are they authority figures? Are they servants? Who is in charge here? Staff? The children? Administrators? No one? Are there open or closed communications channels between staff and the children? Between the children and staff? Among staff personnel? Among the children?

□ *Value systems:* What values and standards are consciously and unconsciously being communicated among and between the children and staff? Sympathy? Empathy? High expectations? Low expectations? Like? Dislike? Acceptance? Rejection? Trust? Mistrust?

□ *Routines, rituals, and regulations:* Are routines, rituals, and behavioral regulations and limits facilitating or frustrating the goals of a program for the individual?

□ *Impact of group processes:* What is the impact of the natural group processes on individuals and subgroups within the milieu? On the total group? Are individual group members cast in the role of a leader? In the role of a follower? In the role of an antagonist? In the role of a scapegoat? In the role of an isolate? In the role of a mascot or pet? In the role of a clown? Can the individual at his or her present stage of development function effectively in a group setting such as this milieu provides?

□ *Impact of the individual's psychopathological characteristics:* What are the effects of abnormal behaviors on the individuals themselves and on others in the milieu? Are these effects positive? Are they negative? Do they result in aggression? In withdrawal? In respect? In pity? In fear?

□ *Personal attitudes and feelings:* What are the staff's attitudes and feelings toward each other and the children? What is the impact of these attitudes and feelings on their behavior and on the behavior of others (staff and children)? Is the impact positive? Is it negative? Is it neutral? Is it productive? Is it destructive?

□ *Overt behavior:* Regardless of the individual's intentions, what are group members really doing to each other? What is their overt behavior? Is their relationship helpful? Is it harmful? Is it supportive? Is it personal? Is it vindictive?

□ *Activities and performance:* Is the activity program, including its structure, designed to facilitate the developmental process? Is it productive? Is it constructive? Is it busywork? Is it tedious? Is it frustrating? Is it boring? Is it wasteful? Is it negative? Is it destructive?

☐ *Space, equipment, time, and props:* Are space, equipment, time, and props available in the environment to adequately conduct the activities in the program?

☐ *Effects of the outside milieu:* What is the effect of information, visits, news, telephone calls, and the like, from persons on the outside on the individual or group?

☐ *Effects of the nonimmedidate milieu:* What are the effects of administrators, nurses, physicians, housekeepers, cooks, and others on the individual or group?

☐ *Limits and enforcement:* Are the behavioral limits within which the individual and group must function established? Are these limits reasonable? Are they enforced? Are they enforced consistently and fairly? How are extremes of behavior handled?

☐ *Program responsiveness:* Is the total milieu adequately and objectively monitored to ensure recognition of nontherapeutic elements? Is the structure of the milieu sufficiently flexible and responsive to allow and encourage modification to reduce or neutralize nontherapeutic elements?

The questions listed under each of the preceding variables that compose a milieu may be systematically responded to by educators wishing to evaluate the therapeutic quality of the program in which they teach.

The therapeutic milieu in any setting, residential or day, must be continuously monitored, discussed, evaluated, and manipulated for the benefit of the child.

Levels Systems

A levels system is an organizational framework designed to shape students' social, emotional, and academic behaviors. Rather than an intervention technique or strategy derived from a single theoretical perspective, a levels system offers a structure within which various interventions may be applied. The interventions implemented in a levels system range in theoretical construct from behavior modification (token economy, positive reinforcement, contingency contracts) to psychodynamic (social-skills curriculum, group and individual counseling, expressive arts interventions). The selection of the interventions is based on the practitioner's skills and the functioning level of each student concerned.

The purpose of a levels system is to increase student responsibility for personal, social, emotional, and academic performance. A student's progress through the various levels is dependent on his or her measurable behavior and achievement. As the student progresses through the levels, the behavioral expectations and privileges change.

Levels systems seem to have originated in residential settings. In 1971, the Holy Cross Program (New York City) used a levels system in an adolescent substance abuse program. A 4-level system including a token economy was used to provide students with positive reinforcement and frequent feedback about their performance, to increase their tolerance for delayed gratification, and to develop their reliance upon self as a source of reinforcement (Coughlan, Gold, Dohrenwend, & Zimmerman,

1973). Levels systems have also been applied with incarcerated adolescents (Reid, 1979) and in residential treatment facilities (Rosenstock & Levy, 1978; Mitchell, 1980; Gable & Strain, 1981).

The few classroom adaptations reported in the literature appear to be derived from the institutional systems referred to in these studies. Gersten (in Swanson & Reinert, 1984) described demonstration classrooms for adolescents at the University of Northern Colorado in which a 5-level system was applied. Recently, levels systems have been suggested for application during the process of phasing out token economies without interrupting student progress (LaNunziata, Hunt, & Cooper, 1984).

To demonstrate this approach to behavior management, this section presents two levels systems which have been used in the public school setting. The first is designed for application with elementary and junior high school students, the second with high school students. The discussion of levels systems concludes with several guidelines for practitioners wishing to design a levels system appropriate for the students and environment in which they work.

CCSEC System

The Clark County Special Education Cooperative Day Treatment Program (Jeffersonville, Indiana) levels system is designed to facilitate the return of elementary and junior high school students from inpatient or residential treatment centers to public school special education services. On entry into the program, the students are generally too severely impaired to profit from education services in the local school district. The Clark levels system is individualized for each student on the basis of the annual goals and short-term objectives written in the student's Individualized Education Plan. The system consists of four levels plus a disciplinary level. The expectations, privileges, and requirements for each level are presented in Table 7.1. Students are responsible for monitoring their behavior with teacher assistance. A staff meeting is conducted each week to review each student's performance and to revise individual expectations. Level changes made at these meetings will go into effect the following week.

Students who fail to meet the requirements of their current level return to the next previous level for a 1-week probationary period. During probation, if a student earns 80 percent of the possible available points, then he or she returns to the higher level. Each level in the system has a minimum length of stay regardless of student behavior. Ground or Disciplinary Level offenses include running away, physically abusing staff and peers, destroying property, setting off the fire alarm, possession of weapons or drugs, and so on. The number of points the student must earn to return from Ground Level to the previous level varies as indicated in Table 7.1.

PALS

The Personal Adjustment Level System (PALS, Hinsdale Illinois South High School), a 5-level system for secondary students, is designed to increase self motivation and ac-

TABLE 7.1
CCSEC levels systems

	Level I	Level II	Level III	Level IV (Transition)	Ground Level
Minimum Length of Stay	9 Weeks	12 Weeks	15 Weeks	9 Weeks (Transition)	3-5 days
Requirements for Maintaining Level Status		80% of possible points. (4 out of every 5 days)	80% of possible points. (4 out of every 5 days)	Meets criteria established by public school SEH teachers.	Level I: 70% pos. pts. Level II: 80% pos. pts. Level III: 85% pos. pts. Level IV: 90% pos. pts.
Requirements for Advancing to Next Level	90% of possible points for 45 out of 60 days. No more than 10 Time-Outs.	90% of possible points for 60 out of 72 days. No more than 6 Time-Outs.	90% of possible points for 75 out of 90 days. No more than 5 Time-Outs.	Meets criteria established by public school SEH teachers.	Same expectations for level below the one student was on prior to offense resulting in Ground Level placement.
Academic Expectations	Starts assignments on command. During weeks 1–5, on task for 15 min. out of each ½ hour. Weeks 6–9, on task for 20 min. out of each ½ hr. (not necessarily consecutively)	Starts & completes assignments within specified time. On-task behavior: Weeks 1–4: 20 Min. Weeks 5–8: 25 Min. Weeks 8–12: 30 Min.	Starts and completes assignments within specified time. Stays on task for 30 minutes at a time.	Meets criteria established by public school SEH teachers.	
Behavioral Expectations	Discusses individual goals & class rules with teacher daily. Demonstrates effort to achieve them.	Independently states individual goals and class rules daily and demonstrates effort to achieve them.	Independently states individual goals & class rules daily & demonstrates effort to achieve them. Involved in process of determining individual goals for him/herself.	Meets criteria established by public school SEH teachers.	States reasons for GL placement and alternative strategies. Same expectations for level below the one student was on prior to offense resulting in GL placement.

202

TABLE 7.1, continued

	Level I	Level II	Level III	Level IV	Ground Level
Social Skills Expectations	Interacts appropriately with 1 peer at a time with adult supervision. Accepts compliments appropriately. Interacts appropriately with adults.	Interacts appropriately with 2 or more peers at a time with adult supervision. Compliments him/herself & others at least once a day. Contributes to discussions in daily class meetings.	Interacts appropriately with 2 or more peers without adult supervision. Compliments him/herself & others at least twice a day. Verbally encourages peers to interact appropriately. Attempts to solve conflicts before asking for help.	Meets criteria established by public school SEH teachers.	Same expectations for level below the one student was on prior to offense resulting in Ground Level placement.
Privileges	Free time in classroom. Special activities determined by teacher.	Unescorted restroom and drink breaks and to and from bus. Setting table for lunch. Special Level II purchases in point store. Using computer during free time. Field trips. Purchasing soft drinks & snacks at specified times. Special activities determined by teacher. Playing Atari once a day with supervision.	Lunch in hospital cafeteria once a week. Running errands within building. Playing Atari in office. Special field trips. Special Level III purchases in point store.	Full time placement in public school SEH class. After a 9 week transition period, mainstreaming will be considered by Case Conference Committee.	Free time earned at teacher's discretion. Scheduled restroom breaks with direct supervision. Eat lunch at separate table. Privilege of using tape recorder, computer, record player, etc., is revoked.

(Adapted from Clark County Special Education Cooperative Day Treatment Program Levels System. Adapted by permission.)

ademic achievement. The goal of the system is reintegration into the mainstream of regular education. Small group and individual counseling sessions are an intregral part of the program. All students on Levels 1 through 4 are required to attend group sessions. Students who fail to attend the group remain at Day 1 of their present levels. Unlike the Clark system, initial level placement is determined by a student support team. Like the Clark system, there are minimum lengths of stay at each level. Students can earn bonus days for appropriate behavior or lose days for suspension and inappropriate behavior. Requirements and incentives for PALS levels are presented in Table 7.2.

The levels systems presented here demonstrate the diversity of this approach to managing students' behavior. Analysis indicates that both systems provide a framework within which various therapeutic interventions and behavior management strategies can be applied. Though they differ in specifics, each system contains (a) a description of each level, (b) criteria for movement from one level to another, and (c) specific behaviors, expectations, restrictions, and privileges for each level. Typically, levels systems are comprised of four to six levels. There is considerable variation in the criteria for movement from level to level. All levels systems have a procedure for evaluating student fulfillment of expectations. This procedure may be a point system, a group meeting of staff and/or students, or minimum stay guidelines.

Designing a Levels System

Practitioners wishing to design a levels system will find the following guidelines helpful.

Step 1: Determine the usual entry-level behaviors of the entering student population. For example, students entering the Clark program generally fail to (a) initiate assignments when requested, (b) attend to tasks more than half the time, and (c) interact appropriately with peers or adults.

As an alternative, an "assessment level" may be written into the system. During a brief (several day) assessment period, a student's functioning can be evaluated and compared to the expectations for the various system levels. Then the student may be placed at an appropriate level rather than being required to progress through those that are inappropriate to the student's present level of functioning.

Step 2: Determine the terminal behavior expectations for the students. For the Clark students, these expectations are the same as the social, academic, and behavioral expectations for the students in the public school system.

Step 3: List at least two but no more than four sets of behavioral expectations of approximately equal distance between the expectations listed in Steps One and Two. In the Clark program, for example, two sets of expectations were developed in the academic area. Between initiating assignments on command and meeting the criteria established by public school teachers, there are criteria which focus on beginning and completing assignments within specified time limits, i.e., being on task for increasing time increments.

TABLE 7.2
PALS

Length of stay	Requirements	Incentives
Level I *20 days* *(or as* *contracted* *w/teacher)*	Personal goal-setting conference. Personal IEP conference. Learn school rules, PALS rules, daily routine. Log in journal daily. Keep record of assignments. Participate in weekly group therapy. Maintain appropriate behavior 70% of the time. Completion of 65% of assignments. Participate in required class activities. Document "Helping others project" on a weekly basis. Maintain stable attendance. Progress on 60% of IEP goals. Contained for all classes except PE. Pass 75% of classes.	In-school field trips. One cafeteria pass per week. Off-campus lunch with teacher. Break time with teacher. Bonus days. Free time in class. Food privileges in classroom.
Level II *30 days*	Log in journal three times each week. Personal IEP conference to review objectives and program. Participate in weekly group therapy. Complete 75% of assignments. Maintain appropriate behavior 75% of the time. Participate in required class activities. Attend regular class for 1–3 classes. Maintain stable attendance. Progress on 75% of IEP goals. Pass all classes.	In-school field trips. Bonus days. 2 Cafeteria passes per week. 2 off-campus lunches with the teacher. Free time in class.
Level III *40 days*	Log in journal weekly. Participate in weekly group therapy. Completion of 85% of weekly assignments. Maintain appropriate behavior 90% of the time. Integration into four academic classes and P.E. Document helping others project. Maintain stable attendance. Progress on 90% of IEP goals. Passing all classes. Participate in required class activities.	Three cafeteria passes per week. Up to four outside lunches with the teacher. Food privileges in classroom. In-school field trips. Outside field trips. Bonus days. Free time in classroom.

TABLE 7.2, continued

Level IV
50 days
	Maintain stable attendance.
	Complete 90% of all
	  assignments.
	Maintain appropriate behavior
	  90% of the time.
	Integrated for all classes.
	Passing all classes.
	Progress on 100% of IEP goals
	  to criteria.
	Contact with special teacher daily.
		Free time in class.
		Cafeteria passes.
		Off-campus lunch and breakfast
		  with the teacher.
		Food privileges in classroom.
		In-school field trips.
		Outside field trips.
		Bonus days.

Level V
(Exit)
25 days
	No progress notes from regular
	  teachers.
	Passing all classes.
	Integrated into all classes.
	Maintain appropriate behavior
	  100% of the time.
	Maintain stable attendance.
		*Student is monitored only.
		  Beginning at day 15 special
		  teacher begins arrangement for
		  permanant regular educational
		  placement.

(Adapted from Personal Adjustment Level System, Hinsdale Illinois South High School. Adapted by permission.)

Step 4: Write the sets of graduated expectations on separate sheets of paper. Label them "Level One" through "Level Four."

Step 5: Consider including a Disciplinary or Ground Level. If such a level is appropriate for the students, describe expectations for this level on a separate sheet of paper. In the Clark system, Ground Level expectations are the same as expectations for the level below the one the student was on when he or she committed the offense.

Step 6: Determine the privileges appropriate for students beginning the program, i.e., Level 1. The students in the Clark program require continuous supervision when initially admitted; thus, privileges are restricted to free time in the classroom and supervised activities.

Step 7: Determine the privileges appropriate for students preparing to terminate the program, i.e., at the highest level. For the students in the Clark program, the terminal privileges are those normally available to students with behavior disorders in the public schools.

Step 8: For each level in Step Three, list appropriate privileges evenly distributed among the levels. Remember to reduce the amount of direct supervision provided for the students as they progress through the levels.

Step 9: Next, consider the following questions to determine the length of stay for each level:

a. Will a minimum length of stay be required at each level?

b. How frequently will a student's status be reviewed? Weekly or biweekly meetings to review placement may be appropriate.

c. Who will review a student's status? Involving students in the evaluation process can be beneficial. Student involvement encourages the development of self-control and decision-making skills. Involving other students provides positive peer support which is particularly beneficial at the secondary school level.

d. What level of appropriate behavior will be required to remain at the various levels?

e. What self-monitoring and teacher monitoring procedures are needed?

Step 10: Determine the appropriate communication systems among staff, parents, and students. A successful levels program requires frequent, positive communication. Communications may be facilitated by group meetings, individual conferences, written notes, or forms.

Caution should be exercised in planning and implementing a levels system. Expectations should be expressed positively. For example, rather than "stops hitting," the same expectation can be expressed positively by saying "keeps hands to self." The latter statement is not only positive but suggests to the student the appropriate alternative behavior.

If a Disciplinary or Ground Level is included in the system, then offenses and their consequences should be reasonable, carefully explained, and fairly administered.

The number of days at each level should be realistic. The student should not be required to remain at a level for so many days that he or she becomes frustrated and begins to resist or "drop out" of the system.

A significant benefit of a levels system is that its structure and routine provide security for students. The system provides workable limits with a theoretical flexibility that allows a levels system to respond to individual and group needs.

The advantages of a levels system parallel those of the positive peer culture (Carducci, 1980): (1) it delivers the teacher from the embattled "me against them" position, (2) it encourages the teacher to respect the strengths and abilities of the students, (3) it lends itself to specific classroom approaches such as grouping, students helping students, and individualized interventions, and (4) it provides a means for dealing with students' defense mechanisms such as projection and rationalization by placing the responsibility for personal behavior on the student.

Biophysical Interventions

In this section several biophysical interventions about which educators should have knowledge are discussed. These include several preventive and curative techniques, such as genetic counseling, proper nutrition, general and specialized physical examinations, medication, and others.

In the majority of these interventions the educator plays an important supportive role to that of the physician and other medical personnel. Consequently an analysis of the educator's functions in referral, collaboration and reporting, the modification of classroom structure and curriculum content, the obtaining of permission to administer medication, and the safeguarding and administering of medication is presented as a conclusion to the discussion of the biophysical behavior management interventions.

In addition to the educator's "need to know," the biophysical techniques are reviewed because the probability exists that some of the behavior problems of children are a direct result of heredity or heredity-environment interactions. In addition, the social-emotional (secondary) effects of many biophysical handicaps on the individual's life-style are of direct concern to educators.

The biophysical frame of reference implies that the source of an individual's behavior problem is an organic defect. There are two known causes of biophysical defects in unborn and newborn children: environment and heredity. Environmental factors of special importance to the health of the child are maternal factors (metabolic disorders, maternal age, and number and frequency of pregnancies) and factors that affect the mother during pregnancy (viral diseases and infections, venereal disease, drugs, alcohol, tobacco, diet, and injuries). In addition, the larger environment may have an effect on the child as a consequence of pollution, radiation, and the like.

Heredity, or the transmission of the characteristics or traits of the parents to the child, is a factor in some birth defects. Hereditary characteristics are transmitted from parents to child by means of the chromosomes. Chromosomes are present in every human cell, including the ovum and sperm. Chromosomes are composed of genes, the units of heredity (Redding & Hirschhorn, 1968). The inherited characteristics of a child are determined by the composition and manner in which the gene-carrying chromosomes from the parents combine at the time of conception.

It is generally agreed that birth defects are best reduced or controlled by preventive, rather than curative, techniques. Among the curative interventions available are chemical regulation, corrective surgery, and rehabilitation through training.

Chemical regulation includes such familiar interventions as medication and diet. Corrective surgery is frequently effective in reducing the debilitating effects of clubfoot, cleft lip and palate, and some vision, hearing, and speech problems, among others. Cosmetic surgery is a valuable aid in reducing the effects of observable deformities on the individual. Rehabilitation and training services have a significant positive impact on the life of the mentally retarded, blind, deaf, mute, physically handicapped, learning-disabled, or behavior-disordered individual.

Several biophysical interventions are discussed below.

Genetic Counseling

Genetic counseling involves providing an estimate of the probability of the occurrence of a disease or defect for a particular unborn individual (Kameya, 1972). The major goal of genetic counseling is the prevention of birth defects. The genetic counselor cannot predict with exactitude the occurrence of a defective child but can predict the probability of occurrence of some abnormalities in the offspring of specific parents and parents-to-be.

As a consequence of its capacity to predict the probability of birth defects, genetic counseling has raised some important ethical issues in contemporary society:

☐   Should a defective child be aborted?

☐   Do parents have an inalienable right to knowingly produce a defective child?

It should be remembered that the genetic counselor provides medical information on the *probabilities* that a defective child will be born. The counselor is *not* the ultimate decision maker. The parents must make the final decision concerning the unborn child (Shaw, 1974).

Prenatal Care

Prenatal care involves a variety of examinations and interventions designed to ensure that the unborn child develops normally in a healthy environment. By means of prenatal care, the parents and physician cannot only determine the growth and development patterns of the unborn child but are also in a position to immediately intervene if there are indications of problems. Prenatal care includes consideration of the mother's diet, exercise, and personal hygiene as well as the emotional status of both parents, especially the mother.

Postnatal Care

Postnatal health care is essential for the continued health and well-being of every child. There is in our society a high risk of injury, illness, and infection during childhood and adolescence. All children should be examined by a physician at least annually. Conscientious health care permits the family physician and parents to guide the child through the developmental years and to recognize and intervene if abnormalities develop. Postnatal care includes vision, hearing, and dental care.

Medical Examinations

Differential diagnoses among children with behavior disorders, minimal brain damage, hyperkinesis, a specific learning disability, and similar syndromes require a thorough medical examination. And, because there is no single test or combination of tests that conclusively rules out organic disease (Schulman, 1967), the full physical evaluation includes a variety of tests.

For example, the ideal evaluation for a suspected hyperactive and/or hyperanxious child is a collaborative effort by the parents, teachers, school psychologist, and physician (Renshaw, 1974). The parents' contributions includes a family history and the child's medical, developmental, and behavioral histories. The teacher reports on the child's learning capacity and style and behavioral and perceptual difficulties. The school psychologist contributes the results of a psychological evaluation. The physician's evaluation includes information on the pregnancy, a family history, and a history of the child's birth, neonatal years, development, and behavior.

A full physical examination includes laboratory tests (blood and urine), a skull X-ray examination, and a neurological examination, including an electroencephalogram (EEG), if needed. The physician may prescribe medication on a trial basis as part of the diagnostic process.

A general physical examination is performed to *exclude* the possibility of diseases involving bodily systems that could account for the child's difficulties (Millichap, 1975). The neurological examination is performed to determine the probability of neurological malfunction and includes an evaluation of the individual's gait, coordination, deep tendon reflexes, muscular power and tone, handedness, sensory perception, speech, vision, and hearing. The EEG may be included in this examination.

The EEG, or brain wave recording, consists of simultaneous records of electrical discharges from several parts of the the brain. Occasionally the results of the EEG are used by educators to determine an exceptional child's educational placement. This is an unwise procedure (Bakwin & Bakwin, 1960; Renshaw, 1974). The EEG retains its experimental status. In the following, Renshaw cautions those responsible for interpreting a child's EEG:

> Electroencephalography is expensive, needs serial followup, and may be of value, particularly in ruling out seizure disorders which require specific treatment. It may show up focal discharges diagnostic of subdurals or of masses. It may be "nonspecific abnormal" as it is in 10–30% of "normal" elementary school children and 30–80% of hyperkinetic reaction children. The very wide range in reported percentages reflects a still controversial state concerning its specificity in hyperkinetic reaction.
>
> Total reliance on the EEG for diagnosis is a medical mistake. For completeness of a thorough medical work-up, an EEG should be done. (p. 106)

Nutrition

Nutrition (or malnutrition) is defined as the relationship of nutrient intake to bodily needs (Kameya, 1972). In general, exact scientific relationships have not been demonstrated to exist between specific nutrients and specific behavior problems in children. However, a logical relationship between these factors in all probability does exist. Research has amply demonstrated the relationships between several nutrients and specific disorders of a physical nature.

Knapczyk (1979) noted three major diet-related conditions related to behavior disorders. These are (1) hypoglycemia, (2) vitamin/mineral deficiencies, and (3) allergies. Children with hypoglycemia may become either lethargic, unmotivated, and withdrawn, or hyperactive and inattentive. Vitamin/mineral deficiencies are related to hyperactivity. Various specific food and food additives are related to allergic reactions in children.

It is hardly disputable that children suffering from malnutrition are neither happy nor productive. The malnourished child manifests signs of fatigue, sleepiness, and irritability and appears to lack motivation. Such a child is prone to infections, diseases, and injuries.

The importance of proper nutrition for children cannot be overemphasized. When parents are unable to provide for their children in the home, the school—using local, state, and federal funds—must provide needy children with lunch and breakfast. Malnourishment is not confined to a specific socioeconomic group.

Diet

There is currently considerable activity and publicity on the effects of diet control on the hyperactive behaviors of children. Feingold (1973, 1975) hypothesized that naturally occuring salicylates and artificial food additives may cause the hyperkinetic syndrome in children who have a genetically determined predisposition.

Elimination of these substances from a child's diet would eliminate the symptoms of the hyperkinetic syndrome. Feingold claims that 48 percent of his patients were effectively treated by the diet and that symptoms can be reversed within a few hours if the diet is broken. Cook and Woodhill (1976) supported Feingold's claim in a clinical study of fifteen hyperkinetic children. The parents of ten children were "quite certain" and those of three others were "fairly certain" their child's behavior improved with the diet and relapsed when the diet was broken. Cook and Woodhill cautioned against the generalization of their finding because the sample was limited and the study did not meet rigorous research standards.

In a study of 59 children, Brenner (1977) reported that of 32 children able to tolerate the diet, 11 showed marked improvement as reported by teachers, parents, and physicians. Eight other children were judged "probably improved." No changes were reported in 13 children. In a control group of 27 children, not on the diet, only two were improved without medication after 8 months. Brenner noted that the placebo effect could not be ruled out in the study.

Weiss, Williams, Margen, Abrams, Citron, Cox, McKibben, and Ogar (1980) conducted a challenge study of 22 children with regard to behavioral responses to artificial food colors. Twenty of the 22 children displayed no convincing evidence of sensitivity to the color challenge as reported by parents. Swanson and Kinsbourne (1980) studied the effects of food dyes on children's laboratory learning performance. Twenty children were classified as hyperactive, 20 were not. Both groups were challenged with food dyes. The performance of the hyperactive children was impaired on the days they received food dyes. Performance of the nonhyperactive children was not affected.

In a review of the pertinent empirical investigations with regard to the Feingold diet, Baker (1980) concluded that the differential results reported by Feingold, parents, and others using the diet may be due to variables other than the eliminated substances. He found that in properly controlled studies, the positive effects of the diet evaporated. At this time, the debate remains unsettled as to whether a diet intervention is truly effective.

Megavitamin Therapy

The term *orthomolecular medicine,* or *megavitamin therapy,* was orginally applied in the treatment of mental disorders, such as schizophrenia, to provide the optimum molecular environment for brain function, especially the optimum concentration of substances normally present in the human body. Megavitamin therapy refers specifically to the administration of large doses of vitamins, particularly nicotinic acid, pyridoxine, calcium pantothenate, and ascorbic acid (Millichap, 1975), and other substances.

Some researchers have claimed positive results for megavitamin therapy (Pauling, 1968). However, according to Kameya (1972) and Millichap (1975), there is scant research evidence to support these claims. A task force of the American Psychiatric Association concluded that the claims of megavitamin therapists have not been confirmed in psychopharmacological research (Millichap, 1975). Educators should be aware that objective evidence of the effectiveness of this therapeutic technique does not exist at this time.

Medication

Although behavior-modifying medications have been prescribed for children and youth with behavior disorders since the late 1930s (Wilson & Sherrets, 1979), the treatment-evaluation process remains complicated (Baldwin, 1973). The physician must not only be concerned with the individual child's personal status, but must evaluate the child's environment, potentially biased evaluations of those associated with the child, and the actual and potential effects of other interventions being applied with the child such as special education.

Several reviews have been published (Baldwin, 1973; Renshaw, 1974; Gadow, 1979) describing the use of medication with children, particularly in the treatment of hyperactivity. These reviews are summarized in the following paragraphs.

Central nervous system stimulants. Stimulants are prescribed for their calming effect on prepubertal children of both sexes. This is called a paradoxical effect. Although at this time the specific reasons for this effect are unknown, stimulants have a calming and quieting effect on some children, whereas an adult is generally stimulated. Trade names of stimulants include Ritalin, Dexedrine, and Cylert.

The sought-for positive effects of the stimulants are (a) increased controlled physical activity, (b) increased goal-directedness, (c) decreased impulsivity and disruptiveness, (d) decreased distractibility, (e) increased attending, (f) improved performance, cognition, and perception, (g) improved motor coordination, (h) improved cooperation, (i) decreased negative and increased positive behavior.

Stimulants have several possible side effects. Students may experience nausea, loss of appetite, and weight loss. There may be a disruption in sleep patterns, with insomnia or infrequent drowsiness both observed. Nervousness, depression, and crying are also noted. When the stimulant is first introduced, severe shaking and fear may be observed.

Antianxiety and antipsychotic drugs. These drugs are prescribed for calming effects. Trade names include Mellaril, Thorazine, Librium, Miltown, and Equanil among others. Mellaril and Thorazine are the most frequently prescribed tranquilizers for children.

Desired positive effects of tranquilizers are increased calmness and improved behavior and social functioning. Possible negative effects include nausea, drowsiness, dry mouth and nasal congestion, nervousness, rashes, increased appetite and weight gain.

Anticonvulsants and antihistamines. Anticonvulsants are used to treat children whose behavior and learning problems are complicated by seizures. Trade names for these medications include Dilantin, Mysoline, and Valproic Acid among others.

Antihistamines are used to counteract the effects of various allergies. Trade names include Benadryl, Vistaril, and Phenergan. According to Renshaw (1974), these medications are exceptionally safe. They are often prescribed for their sedative effects on children in pain and as a nighttime sedative.

In summary, teachers should remember that although properly prescribed and monitored medication can have a beneficial effect on the child, it cannot (1) compensate for "lost" years of learning, (2) provide the discipline needed to develop acceptable functioning, (3) improve the self-esteem needed for self-acceptance, (4) provide the love the child needs for normal development, or (5) reverse essential deficits, such as mental retardation and cerebral palsy (Renshaw, 1974).

Educator's Role in Biophysical Interventions

The educator plays an important supportive role to medical personnel in the application of biophysical interventions. This supportive role includes (1) referral, (2) collaboration with and reporting of observations to the physician, (3) modification of classroom structure and curriculum content to meet the needs of the child, (4) obtaining permission to administer medication, and (5) safeguarding and administering medication to the child in school.

Referral. The educator is not in a position by experience, training, or function to refer a child directly to a physician. Neither is the educator in a position to suggest the prescribing of medication to a physician for a specific child. In addition, the educator should not attempt to coerce parents to accept any particular biophysical treatment.

It is proper for teachers to inform parents of a child's problems. The school initiates contact with medical personnel on behalf of a particular child only with parental consent. It is suggested that an educator not directly involved with the child in school serve as a contact person and intermediary between the teacher and parents during the referral process (Report of the Conference on the Use of Stimulant Drugs, 1971).

Collaboration with and Reporting of Observations to the Physician. A primary role of the teacher in biophysical interventions is the provision of current and objective feedback to the physician on the observable effects of the treatment on the child's behavior and learning (Wilson and Sherrets, 1979). The majority of the present-day medications are experimental substances, the effects of which on a particular child cannot be predicted with exactitude. Thus meaningful feedback to the prescribing physician will assist in maximizing the positive effects of medication. The teacher, a trained observer who is with the child throughout the day, is in an excellent position to observe the effects of the medication and report, through proper channels, to the physician.

Modification of Classroom Structure and Curriculum Content. During the biophysical treatment process, especially during the beginning weeks, the child's behavior and learning styles may change radically. Consequently, it will be necessary for the teacher to modify, as necessary, both classroom structure and curriculum content to respond to the child's needs. Classroom structure may have to be increased or decreased to permit the child to adjust to his or her "new" behavior. The curriculum may have to be changed to allow the child to learn the knowledge and skills neglected during the "lost" years.

Obtaining Permission to Dispense Medication. The educator must obtain permission to dispense medication in the school when medical personnel (physician and/or nurse) are not available. A child should not be dismissed from school because medical personnel are not immediately available to administer medication. In some circumstances, teachers may dispense medication with proper permission. However, school personnel must investigate and adhere to their state's laws and regulations governing the dispensing of medication in the schools. In some cases, the school may need legal advice. A permission form suggested by Renshaw (1974) is shown in Figure 7.1.

Safeguarding and Administration of Medication. When medication is dispensed in the school, the following guidelines should be adhered to:

1. Proper permission forms, completed by parents and physicians, should be obtained and filed in the child's record folder (see Figure 7.1).
2. All medication should be stored in a central location. This facility should be clean, ventilated, and lighted and should contain a locked cabinet. A water tap is needed. A refrigerator is necessary for some medications.
3. All medication must be properly labeled with the child's name and the physician's name. The label should include directions for use.
4. All medication, including new prescriptions and refills, received from and returned home should be logged in and out of the school. Medication should be inventoried frequently. One individual from the school's faculty or staff should be appointed to inventory the medication and function as a contact person in all communications with parents, physicians, and other medical personnel in relation to medication.
5. A responsible adult must be present when a child takes a medication.
6. A log, to be filled in each time a child takes a medication, should be affixed to the

wall in the medication center. This form is presented in Figure 7.2. The completed forms should be retained in a file.

SUMMARY

In this chapter several biophysical and environmental interventions of relevance to the teacher interested in a broad understanding of behavior management are presented.

School Medication Consent and Directions

Parent permission: Date _____

Child _____Birthdate _____

Address _____Phone _____

School _____Grade _____ Teacher _____

_____

I hereby consent for the above-named school to supervise the medication prescribed below by my physician for my child.

_____

Physician's direction: Date _____

Child _____

Medication and instruction _____

_____

Doctor requests teacher's comments:

Please observe the following _____

Phone _____ Best time to call _____

_____

Physician's signature
Physician/Clinic name

Address _____

FIGURE 7.1
School medication consent form and directions.
From Renshaw, D. C. The hyperactive child, p. 127, Chicago: Nelson-Hall Publishers, 1974.)

Medication Log

Child's name	Date	Time	Medication	Person dispensing medication	Notes

FIGURE 7.2
Medication log.

The careful reader will note that significant overlap exists between the behavior management interventions presented in this and the previous chapter. The educator should seek to synthesize the various conceptual frameworks (theories) and their intervention into a personal perspective of behavior management.

EXERCISES

Quiz

1. The four groups of environmental interventions are:

   a. _____

   b. _____

   c. _____

   d. _____

2. Among the variables to be considered during the process of grouping are:

   a. _____

   b. _____

   c. _____

3. List eight variables to be considered in planning the classroom environment.

   a. _____

   b. _____

   c. _____

   d. _____

   e. _____

   f. _____

   g. _____

   h. _____

4. The three kinds of classroom meetings suggested by Vogel and Smith (1974) are:

   a. _____

   b. _____

   c. _____

5. What is a milieu? List six critical elements the educator should consider in the evaluation of the classroom or school milieu.

   a. _____

   b. (1) _____

(2) _____

(3) _____

(4) _____

(5) _____

(6) _____

6. Define a levels system _____

_____

_____

7. What are the guidelines for planning a levels system?

a. _____

b. _____

c. _____

d. _____

e. _____

f. _____

g. _____

h. _____

i. _____

j. _____

8. The three groups of medication most frequently prescribed for children with behavior problems are:

a. _____

b. _____

c. _____

9. The educator plays an important supportive role to medical personnel in the biophysical interventions. The educator's functions in this supportive role are:

a. _____

b. _____

c. _____

d. _____

e. _____

Projects

1. Write a brief essay (300 words) on the following topics:
   a. The advantages and disadvantages of the environmental interventions.
   b. The advantages and disadvantages of the biophysical interventions from the educator's point of view.
2. Discuss the role of the educator in biophysical interventions.
3. Invite a physician or nurse to discuss biophysical interventions with your class.
4. Survey your community and school to ascertain which, if any, of the environmental interventions discussed in the chapter are applied to assist children with behavior problems.
5. Using the questions presented under the critical elements in the milieu, interview a teacher and principal to determine the character of the milieu in which they function.

REFERENCES

Anderson, N. & Marrone, R. T. (1979). Therapeutic discussion groups in public school classes for emotionally disturbed children. *Focus on Exceptional Children, 12*(1), 1–15.

Baker, R. W. (1980). The treatment of behavior disorders with medication. In S. G. Sapir & A. C. Nitzberg (Eds.), *Children with learning problems.* New York: Brunner/Mazel.

Bakwin, H. & Bakwin, R. M. (1960). *Clinical management of behavior disorders in children.* Philadelphia: W. B. Saunders Co.

Baldwin, R. W. (1973). The treatment of behavior disorders with medication. In S. G. Sapir & A. C. Nitzberg (Eds.), *Children with learning problems.* New York: Brunner/Mazel.

Bayes, K. (1967). *The therapeutic effect on environment on emotionally disturbed and mentally subnormal children.* Surrey, England: Union Brothers.

Brenner, A. (1977). A study of the efficacy of the Feingold diet on hyperkinetic children. *Clinical Pediatrics, 16,* 652–656.

Carducci, D. J. (1980). Positive peer culture and assertiveness training. *Behavioral Disorders, 5*(3), 156–162.

Clark County Special Education Cooperative. (1984). *Day treatment program agreement.* Jeffersonville, IN: Clark County Special Education Cooperative.

Cook, P. S., & Woodhill, J. M. (1976). The Feingold dietary treatment of the hyperkinetic syndrome. *Medical Journal of Australia, 2,* 85–89.

Coughlan, A. J., Gold, S. R., Dohrenwend, E. F., & Zimmerman, R. S. (1973). A psychobehavioral residential drug abuse program: A new adventure in adolescent psychiatry. *International Journal of Addiction, 8*(5), 767–777.

Eskey, M., & Hauser, S. (1984). *Pals (Personal adjustment level system).* Hinsdale, IL: Hindsdale South High School.

Feingold, B. F. (1973). Food additives and child development. *Hospital Practice, 8,* 11.

Feingold, B. F. (1975). *Why your child is hyperactive.* New York: Random House.

Gable, R. A., & Strain, P. S. (1981). Individualizing a token economy system for the treatment of children's behavior disorders. *Behavioral Disorders, 1,* 39–45.

Gadow, K. (1979). *Children on medication: A primer for school personnel.* Reston, VA: Council for Exceptional Children.

Hare, A. P. (1962). *Handbook for small group research.* New York: Free Press.

Hare, A. P., Borgatta, E. F., & Bales, R. F. (1965). *Small groups: Studies in social interaction.* New York: Alfred A. Knopf.

Harth, R. & Morris, S. M. (1976). Group processes for behavior change. *Teaching Exceptional Children, 8*(4), 136–139.

Hewett, F. M. (1968). *The emotionally disturbed child in the classroom.* Boston: Allyn & Bacon.

Kameya, L. I. (1972). Biophysical interventions in emotional disturbance. In W. C. Rhodes & M. L. Tracy (Eds.), *A study of child variance: Vol. 2.*

Interventions. Ann Arbor: University of Michigan Press.

Knapczyk, D. R. (1979). Diet control in the management of behavior disorders. *Behavioral Disorders, 5*(1), 2–9.

LaNunziata, L. J., Hunt, K. P., & Cooper, J. O. (1984). Suggestions for phasing out token economy systems in primary and intermediate grades. *Techniques, 1,* 151–156.

Leissner, A. (1965). Street-club work in New York and Tel-Aviv. *Action-Research Project on Delinquent Street Corner Groups in Tel-Aviv, Israel,* February.

Lewis, W. W. (1967). Project Re-Ed: Educational intervention in discordant child-rearing systems. In E. L. Cown, E. A. Gardner, & M. Zax (Eds.), *Emergent approaches to mental health problems.* New York: Appleton-Century-Crofts.

Long, N. J., Morse, W. C., & Newman, R. G. (1980). Milieu therapy. In N. J. Long, W. C. Morse, & R. G. Newman (Eds.), *Conflict in the classroom: The education of emotionally disturbed children* (4th ed.), Belmont, CA: Wadsworth Publishing Co.

Loughmiller, C. (1965). *Wilderness road.* Austin: University of Texas, Hogg Foundation for Mental Health.

Makarenko, A. S. (1951). *The road to life: An epic of education* (Vols. 2 and 3), Moscow: Foreign Languages Publishing House.

Millichap, J. G. (1975). *The hyperactive child with minimal brain dysfunction.* Chicago: Year Book Medical Publishers.

Mitchell, J. D. (1980). Positive peer culture and a level system: A comparison in an adolescent treatment facility. *Criminal Justice and Behavior, 7*(4), 399–406.

Morris, S. M. (1982). A classroom process for behavior change. *The Pointer, 26,*(3) 25–28.

Morse, W. C., & Wineman, D. (1957). Group interviewing in a camp for disturbed boys. *Journal of Social Issues, 13*(1), 23–31.

Newman, R. G. (1967). *Psychological consultation in the schools: A catalyst for learning.* New York: Basic Books.

Pauling, L. C. (1968). Orthomolecular psychiatry. *Science, 160,* 265–271.

Redding, A., & Hirschhorn, K. (1968). Guide to human chromosome defects. *Birth Defects Original Article Series, 4*(1), 1–16.

Redl, F. (1942). Group emotion and leadership. *Psychiatry, 5,* 573–596.

Redl, F. (1959). The concept of the life-space interview. *American Journal of Orthopsychiatry, 29,* 1–18.

Reid, I. (1979). Developing a behavioral regime in a secure youth treatment centre. *Bulletin of the British Psychological Society, 32,* 207.

Renshaw, D. C. (1974). *The hyperactive child.* Chicago: Nelson-Hall Publishers.

Report of the Conference on the Use of Stimulant Drugs in the Treatment of Behaviorally Disturbed Young School Children. (1971). *Journal of Learning Disabilities, 4,* 523–530.

Rhodes, W. C. (1967). Psychosocial learning. In E. M. Bower & W. G. Hollister (Eds.), *Behavioral science frontiers in education.* New York: John Wiley & Sons.

Rhodes, W. C. (1968). The disturbing child: A problem of ecological management. In P. S. Graubard (Ed.), *Children against schools.* Chicago: Follett Publishing Co.

Rhodes, W. C. (1972). Overview of interventions. In W. C. Rhodes & M. L. Tracy (Eds.), *A study of child variance: Vol. 2. Interventions.* Ann Arbor: University of Michigan Press.

Rhodes, W. C., & Gibbins, S. (1972). Community programming for the behaviorally deviant child. In H. C. Quay & J. F. Werry (Eds.), *Psychopathological disorders of childhood.* New York: John Wiley & Sons.

Rhodes, W. C., & Tracy, M. L. (1972a). *A study of child variance: Vol. 1. Theories.* Ann Arbor: University of Michigan Press.

Rhodes, W. C., & Tracy, M. L. (1972b). *A study of child variance: Vol. 2. Interventions.* Ann Arbor: University of Michigan Press.

Rickard, H. C., & Lattal, K. A. (1969). Group problem-solving in a therapeutic summer camp: An illustration. *Adolescence, 4*(15), 319–332.

Rickard, H. C., Serum, C. S., & Wilson, W. (1971). Developing problem-solving attitudes in emotionally disturbed children. *Adolescence, 5*(24), 451–456.

Rosenstock, H. A., & Levy, H. J. (1978). On the clinical superiority of the level system. *Journal of the*

National Association of Private Psychiatric Hospitals, 9(3), 32–36.

Schulman, J. L. (1967). *Management of emotional disorders in pediatric practice.* Chicago: Year Book Medical Publishers.

Shaw, M. W. (1974). Genetic counseling. *Science, 184,* 751.

Shea, T. M. (1977). *Camping for special children.* St. Louis: C. V. Mosby Co.

Shea, T. M. (1978). *Teaching children and youth with behavior disorders.* St. Louis: C. V. Mosby Co.

Shea, T. M. & Bauer, A. M. (1987). *Teaching children and youth with behavior disorders* (2nd ed.). Englewood Cliffs, NJ: Prentice-Hall.

Stickney, S. B. (1968). Schools are our community mental health centers. *American Journal of Psychiatry, 124,* 1407–1414.

Swanson, J. M. & Kinsbourne, M. (1980). Food dyes impair performance of hyperactive children on a laboratory learning test. *Science, 207*(28), 1485–1486.

Swanson, H. L. & Reinert, H. R. (1984). *Teaching strategies for children in conflict.* St. Louis: Mosby Co.

Valett, R. E. (1969). *Programming learning disabili-*ties. Belmont, CA: Fearon Publishers.

Vogel, E. E., & Bell, N. W. (1960). The emotionally disturbed child as the family scapegoat. In N. W. Bell & E. E. Vogel (Eds.). *A modern introduction to the family.* New York: Free Press.

Vogel, J., & Smith, A. R. (1974). Rx for change: The classroom meeting. *Learning, 2*(7), 69–72.

Wagner, M. (1972). Environmental interventions in emotional disturbance. In W. C. Rhodes & M. L. Tracy (Eds.), *A study of child variance: Vol. 2. Interventions.* Ann Arbor: University of Michigan Press.

Weinstein, L. (1968). Project Re-Ed: Schools for emotionally disturbed children—effectiveness as viewed by referring agencies, parents, and teachers. *Exceptional Children, 35,* 703–711.

Weiss, B., Wiliams, J. H., Margen, S., Abrams, B., Citron, L. J., Cox, C., McKibben, J., & Ogar, D. (1980). Behavioral responses to artificial food colors. *Science, 207*(28) 1487–1488.

Wilson, J. E., & Sherrets, S. D. (1979). A review of past and current pharmacological interventions in the treatment of emotionally disturbed children and adolescents. *Behavioral Disorders, 5*(1), 60–69.

CHAPTER EIGHT

Parent Training and
Home-School Behavior Management

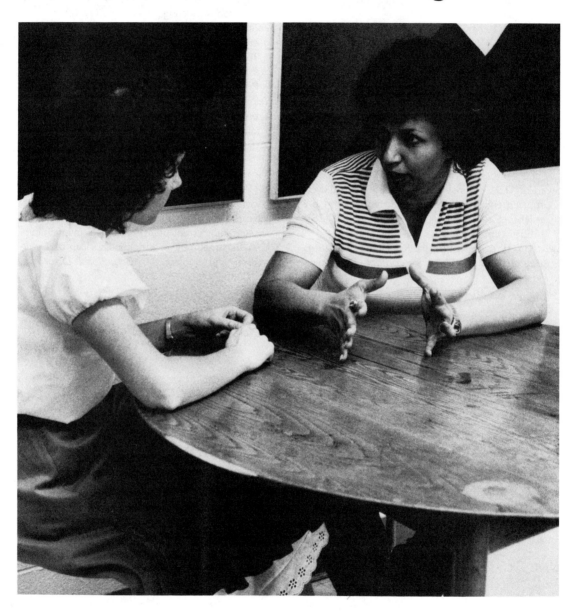

Mr. and Mrs. Wagnal arrived at the counseling center for their appointment with Dr. Murphy promptly at 3 PM. They were visiting the center to consult with Dr. Murphy, a psychologist, concerning the behavior problems of their 3-year-old son, Dennis. Dennis is their first child.

The Wagnals were disturbed about Dennis because of his poor eating habits, his lack of interest in other children, his frequent tantrums, and his toilet training problems. They reported that Dennis would eat only pickles, potato chips, chocolate candy, white bread, and frankfurters. He drank only water and cola. Needless to say, the Wagnals were concerned about Dennis's physical well-being.

Mrs. Wagnal stated that she had tried "everything" in an effort to bladder train Dennis. She had placed him on a rigid drinking schedule to control his liquid intake; she had awakened him every hour throughout the night and took him to the bathroom; she had set an egg timer to remind her to take him to the bathroom each hour throughout the day; and she had even purchased a musical potty chair. All of this had no influence on the boy's behavior.

The Wagnals' greatest concern was Dennis's behavior toward other children. Whenever another child of Dennis's age visited the home, Dennis would ignore the other child until he or she began playing with one of his toys. When the other child touched his possessions, Dennis immediately had a tantrum. He would kick and scream until the other child was removed from the home.

The Wagnals were desperate for help. Neither parent had relatives to whom they could turn for help with Dennis.

The Wagnals realized their need for some training and counseling if they were to help Dennis.

Mr. and Mrs. Mitchell arrived at Room 210 of Collinsdale Junior High School promptly at 7:30 PM. They were to confer with Mr. Boyle, their 13-year-old daughter Eileen's homeroom teacher. This was the first time they had been summoned to a conference because of one of their children.

Neither parent was anxious to visit with Mr. Boyle. Eileen's last report card contained two Fs, three Cs, and a B. Her conduct grades were at the bottom of the school's 5-point scale. In addition to the report card, the Mitchells had received a dozen or more negative notes from Eileen's teachers.

They had yelled and hollered, scolded and punished, and even grounded Eileen during the preceding 3 months without effect. The Mitchells realized that without cooperation from their daughter's teachers they could not successfully help her.

There must be some techniques available for implementation to increase the consistency with which the home and school could manage Eileen's behavior and academic performance.

223

After studying the literature on parent education and training from a variety of theoretical and methodological perspectives, Clements and Alexander (1975) concluded: "Extensive research demonstrates unequivocally that children learn more, adjust better, and progress faster when parent training is effected" (p. 7).

Parent training is an integral part of a successful home-school management program. According to Beale and Beers (1982), there are three broad categories from which to work with parents. They are (1) parent education, (2) parent involvement, and (3) parent-teacher communication. These may be rephrased as (1) "teach them what they need to know," (2) "bring them in and put them to work," and (3) "I talk, you talk, we talk."

The primary purposes of this chapter are to present a systematic methodology designed to facilitate (1) the effectiveness with which parents manage their children's behavior in home and community settings, (2) cooperation between the parents and teacher in the implementation of effective behavior management interventions on behalf of the child for whom they have a shared responsibility, and (3) the teacher's efforts to plan and conduct a parent training program.

The parent training perspective presented here is but one of many discussed in the literature. Extensive references to other approaches, such as those developed by Dinkmeyer and McKay (1973), Shea and Bauer (1985), Croft (1979), Kroth and Simpson (1977), Winton (1986), Homan (1977), and Webster (1977), as well as references to several other methods of conducting parent education and training, are presented at the end of the chapter. The reader should find these references an excellent point of departure for a comprehensive study of parent education and training.

The following are discussed in the chapter:

- [ ] The need for and desirability of parent education and training
- [ ] The reactions, problems, and needs of parents of children with behavior problems and handicapping conditions
- [ ] An overview of the purposes and objectives of parent training and the specific objectives of the program presented in this chapter
- [ ] Assessment techniques used to aid parents in selecting target behaviors
- [ ] A list of potentially effective reinforcers available in the home
- [ ] An 8-session behavior modification training course for parents
- [ ] Several techniques to facilitate home-school communication and thus the effectiveness of cooperative behavior management programs

Need for and Desirability of Parent Education and Training

There remains among present-day regular and special education teachers, as well as educational administrators and other professionals, skepticism concerning the need for and desirability of school-sponsored programs for parents. Our experience, however, as parents and educators, indicates that parent education and training is a necessary component of a comprehensive school service program.

Clements and Alexander (1975) agree:

> It is unnecessary to revisit the already proven axiom that parents are effective change agents in the lives of exceptional children. It is, perhaps, equally as extravagant to indulge in outlining the boundaries of social and academic learning and perpetuate the pseudo-issue of who governs which set of constructs when, in reality, these are shared and inter-active responsibilities. We must instead face an important issue in the third quarter of the twentieth century; parents are moving both physically and intellectually back into the mainstream of American education. (p. 1)

The question is not whether parent training is needed but how educators can effectively and efficiently conduct parent programs for the ultimate benefit of all children. Clements and Alexander suggest that the teacher is the school-based professional primarily responsible for parent services. All teachers of regular and special classes must acknowledge their responsibility and take steps to provide appropriate programs for parents.

As part of the Rutland Center's Early Childhood Project, Wood (1975) and her associates offer a parent program with two primary goals: to provide parents with information relative to the needs of their children and to assist them in practical ways in their efforts to meet their children's needs.

Gardner (1974) maintains that cooperative home-school endeavors are more effective in responding to the needs of behavior-disordered children than are school endeavors alone. He states that parents require the assistance of school personnel in efforts to manage their children's behavior:

> Many parents do need assistance in recognizing that what they are doing may create additional problems for the child. Many could benefit from guidance in modifying the manner in which they interact with or respond to their children. They do not need the teacher to place blame on them or to lecture them on what they have done wrong or how they have created the child's problem. They do require information, guidance, and support. They need information about how specific and general problems can be approached and how their day to day interactions with their child can contribute to the child's development. They do not need generalities about being a good parent. They do need specific, concrete, and practical suggestions about how they can best promote optimal adjustment for their child. (p. 316)

The Pathfinder School (Susser, 1974) perceives parents and educators as partners. According to Susser, success in the classroom is lasting only if there is 24-hour-a-day follow-through; the approach of school and home, teacher and parent, must be consistent.

Karnes and Zehrbach (1972) have suggested that programs for handicapped children can be significantly improved if parents are meaningfully involved in them.

Opinions relative to the need for and desirability of programs for parents are not exclusively the domain of professionals. Many parents are aware of their need for education and training. In *Heartaches and Handicaps: An Irreverent Survival Manual for Parents,* Stigen (1976) writes repeatedly of her need for assistance through meaningful education and training. She discusses the inadequacy of the guidance and supportive services for parents offered by hospitals, schools, clinics, and other social service agencies.

Kratoville (1975a, 1975b) and Jogis (1975), both parents of handicapped children, have described their need for sensitive, practical assistance in their role as primary therapist for their children. These parents noted a lack of meaningful assistance and understanding of their problems by professionals in hospitals, schools, clinics, and community agencies. They discovered the obvious lack of training and sensitivity of professionals toward parents.

The opinions of the parents and professionals just cited and those of many others, including parents and teachers involved primarily with nonhandicapped children, lead us to the following conclusions (Shea and Bauer, 1985):

1. Both parents and professionals recognize the need for parent education and training.
2. Parent programs are desirable because they not only respond to the needs of the parents but also have a significant positive effect on the children.
3. The teacher, a specialist in instructional processes and behavior management techniques, is the logical professional to coordinate and conduct parent programs in cooperation with the school counselor, psychologist, or social worker.
4. Children benefit most when the behavior management approaches of the home and school are consistent.
5. Parent programs must be practical, concrete, specific, and meaningful to the parents.

Although the literature cited is primarily concerned with children administratively classified as handicapped, the conclusions drawn from the literature are relevant to all children and their parents. "Normal" children also have problems and are frequently a behavior management concern to their parents.

Parents' Reactions, Problems, and Needs

The parents of a child with a problem are first and foremost human beings, and like all human beings they react as individuals to the problems of loved ones. A particular parent's reaction is in large part determined by that individual's personal characteristics, life experiences, education and training, expectations, socioeconomic circumstances, and a variety of other variables. The parent's reaction is influenced by the characteristics of the child and the specific problem and, to some degree, by the educator's reaction to the problem (Shea & Bauer, 1985).

Educators should keep in mind that parents with problem children are not necessarily "problem parents" (Denhoff, 1960). They do not necessarily need personal counseling. The majority are normal persons who are responding in a normal manner to unanticipated trauma.

Ross (1964) discussed parental reactions to the birth or diagnosis of a child with exceptionality from a psychoanalytic perspective. The recognition of a handicap in a child causes an increase in the parents' level of anxiety. This anxiety appears to be caused by recognition of the unanticipated discrepancy between the parents' expectations for the child and the way the child is in reality. In their efforts to control anxiety, the parents employ one or more of a broad range of defense mechanisms. These defenses are used to regain emotional equilibrium, which has been threatened by the crisis. Although the defense mechanisms are applied for positive reasons, that is, the regaining of emotional equilibrium, they may be destructive to the individual parent and child if they are overused or if they become habitual. According to Ross, counseling and similar supportive therapeutic services are required to aid parents in dealing with their initial anxiety and consequent defensive reactions resulting from their child's problem.

A crisis reaction to a child's problems is not the exclusive province of parents of children classified as deviant, special, exceptional, or handicapped (Gordon, 1976). Emotional reactions to problems with a child are a natural human response for any parent confronted with a crisis or perceived crisis. Also, all parents do not employ the same defense mechanisms. Parental reactions are as varied as the individual parents confronted with a crisis situation (Gordon, 1976).

Among the defense mechanisms parents may apply in response to their recognition of a problem with a child are:

- *Self-doubt:* The parents may react to the child's problem with self-doubt. They may doubt their worth as human beings and as parents. Their self-worth may be in doubt because of a perceived inability to give birth to or raise a child according to their expectations and the expectations of society.
- *Unhappiness and mourning:* The parents may react to the child's handicap with extreme unhappiness. The child's problem is perceived as so severe that the parents' joy of life is gone. It is impossible for them to smile, laugh, converse, or take an active part in any of life's common pleasures. In the extreme, this parental reaction is similar to the mourning that occurs after the death of a loved one.
- *Guilt:* Because of the uncertain cause of their child's problem, many parents feel guilty. They believe that the child's problem is their fault. Many times parents will go to extreme lengths to find a reason for the child's difficulty and may discover some small insignificant personal behavior or incident in the past on which to place personal blame.
- *Denial:* The parents may react to the child's problem by denying its existence. They reason that if the existence of the problem is denied, they do not have to concern themselves with it.
- *Projection:* Many parents who recognize the existence of a problem may blame it on another person. They may blame the child's difficulty on a physician, nurse, caseworker, counselor, baby-sitter, or teacher. Occasionally they will project blame onto their spouse or other children.

☐ *Withdrawal:* The parents may react to the child's problem by withdrawal, believing that they can find a solution if they give the problem sufficient time and personal consideration. In some cases such withdrawal leads to depression requiring professional attention to restore normal functioning.

☐ *Avoidance and rejection:* To some parents the birth or diagnosis of an exceptional child is so traumatic that they avoid contact with the child; they are unable to feed, clothe, or play with the child.

☐ *Embarrassment and social isolation:* Many parents of handicapped children are embarrassed by them. In some cases this embarrassment leads to social isolation. Neither parent nor child leaves the home for shopping, walks, visits, or entertainment. These parents choose to avoid embarrassment by not participating in social situations that may result in curious stares or questions concerning the child or the child's behavior.

☐ *Hostility:* Some parents report feelings of hostility and, on occasion, overt anger toward others who stare or ask questions about the child. The object of this hostility and anger may be anyone: a passenger on a bus, a person in the street, a friend, a neighbor, or a relative.

☐ *Overdependency and helplessness:* The parents may react with overdependency on their spouse, a child, a relative, or a professional. They are helpless to make any decision concerning the child's future.

☐ *Confusion:* Most parents are confused by the child's problem. They are confused about the cause of the problem, its normal course, and its treatment. Such confusion is largely a result of a lack of factual information and guidance from professionals responsible for providing such services.

☐ *Frustration:* Many parents who have decided on a course of action that is appropriate for their child become frustrated in their efforts to obtain services. They are confronted with insensitive and inadequately trained professionals. They are frustrated by the lack of appropriate services in the community.

The educator must recognize that many of the foregoing emotional reactions are not under a parent's conscious control. Parents must be aided in dealing with their emotional reactions before they can fully participate in and benefit from a training program.

Effective parent educators realize that they need a variety of counseling and instructional skills. They must learn to listen to the meaning behind the parents' words, as well as the words themselves (Lichter, 1976). They must be sensitive to the parents' feelings. They must be able to empathize with the problems confronting the parents and child. Although parent educators must approach their task with honesty and forthrightness, they must not be cruel, give the impression that the parents, child, and problem are hopeless, or indicate that they have all the answers. Parent educators must have sufficient confidence in their teaching ability to permit parents to develop confidence in them—and through them, in themselves.

Purposes and Objectives of Parent Training

McDowell (1976) has classified parent programs under three headings: (1) informational, (2) psychotherapeutic, and (3) training.

The informational program is designed primarily to present knowledge to parents about a variety of topics. Among the focuses of such informational programs are (1) child-raising techniques, (2) child development, (3) educational program designs, objectives, and procedures, (4) the causes, effects, and treatment of handicapping conditions, and (5) techniques of behavior management. The primary purpose of these parent programs is the transmission of information.

The psychotherapeutic strategy is employed to assist parents in their efforts to deal with personal feelings and conflicts resulting from the child's problem. It is assumed that parents must adjust to the emotional crisis before they can plan and implement an action program.

Parent training programs are designed to assist parents' efforts to effectively interact with and manage the behavior of their children. These programs can be exemplified by several contemporary parent training programs. Parent effectiveness training (Gordon, 1970) focuses primarily on assisting parents in establishing effective and positive communications with children. The C-Group strategy (Dinkmeyer and McKay, 1973) focuses on training parents to solve practical child management problems. Both programs are action oriented. They necessitate parental involvement and commitment. In these programs it is assumed that once parents have learned appropriate and effective problem-solving skills and have made them a habit, they will continue to apply them in the management of child behavior.

The program for parent-teacher cooperation in child management presented in this chapter can be classified as a parent training program. It focuses primarily on training and implementation of behavior management techniques as an effective and efficient means of managing behavior. As a consequence of this focus, the program is limited in its effectiveness with those parents in need of psychotherapeutic or basic informational services.

Objectives of the Parent Training Program

The specific objectives of the parent training program presented in this chapter are:

☐ To increase the parents' knowledge of the techniques of behavior modification.
☐ To increase the parents' skills in the application of behavior modification techniques in the management of their children's behavior.
☐ To provide both the parents and the teacher with a common perspective of child behavior management and facilitate cooperative child behavior management efforts.

These objectives are attained by instructing the parents in behavior modification techniques and by assisting the parents' application of these techniques in home and home-school behavior management interventions.

The steps in the behavior change process applied in the parent training program are identical to those presented in Chapter 3. These steps are repeated here for reader convenience. Those wishing to review in depth the steps in the behavior change process are referred to Chapter 3. The steps are:

Step 1: Selecting a target behavior.
Step 2: Collecting and recording baseline data.
Step 3: Identifying appropriate reinforcers.
Step 4: Implementing an intervention and collecting and recording intervention data.
Step 5: Evaluating the effects of intervention.

It must be remembered that in parent training the teacher is generally once removed from direct observation of the child's behavior in the home setting; thus the teacher must rely on the parents' observations and reports. Consequently assessment strategies must be implemented to facilitate the parents' selection and objectification of a target behavior.

In addition, reinforcers applied in the home setting differ somewhat from those available and applicable in the school; thus attention is given to the parents' recognition and application of home reinforcers.

Selecting the Target Behavior: Assessment Techniques

To be of practical assistance to parents wishing to improve their behavior management skills, the educator must obtain specific information about the child and the problem. The information needed by the teacher includes (Blackham and Silberman, 1975):

☐ The history of the problem
☐ Specific areas of conflict
☐ A description of the behavior that makes it receptive to direct observation and measurement
☐ The identity of the person or persons present when the behavior occurs
☐ Reinforcers that appear to maintain the behavior
☐ The roles and responsibilities of the parents and other family members in the child's life
☐ Parental expectations and behavior requirements and the reasonableness of these expectations and requirements
☐ Methods presently used in attempts to change the behavior
☐ Rewards that are available or that can be made available in the home
☐ Observational data on the rate or frequency of the behavior

Blackham and Silberman have suggested four methods for obtaining data on parent-child interactions and problem areas:

1. Direct observation of the child and other family members in the home
2. Direct observation of the child and other family members in the clinic or school setting
3. Parental observation of the child's interaction within the family at home and the reporting of the resultant data to the educator
4. A personal interview with the parents and child

As a result of the administrative organization of the public school system, the first two methods are not feasible; that is, the teacher is usually unable to spend the needed time observing parent-child interaction in either the home or the school. The third and fourth methods are most practical and can be implemented by means of the psychosituational assessment interview.

Psychosituational Assessment Interview

The psychosituational assessment interview is primarily an information-gathering technique. The interview focuses primarily on obtaining from the parent or parents descriptive data about the child's behavior and the circumstances surrounding it.

The psychosituational assessment interview is not a conversation between parents and educator.

> A conversation is a two-way exchange of information in which all parties involved may contribute equally or alternately to the flow of the communication. The implicit rules of a social conversation state that all parties have a responsibility for keeping the exchange from coming to a standstill, periods of silence are avoided, "personal" topics are generally taboo, and the content of the conversation may range widely as the participants introduce new topics in association to something another may have said.*

The assessment interview is

> ... a specialized pattern of verbal interaction—initiated for a specific purpose, and focused on some specific content area, with consequent elimination of extraneous material. Moreover, the interview is a pattern of interaction in which the role relationship of interviewer and respondent is highly specialized, its specific characteristics depending somewhat on the purpose and character of the interview.†

---

*From Ross, A. O. *The exceptional child in the family: Helping parents of exceptional children.* New York: Grune & Stratton, Inc., 1964, p. 76. Reprinted by permission.

†From Kahn, R. L., and Cannell, C. F. *The dynamics of interviewing: Theory, technique, and cases.* New York: John Wiley & Sons, Inc., 1957, p. 16.

The psychosituational assessment interview technique was designed by Bersoff and Grieger (1971) and applied by Shea and others (1974). The purpose of the interview is to analyze the unacceptable behavior and uncover the antecedents and consequences that elicit, reinforce, and sustain it. This information about the child is elicited from the parent or parents and contributes to decisions concerning interventions to modify the behavior.

The model of behavior applied to this technique is a departure from the predominant perspective that the personality is composed of needs and traits that predispose the individual to respond in predetermined ways. Such a perspective leads to the assumption that behavior is independent of the situation, and emphasis is on "fixing" the individual rather than restructuring the setting in which the behavior occurs. Bersoff and Grieger proposed that, rather than viewing behavior in such a manner, one should regard it as the individual's inability to respond in certain ways in certain situations. In their model behavior is seen as a function of prior learning and the stimulus situation.

By means of the psychosituational assessment interview, it is possible to determine to what extent the behavior is reinforced and maintained by the environment and to what extent it may be modified by the manipulation of the environment. Thus the primary aspects of the setting in which the behavior occurs are analyzed in the interview. These aspects are (1) the child's behavior, (2) the environmental variables surrounding the behavior, and (3) the attitudes and expectations of the parents.

Behavior refers to the actual behaviors for which the child was referred, including the antecedents and consequences of that behavior, that is, teacher, parental, and peer responses. *Environments and situations* refers to the specific places and circumstances in which the behavior occurs, including the presence of significant others. *Attitudes and emotions* refers to the beliefs and feelings of the referring agent, that is, the parent or parents.

A parent's concern about a child's behavior may be based on irrational ideas and attitudes that lead to unwarranted expectations, demands, and feelings, all of which result in inappropriate actions toward the child following emission of the target behavior. *Expectation* has a dual meaning: It refers to the specific performance that the adult would like the child to achieve (short-term goals) and to the long-range aspirations that the adult has for the child.

The four major tasks to be accomplished during the interview are (1) defining the target behavior(s), (2) explicating specific situations in which the behavior occurs, (3) uncovering the contingencies that seemingly sustain the behavior, and (4) detecting any irrational ideas that make it difficult for the parent or parents to objectively understand, accept, and modify the behavior.

Defining the target behavior involves analyzing the following: (1) its *frequency rate,* the number of times the behavior occurs within a particular time period; (2) its *intensity,* the strength or force of the behavior; and (3) its *duration,* the length of time that the behavior is maintained. A careful analysis of the problem within a behavioral framework helps delineate and define it so that it becomes remediable. This process helps the parents check their perceptions and focus on the relevant problem.

Obtaining information about the specific situations in which the behavior occurs is important because behavior is considered a function of interaction between the learned response of the child and the situation in which the behavior occurs. This information helps the interviewer plan the intervention.

Exploring the contingencies and consequences (results) of the behavior is the next interviewer task. The parents must be aware that *they are part of the problem* and may have a role in sustaining the behavior.

Finally, the interviewer must be aware of the parent or parents' irrational and unrealistic ideas about the child. The following irrational ideas of parents are frequently apparent:

1. The notion that the child is infallible and has wide-ranging competence. When the parents' expectation is that the child is competent in all respects, inefficiency in one or two areas of school functioning is regarded as general failure.
2. The maintenance of absolutistic, unsupportable, and unreasonable expectations of the child. These ideas are usually expressed in "ought" and "should" terms. A parent may say, "He should be able to sit longer" or "He ought to know better."
3. The feeling that it is helpful to become angry over the child's misbehavior. This feeling may lead to guilt and anxiety on the part of the parents that may further interfere with parent-child interactions.
4. The belief that the child is blameworthy and needs to be punished for misdeeds. The failure to accept things as they exist inhibits rational problem solving.

It is recommended that both parents be present at the interview. A joint interview is desirable because differing perceptions and inconsistencies in parental behavior management strategies can be uncovered. It also allows the interviewer to gauge the amount and frequency of mutual support that the parents provide to each other.

The psychosituational assessment interview may be a single session or a series of sessions. If the interviewer is primarily concerned with obtaining data in an effort to design an intervention that includes parental participation, two or three sessions may be sufficient. However, frequently the strategy can be applied in an ongoing intervention program.

To assist the parent, the interviewer may suggest that the parents gather behavioral data. A form for this purpose is presented in Figure 8.1, along with instructions for completing the form.

Frequently parents find it difficult to estimate the number of times during a specified period of time that the misbehavior occurs.

The following are specific interviewer tasks:

1. Establish rapport with the parent or parents.
2. Have the parents specify the target behavior(s), that is, the specific behavior(s) that are disturbing to them. Explore the frequency, intensity, and duration of the behavior.

Behavior Log Form

Target behavior _____

Child _____

Observer _____

Date	Time		Antecedents	Consequences	Applied interventions	Comments
	Begins	Ends				

FIGURE 8.1
Parents' behavior log for home use.

Behavior Log Form

INSTRUCTIONS

1. Complete the top portion of the form, that is, the target behavior to be observed, the child's name, the observer's name, and date.

2. Write *day* and *date* of the first observation in first column, for example, M/8/3 or Th/11/3.

3. Upon each occurrence of the target behavior write the time it begins and ends in the second and third columns, respectively. If the target behavior is nearly instantaneous, write the time of the occurrence in the second column.

4. Upon each occurrence of the target behavior, write what happened immediately *before* the behavior in the fourth column.

5. In column six write what you or another person interacting with or supervising the child did to either *encourage* or *discourage* the behavior. If there was no reaction to the behavior, it should be noted in this column.

6. In column seven write any comments you have regarding the occurrence of the behavior that are out of the ordinary, for example, child was tired, grandmother was visiting, bad day in school, marital conflict occurring, and so on.

It is recommended that a behavior log be maintained for a minimum of 1 week before an intervention is implemented.

FIGURE 8.1, *continued.*

Example Questions
- ☐ What exactly does the child do that you find unacceptable or annoying?
- ☐ What exactly does the child do that makes you say he or she is hyperactive, nonresponsive, or disobedient?
- ☐ What else does the child do that makes you say he or she is hyperactive, nonresponsive, or disobedient?
- ☐ In the course of an hour (day) how often is the child hyperactive, nonresponsive, or disobedient?

3. Have the parents delineate the specific situations and environments in which the behavior occurs. Establish where the behavior takes place and who is present when the behavior occurs.

Example Questions
- ☐ Where does this behavior occur? In the house? In the yard? On the playground? In a store?
- ☐ Does it occur when the child is working on a particular project? With a particular group? While watching TV? When getting ready to go to bed? When getting up in the morning?
- ☐ Who is present when the behavior occurs? Mother? Father? Brothers? Sisters? Playmates? Visitors?

4. Explore the contingencies that may stimulate and sustain the behavior. Determine what happens immediately before and after the behavior occurs, that is, the antecedents and consequences of the behavior.
   Example Questions
   ☐ What happens just before the behavior occurs?
   ☐ What happens just after the behavior occurs?
   ☐ What do you usually do when the child engages in this behavior?
   ☐ How do other people indicate to the child that the behavior is unacceptable?

5. Attempt to determine the ratio of positive-to-negative interactions between the child and the parents.
   Example Questions
   ☐ Is your relationship with the child usually pleasant or unpleasant?
   ☐ Do you usually praise his or her accomplishments?
   ☐ Do you reprimand the child's failures and ignore his or her success?

6. Explore the methods the parents use for behavior control. Explore the type of punishment and the conditions for application.
   Example Questions
   ☐ Do you punish the behavior?
   ☐ How do you punish inappropriate behavior?
   ☐ Who is responsible for administering the punishment?
   ☐ Do you always use this method of punishment?
   ☐ Which other methods do you use?

7. Determine to what degree the parents are aware of how praise or punishment is communicated and its effect on the child's behavior.
   Example Questions
   ☐ Can the child tell when you are angry? How?
   ☐ Can the child tell when you want him or her to stop doing something? How?

8. Explore the manner in which expectations and consequences are communicated by the parents to their child.
   Example Questions
   ☐ Are the rules you expect the child to follow clearly spelled out?
   ☐ Does the child know what you expect him or her to do?

9. Detect irrational and unrealistic ideas that make it difficult for the parents to understand, accept, or modify the child's behavior. Be alert for and explore irrational ideas that may be expressed by the parents. Restate irrational ideas but avoid reinforcing them.

10. Conclude the session by restating the unacceptable behavior and presenting the desirable behavior. You may suggest that the parents keep a log of the child's behavior. (Refer to Figure 8.1.) Explain to the parents how the log should be used. You may suggest one or two techniques for changing the behavior. (This is only done if additional sessions are prohibited.) Make arrangements for a future meeting.

A careful reading of the parent-teacher psychosituational assessment interview that follows will clarify the use of this technique.

Parent-Teacher Interview

T: Good afternoon, Mr. _____.

P: Hello, Mrs. _____, how are you?

T: Fine, thank you. Glad to meet you. Sit down, please. I'm Mark's special education teacher this year, and I'd like to ask you some questions about Mark. Let's see. He's 9 years old, and he's presently in Mrs. Lee's class—that's third grade.

P: Yes.

T: Mrs. Lee has told me that Mark does rather well in some of his subjects. He's particularly good in math. He enjoys that very much. He has a little bit of difficulty with reading and writing, however. And behaviorally, she finds some problems with him leaving his seat frequently. He's rather active in the classroom.

P: Yeah, she's not the only one who has problems with him.

T: I see.

P: He's a bad boy. We have trouble with him at home all the time.

T: Oh, you do?

P: Yeah, I'm, well, I know Mrs. Lee does, too, because my wife tells me that Mrs. Lee calls, and the principal calls about him and about sending him home from school all the time. My wife should be here today—she really spends most of the time with Mark, but she didn't want to come because she wasn't feeling very good. I drive a truck, and I'm on the road most of the time. I don't see much of him.

T: It was very nice of you to come today.

P: Well . . . thank you.

T: I'd like to ask you some more questions about Mark's behavior at home. You said that he seems to . . . you have some trouble with him, too. Would you explain that to me a little?

P: He fights all the time. He's just always getting in fights. Like I said, I'm gone a lot, but my wife tells me that she has trouble with him all the time. Fights with his brothers, and every once in a while he fights with the neighbors—he is just always getting into trouble. That seems to be about it.

T: Fighting seems to be the biggest problem.

P: Oh, yeah, he fights all the time. Always in trouble.

T: Could you give me an example of how one of these fights occurs?

P: Well, my wife was telling me last night that he and the older boy were playing Chinese checkers, and he lost. Mark lost, and Bill picked up a handful of—not Bill, but Mark— picked up a handful of marbles and threw them at Bill and went at him with his fists.

T: He became so agitated by losing that he started a fight.

P: He can't lose . . . he just goes . . . losing . . . he fights. That's just automatic—one, two. He just can't stand to lose. As long as he's winning, he gets along fine.

T: Are there any cases you can tell me about when he wins—how he acts?

P: Well, I take the boys fishing in the spring and in the summer.

T: That's nice.

P: Oh, yeah. I like to fish. Actually it's comforting and its lot of fun. We enjoy it—being out—and usually Mark, when he goes with us, he catches most of the fish.

T: Oh, really.

P: Oh, yeah. And, yeah, he has a good time then, bragging around and measuring, comparing the size of his fish and the other boys' fish and boasting about it. Yeah, he likes that.

T: He doesn't seem to fight much when you go fishing, does he?

P: Well, it all depends. Now, if one of the other boys catches a bigger fish or more fish, then he'll fight. He'll go at them, hit them, holler at them. Yeah, he can't stand to lose.

T: But if he's winning, and especially when he's fishing, he must enjoy that—going with you.

P: Yeah, he likes to go fishing. We have a good time.

T: Do you ever go with him by yourself?

P: We all go fishing. I tried to get my wife to go, but she doesn't care much for fishing. She doesn't like to bait the hook. You know how women are.

T: Oh, yes. So fishing is one thing that Mark really enjoys, especially when he's winning. And he's pretty good at it, from what you say.

P: That's right.

T: He must have had some good training. Let's talk about the fighting that goes on at home. Could you tell me a little bit more about it? You said that if losing is involved, then he seems to fight.

P: Yeah, that's right.

T: One example was with the Chinese checkers and his older brother. Could you give me any other examples?

P: Yeah, if he thinks one of the other kids gets more ice cream—like his younger brother —he'll poke him and start a fight. You know. It's really bad. My wife says that he's on the younger boy all the time at home, and she has to spank him or send him out of the house or send him up to bed, and it keeps going on. He's really a bad boy at home.

T: And you say he fights all the time. It probably seems like it's all the time because it's rather upsetting.

P: She's always complaining about it.

T: Do you have any idea of how often exactly this happens? Once a night, twice a night, once a week?

P: Well, it may be two or three times a week.

T: Two or three times a week?

P: Yeah, about two or three times a week—mainly because he wins the other 2 or 3 days.

T: Oh, I see.

P: Yeah, he's pretty good.

T: On the winning days he's really not that much of a problem?

P: No problem. As long as he's winning, he gets along with everyone really well.

T: Let's talk about these fights a little. You mentioned that he gets into almost real fisticuffs. Do you mean that he actually punches?

P: Not *almost*. He really does. Punches. And he keeps punching until the other kid gives up.

T: That's how the fight usually is settled?

P: That's how it's settled, unless one of the adults steps in and stops it.

T: By one of the adults, I assume you mean yourself or your wife.

P: My wife is home most of the time—she does this. When I'm home, I'm watching television, and if he starts a ruckus, I stop it right away. I don't let anything go on. I stop it unless it's a tight inning, and then I may wait until the action's over and then I stop it. But it doesn't stop until I stop it.

T: You mentioned shaking him to stop it.

P: Yeah, I shake him.

Parent Training and Home-School Behavior Management

T: Does that seem to work?

P: Well, you know, shake them till their teeth rattle—that straightens them out. That's what my daddy always said.

T: Do you use any other forms of punishment besides shaking?

P: Well, if that doesn't work, yeah, sure. I spank them when I feel that I should, and sometimes I just send them out of the house.

T: How long do these fights last? Just until . . . someone gives up? Maybe a minute? Two, 5 minutes?

P: If an adult's not there, sometimes they'll go on sometimes 5 or 10 minutes, 15 minutes. If an adult's there, of course, the adult stops it. Or an older kid can stop it, but they usually like to watch the fight.

T: Do you think what you're doing—this shaking and spanking—has changed his behavior any? Has it stopped the fighting?

P: It stops it then.

T: It stops it for that time?

P: Yeah.

T: When he loses, he fights, and when he fights, it's physical. It's dangerous to the other person.

P: Sometimes he yells and just hollers and screams at the other kids. One time he hit his older brother with a chair because he was losing the fight. And I mean, he really gets violent. He really wants to win.

T: These fights, even though they are violent, last sometimes less than 5 minutes? Sometimes up to 15 minutes?

P: Yeah, that's about right.

T: And they seem to happen two or three times a week?

P: Yeah, that's about right.

T: But it seems like, otherwise, the rest of the time he's really pretty agreeable and easy to get along with. Things seem to go all right as long as he's winning.

P: As long as things are going his way and nobody steps on him or steps on his toes, he's all right.

T: Fine. Most of the time when you're dealing with Mark, is it a pleasant interaction or are there problems? Let's say for the most part.

P: See, I'm not home very much, and when I'm home I like to do what I like to do. I like to watch television and sports and so forth. And you know, of course, we do go fishing in the spring and summer, and then we get along fine—unless, of course, someone catches more fish than he does. But when I'm home, I like to watch television. I really don't pay that much attention to the kids. But my wife says that, you know, some days he can be very nice. But most of the time he's a bad, rotten kid.

T: Well, I think maybe we should start to work on this fighting behavior. I could help you with some suggestions.

P: Well, I'll tell you, we'd appreciate anything you could suggest.

T: Well, one thing I think would be a good idea is if you and your wife could keep what we call a log. We train our teachers to keep this. All it is, is that you would write down every day whether or not there was a fight. Then, what time the fight occurred, what the behavior was just before the fight happened, and how it was resolved. So, an example of this, which was done by another parent, would show that, like, Monday there was a fight, Tuesday nothing, Wednesday nothing—but Thursday there were two fights. Then, if you and your wife together would keep this kind of log . . .

P: Well, I know what a log is. That's what I do because I'm a truck driver. We keep a log, and I can show my wife how to do it. I can't guarantee she'll do it, but I can show her how, and . . .

T: That would be very helpful.

P: Yeah, fine.

T: I think that you can probably explain it better than I could.

P: Probably so, right.

T: Then maybe in 3 weeks' time, we'll make another appointment for an interview, and you and your wife can come together.

P: Well, I'm not sure that I'll be able to make it because I'm on the road. But I think if my wife has something to talk about and hold onto, why, she'll probably be willing to come and chat with you.

T: Let's see if we can't arrange it for the three of us.

P: All right.

T: I'll do it at your convenience.

P: OK, right.

T: And if you will bring in the log for the next 3 weeks of behavior—how many times he fights—we won't worry about anything else, just the fighting behavior. Until that time, I'd also like you maybe to take some time with Mark alone and let me know how it works out with you just dealing with him individually, apart from his brothers. Just once in a while. I realize that you're very busy, but that may give us some insights.

P: Kind of father-son talks.

T: That kind of thing; that might work out well.

P: I'll try that.

Other Assessment Aids

Several of the behavior checklists and inventories discussed in this section can be helpful in the effort to assist parents in the objectification of their perception of the child's problem. Like the psychosituational assessment interview technique discussed in the previous section, these techniques are of assistance to the parent and teacher wishing to select a target behavior. The instruments are most effectively and appropriately used as part of a battery of assessment instruments. They may be applied in the effort to focus the initial psychosituational assessment interview sessions on specific areas of conflict and behavior.

Among the checklists and inventories found helpful to educators working with parents are:

- ☐ Behavior Problem Checklist (Quay and Peterson, 1967)
- ☐ Devereux Child Behavior Rating Scale (Spivack and Spotts, 1966)
- ☐ Devereux Adolescent Behavior Rating Scale (Spivack, Spotts, & Haimes, 1967)
- ☐ Vineland Adaptive Behavior Scales (Sparrow et al., 1984)
- ☐ Child Behavior Rating Scale (Cassel, 1962)
- ☐ Walker Problem Behavior Identification Checklist (Walker, 1976)
- ☐ Burks' Behavior Rating Scales (Burks, 1977)

In general, the statistical reliability and validity of these inventories, checklists, and scales are questionable. However, if properly applied in conjunction with an interview, they can facilitate efforts to focus the parent or parents' attention on the child's specific behavior problem.

Another technique that can be applied to assist parents in the selection of a target behavior is the Target Behavior kit (Kroth, 1972). The kit applies the Q-sort technique, developed by Stephenson (1953). It can be applied to facilitate the psychosituational assessment interview, that is, to assist the parent or parents in the selection and ranking of the child's behaviors.

The Target Behavior kit contains:

☐ A 9-column target behavior board that is divided into 25 squares. The columns vary in length from 1 to 5 squares. The 5-square column is in the center of the board; the 1-square columns are located on the extreme left and right of the board. The column designations range from "most like me" to "most unlike me," with the "undecided" category in the center of the board. For work with parents, the column designations can be changed to "most like my child," "least like my child," and so on.
☐ Two sets of cards listing 25 observable and measurable behaviors. One set lists home behaviors; the other lists classroom behaviors.
☐ Several blank cards on which additional observable and measurable behaviors may be written.
☐ A manual.
☐ Record sheets.

In completing the behavior-sorting task, the parents are instructed to arrange the cards on the board from the perspective of the child's real or actual behaviors. In a second ranking, they are instructed to arrange the cards from the perspective of the ideal behaviors, that is, "how I would like my child to be." As the parents complete the two sortings, the interviewer notes the discrepancies between their perceptions of the child's real and ideal behaviors. These discrepancies then become material for interview sessions.

Home Reinforcers

In this section a list of potentially effective home reinforcers is presented. These have been found useful to parents needing suggestions on rewards they may apply at home. Additional suggestions are presented in the extensive list of reinforcers in Chapter 3.

Consumable food reinforcers	
Fruits	Cookies
Candies	Cake
Snack foods	Crackers
Gum	Milk
Ice cream	Soda
	Juice

Reinforcing activities in relation to food reinforcers

Baking cookies or a cake with a parent
Preparing dinner with a parent
Operating a toaster, mixer, or another appliance.
Washing dishes or operating the dishwasher
Setting the table for snack time
Serving snacks
Cleaning the table after snack time

Tangible reinforcers

Pencils or pens
Colored, broad-tipped markers
Erasers
Money to purchase desired items
Records
Surprise gifts
Toys
Games
Coloring books
Pads of paper
Books
Jewelry
Clothing
Pets
Pet supplies

Token reinforcers

Points
Stars
Chips
Play money
Check marks

Game activity reinforcers

Playing outdoors alone with friends or a parent
Participating in organized sports
Flying a kite
Participating in table games: checkers, backgammon, cards, and so on
Playing computer games

Social reinforcers

Smiles
Hugs
Pats
Kisses
Attention from parents
Compliments about activities, efforts, appearance

Reinforcing actitivies

Reading or looking at books, magazines, catalogs
Using the home computer
Watching television
Getting additional playtime
Going to the zoo
Fishing
Obtaining and caring for a pet
Spending the night with a friend or relative
Shopping with a parent
Having a friend spend the night
Going to the movies
Using the stereo
Getting telephone privileges
Receiving help from a parent on a homework assignment or chore
Attending a recreational activity or sporting event
Attending or having a party
Staying out later than usual
Accompanying parents instead of remaining with a sitter
Driving the family car
Going for ice cream, hamburgers, french fries
Working on a project with a parent
Visiting a parent's place of work
Joining and participating in a club or team
Taking lessons (music, dance, swimming)
Using the family typewriter
Listening to a story as a parent reads

Parent Training Program

The parent training program presented in this section has two objectives: (1) to train parents in the theory and application of behavior modification principles and practices and (2) to assist parents' efforts to systematically modify selected target behaviors exhibited by their children. Although not a primary objective of the program, a benefit derived by many parents is mutual support and understanding of their child management problems from other members of the group and the educator.

The program includes the three phases: preparation, instructional, and follow-up.

Preparation Phase

Before beginning the instructional phase of the training program, the parent educator should conduct one or more psychosituational assessment interviews with each parent or couple. The objective of these interviews is (1) to determine the parent or parents' needs, interests, and readiness to participate in a formal training program and (2) to clarify at least one behavior they wish to modify.

The individual interview sessions are an excellent time for the educator to discuss the program objectives, organization, and requirements and to invite the parent or parents' participation.

Instructional Phase

The instructional phase of the parent training program includes eight weekly sessions. The 1½-hour sessions are divided into two 40-minute segments and a 10-minute break.

The first 40-minute segment is devoted to brief formal presentations by the educator on the principles and practices of behavior modification. The remainder of this segment is devoted to a question-and-answer session, group discussion, and practice exercises and activities.

The 10-minute break is devoted to informal discussion. Coffee, tea, milk, and soft drinks as well as snacks can be served. These items may be furnished by the educator or by the parents.

The second 40-minute segment of the weekly session is devoted to planning, implementing, and evaluating the parents' behavioral intervention programs. These programs are concerned with the behaviors selected during the preparation phase. During this second segment, time is devoted to participants' reports of their interventions. All members of the group are expected and encouraged to question, discuss, and make suggestions for improving the interventions. A positive and helpful attitude must be maintained by all participants throughout this segment. Maintaining a positive tone in the group is a primary function of the educator.

Meetings are conducted in a mutually agreed-upon location. The educator's or participants' homes are *not* recommended, in large part to avoid potential embarrassment, competition, or inconvenience to the participants. A school, YMCA, YWCA, or community center is an excellent location for meeting. The facility must be accessible to the participants. If necessary, car pools can be arranged among the participants. In some cases child care services will be needed. In addition, the meeting room should ensure the group's privacy. Appropriate adult furnishings are necessary. A worktable should be available.

Group membership is limited to 12 or 14 persons, excluding the educator. Teachers of the parent-members' children can become group members. Groups are open to both women and men. Participation by both parents is desirable.

Attendance should be regular because of the cumulative nature of the material. If parents are unable to attend a particular session, the educator must update them in an individual session. However, absences should be discouraged for the sake of group cohesion.

The educator functions as an instructor and group facilitator during weekly sessions. Although the educator's function as an instructor remains relatively constant throughout the program, parents should be permitted and encouraged to make instructional presentations. The educator's function as group facilitator should diminish as the instructional phase progresses and the participants begin to assert leadership.

Occasionally a team of two educators may present the training program. This is an excellent idea, particularly if one assumes the functions of instructor and the other the functions of facilitator. Of course, success in team teaching assumes personal-professional compatibility as well as fundamental agreement on the subject matter and instructional methods.

Any person who is knowledgeable of the principles and practices of behavior modification, child behavior, and group processes can serve as an educator. This includes both regular and special education teachers, college instructors, counselors, psychologists, nurses, social workers, and others.

The instructional materials needed for the parent training program are this text, especially the work sheets at the back. Each participant should have a copy of the text. Additional instructional aids are suggested in the lesson plans.

Follow-up Phase

Contacts with the parents should not be terminated at the end of the 8-week training program. It is suggested that the educator develop a follow-up plan, maintaining periodic contact with the group and with individual members to reinforce their efforts and assist in the planning and implementation of additional interventions. Contact can be maintained by individual interviews, telephone conversations, and monthly meetings.

The periodic reinforcement offered the participants during the follow-up phase will increase the probability that the skills learned during the training program will not fall into disuse.

Parent Training Lessons

Lesson 1: Introduction to Behavior Modification*

Goals
1. To familiarize participants with the models of causation of human behavior and with the behavior change process
2. To enable participants to exemplify each of the principles of behavior modification
3. To enable participants to complete two or more target behavior selection checklists correctly
4. To enable participants to accurately observe and record a target behavior

Content
1. Models of causation of human behavior
2. Principles of behavior modification
3. Overview of the behavior change process
4. Selecting a target behavior
5. Observing and recording a target behavior

Instructional methods
1. Lecture
2. Discussion
3. Demonstration
4. Completion of a target behavior selection checklist
5. Recording the target behavior rate or frequency

Activities
1. Segment A (40 minutes)
   a. Introduction of the educator and individual participants
   b. Overview of the course organization and content
   c. Brief lecture on contemporary theories of causation of human behavior
   d. Brief lecture or overview of the behavior change process
   e. Lecture on the principles of behavior modification; each participant requested to cite a personal example of each principle (may be written)
   f. Examples of target behaviors presented and explanation of the target behavior selection process; demonstration of how to complete a target behavior selection checklist; each participant requested to select a target behavior and complete a target behavior selection checklist
   g. Procedures for observing and recording target behaviors presented, exemplified, and discussed
2. Break (10 minutes)
3. Segment B (40 minutes)
   a. Target Behavior 1 (home behavior)

---

*Time constraints may necessitate making this lesson into two sessions.

(1) Each participant (or mother and father) presents to the group the target behavior selected during the psychosituational assessment interview of the course preparation phase. Participants also present and discuss the data that they recorded on the behavior log form.

(2) Each participant completes a target behavior selection checklist on Target Behavior 1.

(3) Each participant transfers the data on the behavior log form to an appropriate tally form (see Table 3.2).

Resources*

1. Segment A
   a. Parent educator and individual participants
   b. Chapter 8: Preparation phase of program and lesson titles
   c. Chapter 1: Models of human behavior
   d. Chapter 3: Entire chapter
   e. Chapter 2: Principles of reinforcement
   f. Chapter 3: Selecting a target behavior; target behavior selection checklist (back of text)
   g. Chapter 3: Collecting and recording baseline data
2. Break
3. Segment B
   a. Target Behavior 1
      (1) Behavior log form (back of text)
      (2) Target behavior selection checklist (back of text)
      (3) Chapter 3: Collecting and recording baseline data

Evaluation

1. Quiz on or written examples of the principles of reinforcement
2. Completed behavior log form, target behavior selection checklist, and tally form

Home assignment

1. Observe and record baseline data on Target Behavior 1
2. Read:
   a. Chapter 2: Consequences of behavior; Schedules of reinforcement
   b. Chapter 3: Collecting and recording baseline data

Lesson 2: Consequences of Behavior

Goals

1. To familiarize participants with the consequences of human behavior and the common reinforcement schedules
2. To enable participants to accurately chart baseline data on Target Behavior 1

Content

1. Review of Lesson 1

---

*Where appropriate, the numbers and letters in this section are in agreement with those in the activities section.

2. Consequences of behavior
3. Schedules of reinforcement
4. Collecting and recording baseline data
5. Charting baseline data

Instructional methods

1. Lecture
2. Demonstration
3. Discussion
4. Completion of a behavior chart

Activities

1. Segment A (40 minutes)
   a. Review
   b. Lecture/demonstration on the consequences of human behavior, the common reinforcement schedules, and the procedure of charting baseline data
   c. Discussion of (b)
   d. Examples of baseline data presented; each participant requested to chart example baseline data on a behavior chart
2. Break (10 minutes)
3. Segment B (40 minutes)
   a. Target Behavior 1 (home behavior)
      (1) Each participant charts baseline data collected between Lessons 1 and 2 (Baseline 1 data).
      (2) Participants present their raw data to the group for discussion, clarification, and practice charting.

Resources

1. Segment A
   a. Lesson 1 resources
   b. Chapter 2: Consequences of behavior; Schedules of reinforcement; Chapter 3: Collecting and recording baseline data
   c. Parent educator and participants
   d. Chapter 3: Collecting and recording baseline data; behavior chart (back of text)
2. Break
3. Segment B
   a. Target Behavior 1
      (1) Behavior chart (back of text)
      (2) Behavior tally form used during Week 1

Evaluation

1. Quiz on or written examples of the consequences of behavior and the common schedules of reinforcement
2. Completed tally form and behavior chart

Home assignment

1. Continue observing and recording Baseline 1 data on target Behavior 1
2. Observe and note those things and activities the chlid likes to do during free time
3. Read:

a. Chapter 3: Identifying appropriate reinforcers
b. Chapter 8: Home reinforcers

Lesson 3: Selecting Effective Reinforcers

Goals
1. To familiarize participants with the behavior modification intervention strategies for increasing, maintaining, and decreasing behavior.
2. To enable participants to compile a list of potentially effective home-based reinforcers
3. To enable participants to accurately chart Baseline 1 data on Target Behavior 1
4. To facilitate participants' selection of reinforcers, a reinforcement schedule, and an intervention strategy for Target Behavior 1

Content
1. Review of Lesson 2
2. Selecting potentially effective reinforcers
3. Overview of behavior modification intervention strategies
4. Charting or graphing baseline data
5. Selecting an appropriate reinforcement schedule and intervention strategy

Instructional methods
1. Lecture
2. Discussion
3. Completion of behavior chart
4. Individual/group project

Activities
1. Segment A (40 minutes)
    a. Review
    b. Lecture on selecting potentially effective reinforcers and on behavior modification intervention strategies
    c. Discussion of (b)
    d. Individual/group development of a list of children's rewards observed as home assignment
2. Break (10 minutes)
3. Segment B (40 minutes)
    a. Target Behavior 1 (home behavior)
        (1) Each participant charts Baseline 1 data collected between Lessons 2 and 3.
        (2) Each participant (with educator's assistance) selects reinforcers, a reinforcement schedule, and an intervention strategy to modify Target Behavior 1.

Resources
1. Segment A
    a. Lesson 2 resources
    b. Chapter 3: Identifying appropriate reinforcers; Chapter 4: Entire chapter; Chapter 5: Entire chapter; Chapter 8: Home reinforcers

    c. Parent educator and participants

    d. Chapter 3: Identifying appropriate reinforcers

2. Break
3. Segment B

    a. Target Behavior 1

        (1) Behavior chart (back of text)

        (2) Participant with assistance of parent educator and other participants

Evaluation

1. Quiz on methods of selecting appropriate reinforcers
2. Results of individual/group list of children's rewards
3. Behavior chart on Target Behavior 1

Home assignment

1. Implement intervention strategy for Target Behavior 1 and continue observing and recording data
2. Read Chapter 4: Shaping; Modeling; Contingency contracting

Lesson 4: Strategies to Increase Behavior

Goals

1. To familiarize participants with modeling, shaping, and contingency contracting intervention strategies
2. To enable participants to accurately chart intervention data on Target Behavior 1
3. To enable participants to accurately complete a target behavior selection checklist on Target Behavior 2 (home or home-school behavior)

Content

1. Review of Lesson 3
2. Intervention strategies: shaping, modeling, and contingency contracting
3. Charting intervention data
4. Selecting a target behavior

Instructional methods

1. Lecture
2. Discussion
3. Completion of contingency contract form
4. Completion of target behavior selection checklist
5. Completion of behavior chart

Activities

1. Segment A (40 minutes)

    a. Review

    b. Lecture/demonstration on shaping, modeling, and contingency contracting

    c. Discussion of (b)

    d. Participants requested to present examples of shaping and modeling from home setting (may be written)

    e. Completion of one or more contingency contracts

2. Break (10 minutes)

3. Segment B (40 minutes)
   a. Target Behavior 1 (home behavior)
      (1) Each participant charts or graphs intervention data collected between Lessons 3 and 4 (Intervention 1 data).
      (2) Participants discuss charts.
   b. Target Behavior 2 (home or home-school behavior)
      (1) Each participant completes a target behavior selection checklist.
      (2) Participants discuss checklists.

Resources

1. Segment A
   a. Lesson 3 resources
   b. Chapter 4: Shaping; Modeling; Contingency contracting
   c. Parent educator and participants
   d. Same as (c)
   e. Contingency contract form (back of text)
2. Break
3. Segment B
   a. Target Behavior 1
      (1) Behavior chart (back of text)
      (2) Parent educator and participants
   b. Target Behavior 2
      (1) Target behavior selection checklist (back of text)
      (2) Parent educator and participants

Evaluation

1. Quiz on or written examples of shaping and modeling
2. Completing contingency contract forms
3. Behavior chart on Target Behavior 1
4. Target behavior selection checklist on Target Behavior 2

Home assignment

1. Observe and record Intervention 1 data on Target Behavior 1
2. Observe and record Baseline 1 data on Target Behavior 2
3. Read Chapter 4: Token economy

Lesson 5: Strategies to Increase Behavior—Cont'd

Goals

1. To familiarize participants with the token economy intervention strategy
2. To enable participants to accurately chart Intervention 1 data on Target Behavior 1
3. To enable participants to assess the effectiveness of the behavior change program for Target Behavior 1
4. To enable participants to plan an evaluation of Target Behavior 1 by means of observing and recording new baseline data following the intervention (Baseline 2 data)

5. To enable participants to chart Baseline 1 data on Target Behavior 2

Content

1. Review of Lesson 4
2. Token economy intervention strategy
3. Charting data
4. Assessing intervention effectiveness
5. Planning evaluation phase (charting Baseline 2 data)

Instructional methods

1. Lecture
2. Discussion
3. Completion of behavior charts

Activities

1. Segment A (40 minutes)
   a. Review
   b. Lecture/demonstration on token economy
   c. Discussion of (b)
   d. Participants requested to present an example of a home token economy including target behavior(s), reinforcement schedule, reward menu, and proposed point card or tally form (may be written)
2. Break (10 minutes)
3. Segment B (40 minutes)
   a. Target Behavior 1 (home behavior)
      (1) Each participant charts or graphs Intervention 1 data collected between Lessons 4 and 5.
      (2) Each participant assesses the effectiveness of the intervention by analyzing the behavior chart.
      (3) Each participant plans an evaluation phase based on Baseline 2 data.
   b. Target Behavior 2 (home or home-school behavior)
      (1) Each participant charts or graphs Baseline 1 data collected between Lessons 4 and 5.

Resources

1. Segment A
   a. Lesson 4 resources
   b. Chapter 4: Token economy
   c. Parent educator and participants
   d. Participants
2. Break
3. Segment B
   a. Target Behavior 1
      (1) Behavior chart (back of text)
      (2) Participant with assistance of parent educator and other participants
      (3) Same as (2)
   b. Target Behavior 2
      (1) Behavior chart (back of text)

Evaluation
1. Quiz on or written examples of token economy
2. Behavior chart on Target Behavior 1
3. Behavior chart on Target Behavior 2

Home assignment
1. Observe and record evaluation (Baseline 2) data on Target Behavior 1
2. Observe and record Baseline 1 data on Target Behavior 2
3. Read:
    a. Chapter 5: Extinction; Time-out; Reinforcement of incompatible behaviors
    b. Chapter 8: Aids to communication

Lesson 6: Strategies to Decrease Behavior

Goals
1. To familiarize participants with extinction, time-out, and reinforcement of incompatible behaviors intervention strategies
2. To familiarize participants with the aids to communication between home and school
3. To enable participants to chart evaluation (Baseline 2) data and plan the reimposition of the intervention (Intervention 2) for Target Behavior 1
4. To enable participants to chart Baseline 1 data and plan the specific reinforcers, reinforcement schedule, and intervention strategy to modify Target Behavior 2

Content
1. Review of Lesson 5
2. Extinction, time-out, and reinforcement of incompatible behaviors intervention strategies
3. Aids to communication
4. Charting or graphing data
5. Planning the reimposed intervention (Intervention 2) phase for Target Behavior 1
6. Planning the initial intervention (Intervention 1) phase for Target Behavior 2

Instructional methods
1. Lecture
2. Discussion
3. Completion of behavior charts

Activities
1. Segment A (40 minutes)
    a. Review
    b. Lecture/demonstration on extinction, time-out, and reinforcement of incompatible behaviors
    c. Lecture/demonstration on aids to communication
    d. Discussion of (b) and (c)
    e. Participants requested to present examples of extinction, time-out, and reinforcers (may be written)

2. Break
3. Segment B (40 minutes)
  a. Target Behavior 1 (home behavior)
    (1) Each participant charts Baseline 2 data collected between Lessons 5 and 6.
    (2) Each participant compares Baseline 2 data with Baseline 1 and Intervention 1 data.
    (3) Each participant plans the reimposition of the intervention strategy.
  b. Target Behavior 2 (home or home-school behavior)
    (1) Each participant charts Baseline 1 data collected between Lessons 5 and 6.
    (2) Each participant selects a reinforcement schedule, reinforcers, and an intervention strategy to modify Target Behavior 2.

Resources
1. Segment A
  a. Lesson 5 resources
  b. Chapter 5: Extinction; Time-out; Reinforcement of incompatible behaviors
  c. Chapter 8: Aids to communication
  d. Parent educator and participants
  e. Participants
2. Break
3. Segment B
  a. Target Behavior 1
    (1) Behavior chart (back of text)
    (2) Participants
    (3) Participant with assistance of parent educator and other participants
  b. Target Behavior 2
    (1) Behavior chart (back of text)
    (2) Participants

Evaluation
1. Quiz on or written examples of extinction, time-out, reinforcement of incompatible behaviors, and aids to communication
2. Behavior chart on Target Behavior 1
3. Behavior chart on Target Behavior 2

Home assignment
1. Observe and record behavior data on the reimposed intervention (Intervention 2) for Target Behavior 1
2. Observe and record behavior data on the initial intervention (Intervention 1) for Target Behavior 2
3. Read Chapter 5: Punishment; Desensitization.

Lesson 7: Strategies to Decrease Behavior—Cont'd

Goals
1. To familiarize participants with punishment and desensitization intervention strategies

2. To enable participants to chart Intervention 2 data on Target Behavior 1
3. To enable participants to chart Intervention 1 data on Target Behavior 2

Content

1. Review of Lesson 6
2. Punishment and desensitization intervention strategies
3. Charting data

Instructional methods

1. Lecture/demonstration
2. Discussion
3. Completion of behavior charts

Activities

1. Segment A (40 minutes)
   a. Review
   b. Lecture/demonstration on punishment and desensitization
   c. Discussion of (b)
   d. Participants requested to present examples of punishment and desensitization (may be written)
2. Break (10 minutes)
3. Segment B (40 minutes)
   a. Target Behavior 1 (home behavior)
      (1) Each participant charts Intervention 2 data collected between Lessons 6 and 7.
      (2) Each participant compares Intervention 2 data with previously collected data: Baseline 1, Intervention 1, and Baseline 2 data.
   b. Target Behavior 2 (home or home-school behavior)
      (1) Each participant charts Intervention 1 data collected between Lessons 6 and 7.

Resources

1. Segment A
   a. Lesson 6 resources
   b. Chapter 5: Punishment; Desensitization
   c. Parent educator and participants
   d. Participants
2. Break
3. Segment B
   a. Target Behavior 1
      (1) Behavior chart (back of text)
      (2) Participants
   b. Target Behavior 2
      (1) Behavior chart (back of text)

Evaluation

1. Quiz on or written examples of punishment and desensitization
2. Behavior chart on Target Behavior 1
3. Behavior chart on Target Behavior 2

Home assignment

1. Observe and record behavior data on Intervention 2 for Target Behavior 1
2. Observe and record behavior data on Intervention 1 for Target Behavior 2
3. Read Chapter 9: Some guidelines for application; Some principles concerning individual rights of children.

Lesson 8: Ethical and Effective Application

Goals

1. To familiarize participants with the principles concerning the individual rights of children
2. To enable participants to chart Intervention 2 data for Target Behavior 1
3. To enable participants to plan the phasing out of the intervention imposed on Target Behavior 1
4. To enable participants to chart Intervention 1 data for Target Behavior 2 and assess the effectiveness of the intervention
5. To enable participants to plan the remainder of the behavior change program for Target Behavior 2, which may include Baseline 2 data, Intervention 2, and phasing out
6. To establish procedures for follow-up of course participation

Content

1. Review of Lessons 1 through 7
2. Principles concerning the individual rights of children
3. Charting data
4. Planning intervention phases and phasing out

Instructional methods

1. Lecture/demonstration
2. Discussion
3. Completion of behavior charts

Activities

1. Segment A (40 minutes)
   a. Review
   b. Lecture/demonstration on the principles concerning the individual rights of children
   c. Discussion of (b)
   d. Participants requested to present examples of the principles (may be written)
   e. Plans agreed on for course follow-up activities
2. Break (10 minutes)
3. Segment B (40 minutes)
   a. Target Behavior 1 (home behavior)
      (1) Each participant charts Intervention 2 data.
      (2) Each participant plans the phasing out of the intervention.
   b. Target Behavior 2 (home or home-school behavior)

(1) Each participant plans the remainder of the behavior change program, which may include Baseline 2 data, Intervention 2, and phasing out.

(2) Discussion of (1).

Resources

1. Segment A
   a. Lessons 1 through 7 resources
   b. Chapter 9: Some principles concerning individual rights of children
   c. Parent educator and participants
   d. Participants
   e. Parent educator and participants
2. Break
3. Segment B
   a. Target Behavior 1
      (1) Behavior chart (back of text)
      (2) Participant with assistance of parent educator and other participants
   b. Target Behavior 2
      (1) Participant with assistance of parent educator and other participants
      (2) Parent educator and participants

Evaluation

1. Quiz on or written examples of application of principles
2. Behavior chart on Target Behavior 1 and phasing out plan
3. Behavior chart on Target Behavior 2 and plan for remainder of intervention

Home assignment

1. Continue application of course content and learned skills
2. Attend follow-up session

Aids to Home-School Communication

During the implementation phase of a home-school behavior change intervention, the parents and educator need to communicate precisely and frequently to ensure the integrity of the program. Although it is possible to use telephone conversations and handwritten notes to communicate, the parents and teacher may find these methods imprecise and inordinately demanding of time.

In this section several aids to parent-teacher communication that appear to minimize time and inconvenience for both parties are presented. Many additional aids to parent-teacher communication are found in Shea and Bauer (1985). These methods increase the precision and clarity of communication.

The Passport

The "passport" (Runge et al., 1975) is an effective technique for increasing and maintaining parent-teacher communication and cooperation.

The passport is an ordinary spiral notebook that the child carries daily to and from home and to and from the classrooms in which the child is instructed. The passport is a medium for communications among parents, special teachers, regular teachers, aides, bus drivers, and others concerned with the child's behavior change or academic remediation program. All concerned adults are encouraged to make notations in the notebook.

Before the actual initiation of a behavior change program, the passport procedures are explained to the child, who is told that he or she will be rewarded for carrying the notebook and presenting it to the appropriate adults.

The child is rewarded with points for carrying the passport and for appropriate efforts, accomplishments, and behavior in the home, in the classroom, on the bus, in the gym, and so on. Points may be awarded at home for appropriate behavior and home-study activities. If the child forgets or refuses to carry the "passport," he or she cannot earn points. At the appropriate time, the accumulated points are exchanged for tangible as well as social rewards.

Most elementary school students respond enthusiastically to carrying the passport, receiving points and awards, and reading the comments written about their behavior and achievement by adults.

Parents are introduced to the passport concept and procedures at an evening meeting. At this meeting the method is explained and discussed. Parents' questions and concerns must be appropriately responded to by the teacher. At this session instructions for making notations in the passport are given. Similar meetings or informal discussions should be held with other adults who will be using the passport, such as classroom teachers, special teachers, administrators, bus drivers, and so on.

The guidelines for writing comments in the passport are:

1. Be brief. (Parents are busy, too.)
2. Be positive. (Parents know their child has problems. They don't need to be reinforced.)
3. Be honest. (Don't say a child is doing fine if he is not. However, rather than writing negative notes, write neutral ones or request a parent visit.).
4. Be responsive. (If a parent asks for help, respond immediately.)
5. Be informal. (You are a professional but parents are still your equal.)
6. Be consistent. (If you use the passport, do so consistently and expect the same from the parent.)
7. Avoid jargon. (Parents don't understand educators' jargon. For that matter, do we?)
8. Be careful. (If you are having a bad day, personally, do not project your feelings onto the child or his parents.) (p. 92)*

Points are awarded to the child on the basis of a mutually agreed-on reinforcement schedule and rate. The procedures applied in the passport are similar to those pre-

*From "A Passport to Positive Parent-Teacher Communications" by A. Runge, J. Walker, and T. M. Shea, 1975, *Teaching Exceptional Children*, 7(3), pp. 91–92. Copyright 1975 by The Council for Exceptional Children, 1920 Association Drive, Reston, VA 22091. Reprinted by permission.

sented in the section on the token economy in Chapter 4. Points are recorded on a point card similar to those presented in that section. The card is usually affixed to the inside of the front or back cover of the notebook.

Examples of the types of notations to be made in the passport are presented in Figures 8.2 and 8.3. The first set of examples involves an exchange of information among an elementary school teacher, a bus driver, a physical education teacher, and the child's parents. The second set of examples involves an exchange between an elementary school teacher and parents.

10/25/87
9:00 AM

To: Ms. Dolores

Good day on the bus. Tom sat in his assigned seat and waited his turn to leave the bus. I praised his behavior and gave him two points.

Mr. Parker, Bus Driver

10/25/87
10:30 AM

To: Ms. Dolores

During PE today the group played kickball. Tom was well behaved but had difficulty participating effectively. I awarded him six points. He was praised for his behavior. Can we meet to discuss some means of increasing his participation?

Ms. Minton, PE

10/25/87
2:30 PM

To: Mr. and Mrs. Hogerty

As you can see from the notes above, Tom had a good day at school.

He received 89% on his reading test this morning. That's real progress. Please praise him for this accomplishment.

This evening, Tom is to read pp. 1–5 in his new reading book.

Even better news! Tom remembered to walk in the hallways today. He is very proud of himself.

I shall talk to Ms. Minton today about increasing Tom's participation at PE. I'll let you know what we decide at parent meeting tomorrow night.

Ms. Dolores

10/25/87
9:00 PM

To: Ms. Dolores

We praised and rewarded Tom for his hard work on the reading test, the bus, and the hallways. You're right, he feels good about himself today.

Tom read pp. 1–5 in the new book with his father. The words he had trouble with are underlined.

We will be at parent meeting tomorrow night.

Mary Hogerty

FIGURE 8.2
Sample passport notations between school staff and parents.

5/5/88

Dear Mr. and Mrs. Barea:

John received 98% on his reading test today. Isn't that terrific? He should be praised for his progress.

Please let him read pp. 1–5 in his new reading book to you this evening.

Even better news! John remembered to walk in the hallways. He was really pleased with himself.

Don't forget—parent-teacher group discussion tomorrow night. See you then.

Ms. Anita

5/6/88

Dear Ms. Anita:

We told John what a good job you said he did on his test.

John read pp. 1–5 in the new book with his father. He had trouble with a lot of the words.

He did his math paper.

Mrs. Barea

5/7/88

Dear Mr. and Mrs. Barea:

John and Mr. Miner, the student teacher, went over the difficult reading words today.

Thanks for marking them in the book.

Please review pp. 1–5 in the reading book again. John also has a math paper to complete.

It was a good day. See you at 7 PM.

Ms. Anita

5/8/88

Dear Ms. Anita

Certainly enjoyed the parent discussion last night. Mr. Barea and I appreciated the explanation of John's report card.

John had his math done when we got home. I checked it. He did a good job on his reading.

Mrs. Barea

FIGURE 8.3
Sample passport notations between parents and teachers.

Daily Report Cards

It is generally true that report cards or grades issued periodically by elementary and secondary schools (and universities) have positive effects on student performance. It is also true that this positive effect is of short duration. During our years as secondary school and university teachers it became obvious that students study more and behave better in the few weeks immediately before and after report cards or grades are issued. Unfortunately this high level of student performance does not persist during those times when report card issuance is not imminent (Kroth, 1975).

It would appear that acceptable levels of student performance, both academic and behavioral, can be maintained if feedback on performance is provided frequently to the student and parents. This proposition has led to several efforts to explore the use of daily report cards with normal and exceptional children at various grade levels (Dickerson et al., 1973; Edlund, 1969; Kroth, 1975; Kroth et al., 1970; Powell, 1980).

In 1969 Edlund designed and implemented a daily reporting system that uses rewards available in the home to improve children's school performance. The system focuses on both academic performance and social-personal behavior.

Edlund's daily report card system is introduced to the parents during individual and small group sessions. In these sessions parents are introduced to the principles and procedures of behavior modification as they applied in the reporting system. Specific attention is given to the daily checklist, principles of reinforcement, selecting rewards, and the application of the Premack principle. This initial training is followed up throughout the program by means of weekly parent-professional conferences or telephone communication.

Before the daily reporting system is implemented, baseline data are gathered by the educator and/or parents on the child's academic performance and social-personal behaviors. Using the baseline data, the reporting system is individualized for the child as a response to his or her particular learning or behavior problems.

Children earn points for completing academic assignments and for acceptable school behavior. Points are recorded on a checklist. Although not presented here, Edlund designed three checklists: (1) a report for academic performance only, (2) a report of personal-social behavior only, and (3) a composite report such as that presented in Figure 8.4.

The teacher awards points in the form of check marks at the end of predetermined periods of time or activities throughout the day. At the end of the day, the teacher reviews the child's checklist and initials it. The checklist is taken home by the child and reviewed by the parents, who initial it. The child returns the checklist to the teacher the following day.

If a child fails to take the checklist home, he is sent back to school for it or a duplicate. A child cannot be rewarded without the checklist.

Rewards for school performance are given to the child at home during the afternoon and evening hours. The rewards are individualized. Care is taken to ensure that the child receives only those rewards that are earned and that are meaningful to him or her. A child who fails to earn rewards is assigned undesirable tasks at home, such as housekeeping chores, yardwork, homework, and so on. Special rewards are given to a child for a "perfect day" or several perfect days.

After several weeks of acceptable academic performance and/or behavior, the reward system is phased out over a period of days or weeks.

Edlund concluded that his daily report card system did improve the children's academic performance and acceptable social-personal behavior. He noted that the desirable behavior continued after the rewards were discontinued. The children learned to respond to the verbal praise and social recognition provided by parents and teachers, which naturally occurred as a result of their high level of performance.

Composite Academic Performance and Personal-Social Behavior Report

DAILY REPORT CHECKLIST

Child's Name _____

	Reading		Spelling		Arithmetic		Health		Social Studies		PE		Initials	
	Acad	Beh	Acad	Beh	Acad	Beh	Acad	Beh	Acad	Beh	Acad	Beh	Parent	Teacher
M														
T														
W														
Th														
F														
M														
T														
W														
Th														
F														
M														
T														
W														
Th														
F														

FIGURE 8.4
Composite behavior checklist for gathering baseline data.

The Edlund daily report card system has been applied successfully with children from kindergarten to high school. It has been used successfully with exceptional children classified as emotionally disturbed, mentally retarded, disruptive, school phobic, truant, economically deprived, and culturally different.

The Teacher-Parent Communication Program (TPCP), a daily report card system, was developed by Dickerson and others (1973). This cooperative parent-teacher communication system is designed to help children improve their in-school academic performance and social behavior in exchange for rewards at home.

During a 4-year period the TPCP was used with over 1000 children, ages 5 to 15 years in regular and special education settings. Although Dickerson and others do not view the program as a "cure-all," it was reported by teachers who used it as effective in modifying social behavior and academic performance.

The TPCP centers around report cards issued by the teacher to the child periodically throughout the school day. The completed cards are taken home at the end of the school day. On the basis of the information on the cards, the parents either reward or do not reward the child's performance. Example report cards are presented in Figures 8.5 and 8.6.

The cards have a space for the teacher's evaluation of the child's academic performance and social behavior. The teacher may make notations on the back of the card if desired. Dickerson and his associates recommend that the teacher's notations be neutral and positive. The cards are dated and signed by the teacher.

Daily Report Card for Grades K to 3

Consider card satisfactory *only* when boxes 1 and 3 are checked.

1. ☺ ☐ Social behavior good

2. ☹ ☐ Social behavior bad

3. ☺ ☐ School work done

4. ☹ ☐ School work not done

_____/_____/_____   _____
      Date   Teacher's signature

FIGURE 8.5
Daily report card.
(From Let the cards do the talking—a teacher-parent communication program by D. Dickerson, C. R. Spellman, S. Larsen, and L. Tyler, Teaching Exceptional Children, *4(4), 1973, pp. 170–178. Copyright 1973 by The Council for Exceptional Children. Reprinted with permission.)*

Daily Report Card for Grades 4 to 6

Consider card satisfactory *only* when boxes 1 and 3 are checked.

1. ☐ Social behavior satisfactory

2. ☐ Social behavior unsatisfactory

3. ☐ Academic work satisfactory

4. ☐ Academic work unsatisfactory

_____/_____/_____   _____
Date   Teacher's signature

FIGURE 8.6

Daily report card.

(From Let the cards do the talking—a teacher-parent communication program by D. Dickerson, C. R. Spellman, S. Larsen, and L. Tyler, Teaching Exceptional Children, *4(4), 1973, pp. 170–178. Copyright 1973 by The Council for Exceptional Children. Reprinted with permission.)*

Although not included on the TPCP card, it may be helpful if the card provided space for the parent's signature and notations. The card could be returned to the teacher on the following school day by the child. Such a procedure would ensure that the parents received the card, that the child was rewarded, and that both parents and teacher were attending to the appropriate objectives.

The cards are issued to the child approximately every 40 minutes throughout the school day. At the end of the day the child usually has 10 completed cards to take home.

Although not included in the Dickerson program, it may be desirable to provide space on the card for identification of the activity in which the child participated during the various time periods. This procedure would help the parents identify more precisely the child's problem subjects and situations. It may also be helpful to both parents and teacher if a master card were developed that presented "at a glance" the totals of the child's 10 daily cards.

With few exceptions, the TPCP cards are not acceptable for rewards unless both social behavior and academic performance are checked acceptable by the teacher. Thus a child who behaves appropriately but fails to do this work acceptably is not rewarded. The reverse of this is also true; that is, a child who completes his work but behaves inappropriately is not rewarded.

The presentation of rewards at home is based on the number of acceptable cards the child earns during the school day. The number of cards needed for a reward is initiated at the child's present level of functioning. This performance level is mutually agreed on by parent and teacher. As the child's overall level of performance improves, the number of acceptable cards needed for rewards is systematically increased.

If an acceptable number of cards are earned, the child is praised and encouraged by the parent. The child is permitted to engage in rewarding activities, for example, a later bedtime hour, television viewing, and the like. Special rewards are available for exceptional performance. If the child fails to earn the acceptable number of daily report cards, after-school and evening activities are restricted or the child is assigned undesirable tasks, such as yardwork, housekeeping tasks, homework, and the like.

The TPCP is initiated by the teacher, who solicits the parents' cooperation and participation. During an orientation conference the teacher explains the program to the parents. The purpose and benefits of the TPCP for the child are discussed. The teacher outlines the duties and responsibilities of child, parent, and teacher. Dickerson and associates prepared the checklist in Figure 8.7 to facilitate parent-orientation. The checklist ensures that all elements of the daily reporting system are reviewed.

After the parents and teacher agree to implement the TPCP, the teacher informs the child and makes him or her aware of the parents' participation. The child is given instructions concerning the purpose, objectives, and functioning of the system. The

---

TPCP Conference Checklist

CHECK LIST OF MAJOR POINTS COVERED IN PARENT ORIENTATION CONFERENCE

1. Ten cards will be sent home each day whether academic work is done or not.
2. One bad check makes a card unacceptable.
3. Cards must be signed by the teacher and free of erasures and extra marks.
4. The minimum number of good cards necessary to earn privileges should be explained.
5. The number of acceptable cards will be increased sometime in the future.
6. The program will at first emphasize the quantity of work and later the quality of work.
7. The backs of the cards should always be examined for notations.
8. Weekend bonuses may be earned for each week the specified number of good cards have been earned.
9. After-school and evening activities should be a direct result of performance in school.
10. Cards not received at home should be counted as unacceptable.
11. Cards should be reviewed with the child as soon as he or she arrives home.
12. The cards should be counted each day.
13. Praise and encourage the child for earning the acceptable number of good cards.
14. *Let the cards do the talking.*

FIGURE 8.7

Parent orientation for daily report cards.

(From Let the cards do the talking—a teacher-parent communication program by D. Dickerson, C. R. Spellman, S. Larsen, and L. Tyler, Teaching Exceptional Children, *4(4), 1973, pp. 170–178. Copyright 1973 by The Council for Exceptional Children. Reprinted with permission.)*

child is encouraged to participate in the process of determining his or her initial acceptable performance level and rewards.

The designers of the TPCP recommend that the daily report card system remain in force as long as the child needs it. However, after several weeks of acceptable performance by the child, the teacher, in cooperation with the parents, should begin to phase out the TPCP. Presumably the rewards for a high level of academic performance and social behavior that naturally occur in the child's school behavior and home environments will maintain the acceptable performance levels without the TPCP.

In *It's Positively Fun* (Kaplan et al., 1974) and *It's Absolutely Groovy* (Kaplan & Hoffman, 1981) a variety of certificates, award forms, and other unique forms are presented. Many of these forms can be used in daily report card programs. The authors provide a brief outline for planning and implementing a daily home-school communication program. These texts are excellent references for professionals wishing to implement a daily report card system.

Kroth and others (1970) presented a parent-teacher communication system that included a daily reporting program as an integral part of a behavior modification intervention. This system provides several specific guidelines for professionals desiring a daily reporting system to focus primarily on student behavior.

The purpose of the daily report card system is to improve parent-professional communication for the benefit of the child. Attention is focused on both social-personal behavior and academic performance.

Teachers wishing to implement a daily report card program should consider several characteristics of the systems presented and individualize these in response to the needs of the children and parents with whom they work.

The mechanism used for reporting (communicating) should be specific and easy to complete. Complex mechanisms requiring extensive time and energy inhibit the conduct and effectiveness of the program.

In our opinion, the daily report card program should accentuate the child's positive social-personal behavior and/or academic performance. The child should be rewarded for attaining the mutually agreed-on objectives of the program and ignored if the objectives are not attained. Punishment should be avoided.

Both parents and teachers must remain cognizant of the fact that the conduct of a daily report card program is a shared responsibility. If either teacher or parents fail to meet their responsibilities, the program's effectiveness is inhibited.

SUMMARY

In this chapter a method that may be applied by the educator interested in training parents in behavior modification procedures and principles is presented. The program is designed primarily to increase parental knowledge and skill in the application of behavior modification techniques. The training program also has the potential to increase parent-teacher cooperation. Although not a primary objective of the program, parents are provided a setting in which they may receive emotional support as they struggle with their child's problem.

EXERCISES

Quiz

1. According to Clements and Alexander (1975), "Extensive research demonstrates unequiv-

   ocally that children _____ more, _____ better, and _____ faster

   when _____ training is effected" (p. 7).

2. List six defense mechanisms parents may apply in response to their recognition of a problem with a child.

   a. _____

   b. _____

   c. _____

   d. _____

   e. _____

   f. _____

3. McDowell (1976) has classified parent programs under three categories:

   a. _____

   b. _____

   c. _____

4. The objectives of the parent training program presented in this chapter are:

   a. _____

   _____

   b. _____

   _____

   c. _____

   _____

5. The psychosituational assessment interview is primarily an _____

   _____technique.

6. The four major tasks to be accomplished in the psychosituational assessment interview are:

   a. _____

   b. _____

   c. _____

   d. _____

7. The phases of the parent training program presented in this chapter are:

a. _____   c. _____

b. _____

8. List five of the eight guidelines for writing comments in the "passport."

a. _____   d. _____

b. _____   e. _____

c. _____

Projects

1. Write a 300-word essay on the topic "Parent Education and Training: A Significant Component of the School Service Program."
2. List 25 home reinforcers not presented in the chapter. Classify these as social or tangible.
3. Conduct a psychosituational assessment interview in which a classmate plays the role of a parent. Record and analyze the interview.
4. Obtain, study, and write a report for verbal presentation to your class on one of the checklists and inventories listed in the chapter. As part of the verbal presentation, demonstrate to the group the administration of the instrument.
5. Using one of the lesson plans in the chapter, prepare, present, and evaluate a parent training session. Your classmates can role play as parents.

REFERENCES

Beale, A., & Beers, C. S. (1982). *What do you say to parents after you say hello? Teaching Exceptional Children, 15*(1), 34–38.

Bersoff, D. N. & Grieger, R. M. II (1971). An interview model for the psychosituational assessment of children's behavior. *American Journal of Orthopsychiatry, 41*(3), 483–493.

Blackham, G. J., & Silberman, A. (1975). *Modification of child and adolescent behavior* (2nd ed.). Belmont, CA: Wadsworth Publishing Co.

Burks, H. F. (1977). *Burks' behavior rating scales: Manual.* Los Angeles: Western Psychological Services.

Cassel, R. N. (1962). *The child behavior rating scale: Manual.* Los Angeles: Western Psychological Services.

Clements, J. E., & Alexander, R. N. (1975). Parent training: Bringing it all back home. *Focus on Exceptional Children, 7*(5), 1–12.

Croft, D. J. (1979). *Parents and teachers: A resource book for home, school, and community relations.* Belmont, CA: Wadsworth Publishing, Co.

Denhoff, E. (1960). The impact of parents on the growth of exceptional children. *Exceptional Children, 26*(5), 271–274.

Dickerson, D., Spellman, C. R., Larsen, S., & Tyler, L. (1973). Let the cards do the talking—a teacher-parent communication program. *Teaching Exceptional Children, 4*(4), 170–178.

Dinkmeyer, D., & McKay, G. D. (1973). *Raising a responsible child: Practical steps to successful family relationships.* New York: Simon & Schuster.

Edlund, C. V. (1969). Rewards at home to promote desirable school behavior. *Teaching Exceptional Children, 1*(4), 121–127.

Gardner, W. I. (1974). *Children with learning and behavior problems: A behavior management approach.* Boston: Allyn & Bacon.

Gordon, S. (1976). A parent's concerns. *The Exceptional Parent, 6*(3), 19–22.

Gordon, T. (1970). *Parent effectiveness training.* New York: Wyden Books.

Homan, W. E. (1977). *Child sense: A guide to loving, level-headed parenthood.* New York: Basic

Books.

Jogis, J. L. (1975). To be spoken sadly. In L. Buscaglia (Ed.), *The disabled and their parents: A counseling challenge.* Thorofare, NJ: Charles B. Stack.

Kahn, R. L., & Cannell, C. F. (1957). *The dynamics of interviewing: Theory, technique and cases.* New York: John Wiley & Sons.

Kaplan, P. G., & Hoffman, A. G. (1981). *It's absolutely groovy.* Denver: Love Publishing.

Kaplan, P., Kohfeldt, J., & Sturla, K. (1974). *It's positively fun: Techniques for managing learning environments.* Denver: Love Publishing Co.

Karnes, M. B., & Zehrbach, R. R. (1972). Flexibility in getting parents involved in the school. *Teaching Exceptional Children, 5*(1), 6–19.

Kratoville, B. L. (1975a). What parents feel. In L. Buscaglia (Ed.), *The disabled and their parents: A counseling challenge.* Thorofare, NJ: Charles B. Stack.

Kratoville, B. L. (1975b). What parents need to hear. In L. Buscaglia (Ed.), *The disabled and their parents: A counseling challenge.* Thorofare, NJ: Charles B. Stack.

Kroth, R. L. (1972). *Target behavior.* Olathe, KS: Select-Ed.

Kroth, R. L. (1975). *Communicating with parents of exceptional children: Improving parent-teacher relationships.* Denver: Love Publishing Co.

Kroth, R. L., & Simpson, R. L. (1977). *Parent conferences: A teaching strategy.* Denver: Love Publishing, Co.

Kroth, R. L., Whelan, R. J., & Stables, J. M. (1970). Teacher application of behavior principles in home and classroom environments. *Focus on Exceptional Children, 1*(3), 1–10.

Lichter, P. (1976). Communicating with parents: It begins with listening. *Teaching Exceptional Children, 8*(2), 66–71.

McDowell, R. L. (1976). Parent counseling: The state of the art. *Journal of Learning Disabilities, 9*(10), 614–619.

Powell, T. H. (1980). Improving home-school communication: Sharing daily reports. *The Exceptional Parent, 10*(5), 824–26.

Quay, H. C., & Peterson, D. R. (1967). *Manual for the behavior problems checklist.* Champaign,

IL: Children's Research Center, University of Illinois.

Ross, A. O. (1964). *The exceptional child in the family: Helping parents of exceptional children.* New York: Grune & Stratton.

Runge, A., Walker, J., & Shea, T. M. (1975). A passport to positive parent-teacher communications. *Teaching Exceptional Children, 7*(3), 91–92.

Shea, T. M., & Bauer, A. M. (1985). *Parents and teachers of exceptional students: A handbook for involvement.* Boston: Allyn and Bacon.

Shea, T. M., Whiteside, W. R., Beetner, E. G., & Lindsey, D. L. (1974). *Microteaching module: Psychosituational interview.* Edwardsville: Southern Illinois University.

Sparrow, S. S., Balla, D. A., & Cicchetti, D. V. (1984). *The vineland adaptive behavior scales.* Circle Pines, MN: American Guidance Service.

Spivack, G., & Spotts, J. (1966). *Devereux child behavior (DCB) rating scale.* Devon, PA: The Devereux Foundation.

Spivack, G., Spotts, J., & Haimes, P. E. (1967). *Devereux adolescent behavior (DAB) rating scale.* Devon, PA: The Devereux Foundation.

Stephenson, W. (1953). *The study of behavior: Q-technique and its methodology.* Chicago: University of Chicago Press.

Stigen, G. (1976). *Heartaches and handicaps: An irreverent survival manual for parents.* Palo Alto, CA: Science & Behavior Books.

Susser, P. (1974). Parents and partners. *The Exceptional Parent, 4*(3), 41–47.

Walker, H. M. (1976). *Walker problem behavior identification checklist: Manual.* Los Angeles: Western Psychological Services.

Webster, E. J. (1977). *Counseling with parents of handicapped children: Guidelines for improving communications.* New York: Grune & Stratton.

Winton, P. (1986). Effective strategies for involving families in intervention efforts. *Focus on Exceptional Children, 19*(2), 1–12.

Wood, M. M. (1975). Services to parents. In M. M. Wood (Ed.), *Developmental therapy: A textbook for teachers as therapists for emotionally disturbed young children.* Baltimore: University Park Press.

CHAPTER NINE

Ethical Issues

Mr. Bauer is the teacher of 26 inner-city, street-wise tenth-grade adolescents. He is having little success teaching the subjects (consumer education and practical mathematics) outlined on the city curriculum guide for the tenth grade. In his opinion very little, if any, formal learning takes place in his classroom. Each school day is filled with verbal and physical aggression among the students. Mr. Bauer is in constant fear for his physical safety. He is anxious throughout the day and emotionally fatigued when he arrives home in the evening.

Although he dislikes his present work assignment, he enjoys teaching. However, he has contemplated leaving the profession for employment in business. Mr. Bauer is desperate for some way to control the behavior of his students.

As usual on Friday after school, Mr. Bauer joins a group of other teachers for a little relaxation and libation at Archie's Place before going home. The conversation turns to behavior problems and behavior management. Several of Mr. Bauer's colleagues who are more effective behavior managers than he offer a variety of interventions they apply with success.

Mr. Glove said: "I punch the little idiots. They cut the bull quick."

Mr. Pine offered: "I carry my paddle, and the first turkey that wiggles a finger gets it. I don't like it, but it works."

Ms. Weeping relates: "I scream at them. I can outshout them. If all else fails, I cry."

Ms. Fox stated: "I don't fool with them. It's in the door—shut up—get to work—and out the door. No discussion, no questions, no group work, and no jokes—no nothing."

Mr. Power brags: "I've got the best solution. This fall I bought an electric wand—you know, a cattle prod. It's cheap and effective. The first kid who opens his mouth when he's not suppose to gets it. One good, fast shock usually does it."

As Mr. Bauer sat in the subway on his way home, he reviewed his colleagues' suggestions. Which, if any, should he use with his students? How to decide?

Ms. Jan was employed as a teacher of elementary school-aged severely behavior-disordered children in a private facility. Although she enjoyed her work and believed she was an effective teacher, she was concerned about one of the interventions her supervisors ordered her to implement. Although they had discussed the intervention and her professional reasons for viewing it as inappropriate and unethical, the supervisor remained adamant about its use.

The intervention was "extinction"—ignoring the head-slapping behavior of Tyrone. Tyrone slapped the sides of his head on an average of 61 times an hour during the school day. He slapped himself with such force that the hair on the side of his head had been pulled out and his temples were swollen and severely bruised.

Ms. Jan recognized that she must do something. But what? She needed her job, and she needed a positive recommendation from her supervisor if she were to be considered for her annual pay raise.

Before implementing the interventions suggested in this text, the reader is encouraged to study and contemplate several important issues concerning behavior management presented in this chapter. These issues are (1) the question of ethics, (2) a continuum of management interventions, and (3) the rights of children. This chapter concludes with a discussion of behavior management as a preventive technique.

The Question of Ethics

Both empirical and nonexperimental inquiry have led to the development of the principles of learning and their resultant interventions for the management of human behavior. It is difficult to entirely refute the findings of experimental studies: the principles of learning presented in Chapter 2 are in operation, and the results of controlled research studies are, in the main, positive.

However, practitioners cannot sweep aside the ethical issues created by the application of these principles to the processes of human learning. The principles of learning have caused confusion, concern, and, in some cases, anxiety among those individuals holding more traditional views of human behavior and human freedom. Many scholars have discussed these issues in a depth that is not possible in this text. The reader is referred to works by Bandura (1969), Bellack and Hersen (1977), Fargo and others (1970), Skinner (1953 and 1971), and Ulrich and others (1966) for an in-depth study of these important issues.

The following are some basic metaphysical questions that all practitioners must address:

☐ What is a human being?
☐ Are human beings free; that is, do we have freedom of choice?
☐ Do we behave in accordance with specific principles of behavior that are observable, measurable, and repetitive?
☐ Can our behavior be changed by external forces?
☐ Who can modify whose behavior?

The reader who admits that control of human behavior is possible must consider the following ethical questions:

☐ Who shall decide who will be the manager of behavior?
☐ Who shall decide whose behavior is to be managed?
☐ How can behavior managers be controlled?
☐ What type of interventions shall be applied?
☐ Who will determine the type of interventions to be legitimized?
☐ To what ends will the interventions be applied?

These basic questions have vast implications for our future (as individuals and as members of the human species) and for the future of society. They must be considered and responded to by the behavior management practitioner.

When these questions are applied to the training of children, they have profound implications for educational practice. The queries are rephrased below to point out these implications, which are not only philosophical issues but also pragmatic issues of immediate importance to educators:

- □ What is a child?
- □ Is a child free to make choices?
- □ Should a child be free to make choices?
- □ Does a child act in accordance with specific principles of behavior that are observable, measurable, and repetitive?
- □ Can a child's behavior be changed by external forces?
- □ Can an educator modify a child's behavior?
- □ Can another child or a parent change behavior?
- □ Who shall determine whose and which behaviors are to be changed?
- □ Which interventions shall be applied in the classroom and school to change children's behavior?
- □ Who will legitimize and monitor the interventions being used to change the behavior of children?
- □ To what ends will the interventions be applied?

That we can and do exert some control over our behavior would not be denied by the majority of researchers and practitioners, both behaviorists and traditionalists.

The central issue, then, appears to focus on the relative influences of our nature and environment on behavior. The behaviorist emphasizes the importance of the external environment in the determination of behavior. The behaviorist maintains that the influence of the environment is systematic, constant, and the prime determinant of behavior. This systematic, constant influence is observable and measurable. As a result, our actions can be explained by means of the principles of behavior (or learning). The principles are derived by applying the scientific methods of discovery to the modification of overt human behavior.

Few would deny that, in general, the majority of persons respond in a predictable manner under specified conditions. For example, if we go to a sports event, we cheer; to a funeral, we cry or sigh; to a college class, we sit passively, praying for the end; and so on.

In addition to the issues of whether and how human beings can be controlled, professionals in psychology, the social sciences, and education have focused attention on the issue of the *means* of control. Many professionals suggest that the overt controls applied to human behavior by means of behavior modification interventions are unacceptable and can lead to unethical practices. These individuals fail to recognize or acknowledge that other, more traditional forms of interventions, such as those reviewed in Chapters 6 and 7, may exert equally potent, although less obvious, control over human behavior. For example, traditional nondirect and direct psychotherapeutic interventions, such as client-centered counseling, individual and group psychotherapy, psychoanalysis, and life-space interviewing, have as their objective a change in the child's behavior or encourage the child to change his or her behavior with the therapist's assistance. The silent, evasive therapist and the permissive teacher influence the chlid's behavior, and this influence limits the child's freedom of choice. Such limiting (or controlling), rather than being denied, should be recognized, evaluated, and monitored for the child's benefit.

The student is urged to devote time to systematic exploration of his or her responses to the questions listed in this section.

A Continuum of Behavior Management Interventions

It is both illegal and unethical for practitioners to impose behavior management interventions that are unnecessary or more restrictive than necessary to change the child's behavior. For example, it would be unacceptable to impose seclusion time-out on a child if observational or exclusion time-out would effectively change the target behavior. Likewise, it would be unacceptable to use a verbal counseling or extinction technique with a child who is physically assaulting other persons or is self-injurious when a more restrictive intervention is needed.

In the first example, seclusion time-out is considered unacceptable because it restricts the child's freedom more than is necessary. In this situation seclusion would be imposed only after the less restrictive time-out procedures, that is, after observational and exclusion time-out, have been systematically applied over a period of time without success.

In the second example, extinction and counseling are inappropriate because they are too benign to change the target behavior and thus protect the child and others from harm. Of necessity, the practitioner must impose a more restrictive intervention, for example, physical restraint, time-out, and so on.

Each classroom, school, and local education agency should conduct a periodic inventory among school and cooperating community agency personnel to determine the behavior management interventions available professionals are competent and willing to apply to change the behavior of children. These interventions may include many of the interventions discussed in Chapters 4 to 7 and many others not reviewed in this text.

The behavior management interventions included on the inventory are then ordered on a continuum. The interventions are placed on the continuum to range from the *least* restrictive to the *most* restrictive with regard to the child's freedom to function in comparison with the average child.

An example continuum using selected behavior modification interventions is presented in Figure 9.1. It is obvious that no continuum of interventions is perfect. The exact location of an intervention on the continuum should be accomplished through discussion and consensus among those responsible for the behavior of children in the school and community, including parents and administrators. The continuum presented in Figure 9.1 is based on the work of Lewellen (1980).

Educational agencies should develop procedures to ensure the ethical and effective use of behavior management interventions. Among the items to be considered when planning the procedures to be used in behavior management are:

1. The behaviors to be targeted for change must be noted in the problem child's individualized education program.
2. The behavior management interventions to be implemented are to be described in the child's IEP. The purpose for which the intervention is imposed must be stated.

Example of Continuum of Interventions

1. *Reinforcement of behavior other than the target behavior:* A reinforcer is given at the end of a specified period of time provided that a prespecified misbehavior has not occurred during the specified time interval.
2. *Reinforcement of an appropriate target behavior:* A reinforcer is given following the performance of a prespecified appropriate target behavior.
3. *Reinforcement of incompatible behaviors:* A reinforcer is given following the performance of a prespecified behavior that is physically and functionally incompatible with the target behavior.
4. *Extinction:* The reinforcer that has been sustaining or increasing an undesirable behavior is withheld.
5. *Stimulus change:* The existing environmental conditions are drastically altered to ensure that the target behavior is temporarily suppressed.
6. *Nonexclusionary time-out:*
   a. Head down on desk or table in work area in which target behavior occurred
   b. Restriction to chair in a separate area of the classroom but able to observe classroom activities
   c. Removal of materials (work, play)
   d. Reduction or elimination of room illumination
7. *Physical restraint.*
8. *Negative practice or satiation:* The target behavior is eliminated by continued and increased reinforcement of that behavior.
9. *Overcorrection:* The repeated practice of an appropriate behavior in response to the exhibition of an inappropriate target behavior.
10. *Exclusionary time-out:*
    a. In-school suspension
    b. Quiet room

FIGURE 9.1
Sample continuum of behavior modification interventions.

The procedures to be applied to evaluate the consistency of application and effectiveness of the intervention are stated.

3. Initially the least restrictive intervention feasible is to be applied unless, in the judgment of the IEP team, to do so would be ineffective. The intervention is to be selected or designed through the process of consensus among the team members including the student's parent(s) or parent surrogate(s). During the meeting the team may list subsequent and more restrictive interventions to be imposed if the initial intervention is demonstrated to be ineffective.

4. Data collection procedures are to be developed before the implementation of the intervention. These procedures are applied by the practitioner throughout the time during which the intervention is imposed. A written record of the data collected is to be enclosed in the student's file.

5. Initial and all subsequent techniques are to be imposed for a specified number of school days before being changed or discontinued.

6. Documents on the student's behavior management plan and its application are to be available in the student's IEP file for periodic review by appropriate persons.

Procedures such as those just mentioned safeguard the child from potential mistreatment and the practitioner from potential charges of wrongdoing.

The Rights of Children

In 1969 Allen proposed three legal principles to guide individuals in the helping professions in their actions toward clients (children and adults). These principles serve as the foundation of all behavior management decisions made by teachers of both regular and special education students.

They are (1) the principle of normalization, (2) the principle of fairness, and (3) the principle of respect for the dignity and worth of the individual.

Principle of Normalization

To let the handicapped person obtain an existence as close to the normal as is possible. (Nirje, 1967; cited by Allen, 1969)

When applying this principle, the practitioner must use as a point of reference the child's real environment (including the behavior of the children and adults within it) as well as the ideal democratic environment. This principle demands understanding of the similarities and differences among various groups in society. The practitioner must base decisions on knowledge of the individual child's growth and development, needs, desires, strengths, and disabilities.

Before implementing an intervention, the practitioner must respond to the following queries: Will the implementation of this specific behavioral intervention facilitate the child's movement toward the normally anticipated and observed behavior in this setting, or will it simply eliminate the child (and the behavior) as an inconvenience or annoyance to others in the environment, that is, the child's teacher, peers, administrators, and parents?

Many children who attend classes for retarded, disturbed, and learning-disabled children are in those classes simply because they are different; that is, they are black, Spanish-speaking, slow, nonreaders, poor, and so on. These children may be segregated primarily because they are an annoyance or inconvenience to others. In this "special placement," their opportunity to obtain "an existence as normal as possible" is grossly inhibited, if not totally frustrated.

Principle of Fairness

> Fundamental fairness—due process of law—requires that in decision-making affecting one's life, liberty, or vital interests, the elements of due process will be observed, including the right to notice, to a fair hearing, to representation by counsel, to present evidence, and to appeal an adverse decision. (Allen, 1969)

Although this principle is phrased in legal terminology, it can be simply stated: "Is the intervention I have selected to change this child's behavior fair to the child as an individual?"

At times interventions are arbitrarily applied on the whim of a practitioner without concrete evidence that the child is, in fact, exhibiting the target behavior. Frequently interventions are applied that only serve to prohibit the child from finding *any* success in school. For example, a child who had difficulty learning French grammar is prohibited from going to recess, playing on the school athletic teams, and so on. This child may only be capable of meeting success in these prohibited activities. As do all humans, the child has a need for success. Interventions such as these are unfair.

Unfairness is evidenced frequently when a practitioner refuses to apply an intervention that is obviously needed if the child is to function in school. For example, frequently we are confronted with practitioners who will not use tangible rewards simply because they do not "believe in them." Yet the child whom they are attempting to help is found to respond only to tangible rewards.

Other examples of unfairness might include:

☐ Refusal to try to modify a child's behavior systematically
☐ Arbitrary placement of a child in a special therapy or instructional program without first attempting classroom interventions
☐ Unwillingness of teachers to provide needed services or request consultation because they believe that seeking help is a sign of incompetency

If the principle of fairness is to be implemented, we must begin all decisions from the point of view of the child's welfare: "What does this child need?"

Principle of Respect for the Dignity and Worth of the Individual

One's right to be treated as a human being, and not as an animal or a statistic. (Allen, 1969)

In our actions toward children, are we demonstrating respect for them as human beings? All interventions must be judged against this question. When the intervention is evaluated from this point of view, we find that many common "therapeutic" practices violate the principle of respect. The following are examples:

- □ Physical punishment (spankings, slaps, paddlings)
- □ Psychological punishment (sarcasm, embarrassment, name calling)
- □ Deprivation (prohibiting a child normal opportunities for success)
- □ Segregation (arbitrary special-class placement)
- □ Isolation (inconsistent, long-term use of time-out and restraint)
- □ Medication (capricious use of symptom-control medications)
- □ Extrahuman punishment (use of restraints, electric shockers)

All of these interventions have been used and remain in use in our society. Generally they are applied by individuals who justify the use of any means to attain their end. All of these interventions have been justified by some as the "only way" to accomplish an objective. These techniques are used (and justified) frequently simply because they are convenient, efficient, and seemingly effective.

It cannot be denied that a beaten child will obey, that an electric cattle prod will get a child to pay attention, and that segregation and isolation will reduce conflict. However, practitioners must establish limits on the interventions that can be applied with children. We must judge these interventions in the light of this third principle; that is, could or do the interventions inflict damage on the individual child or relegate the child to a less-than-human classification?

It is absolutely necessary that all behavior management practitioners develop a value system that incorporates the principles of normalization, fairness, and respect for the dignity and the worth of the child. This value system must avoid the pitfall of justifying "any means to attain a desired end."

We should remember that any intervention can be misused and abused if the person using it lacks an ethical system of personal and professional values. Practitioners must never be allowed to forget that knowledge is power and that with power comes the responsibility to apply that power for the benefit of all persons.

The Council for Exceptional Children's Delegate Assembly (1983) adopted standards for the ethical application of behavior management interventions. These standards are:

1.2.1. Special education professionals participate with other professionals and with parents in an interdisciplinary effort in the management of behavior. Professionals:
  1.2.1.1. Apply only those disciplinary methods and behavioral procedures which they

have been instructed to use and which do not undermine the dignity of the individual or the basic human rights of exceptional persons (such as corporal punishment).

1.2.1.2. Clearly specify the goals and objectives for behavior management practices in the exceptional person's Individual Education Program.

1.2.1.3. Conform to policies, statutes, and rules established by state/provincial and local agencies relating to judicious application of disciplinary methods and behavioral procedures.

1.2.1.4. Take adequate measures to discourage, prevent, and intervene when a colleague's behavior is perceived as being detrimental to exceptional persons.

1.2.1.5. Refrain from aversive techniques unless repeated trials of other methods have failed and then only after consultation with parents and appropriate agency officials. (p. 9)

For an in-depth discussion of the legal implications and restrictions on the application of behavior modification interventions, the student is referred to an excellent text by Martin (1975). In addition to the standards and principles discussed above, educators must obey applicable state and local laws and regulations governing the use of behavior management interventions.

Behavior Management Prevention

Most of the behavior management literature is concerned with the remediation of academic and behavior problems in the home, school, institution, and clinic. Efforts have generally been directed toward the increase of acceptable and decrease of unacceptable behaviors. Very few research reports and position statements have focused on the maintenance of the acceptable behaviors of normally functioning children.

There are many opportunities in the classroom to prevent the development of inappropriate behavior by systematically maintaining the existing acceptable behavior. If teachers understand and apply the principles of behavior management (presented in Chapter 2) as part of their normal teaching methodology, many potential problems and conflicts can be avoided.

Concerned teachers monitor and evaluate their personal teaching behaviors and the learning behaviors of their classroom groups. They do this by systematically evaluating the teaching-learning process. They recognize that children need positive reinforcement (rewards) and that only the child being rewarded can indicate with certitude what is rewarding.

Experienced practitioners understand that they can and do reinforce inappropriate behavior on occasion. Consequently they attempt to reward only appropriate behaviors. They realize that the younger, less experienced child needs to be immediately reinforced for exhibiting appropriate behavior. They also recognize that delayed rewards are more desirable, from a societal point of view, than immediate rewards and that social rewards are more desirable than tangible rewards. They always give the child social reinforcement in conjunction with tangible rewards.

Prevention-minded practitioners recognize that new behaviors must be rewarded more frequently and more consistently than established behaviors and that although continuous reinforcement is necessary when a new behavior is being established, intermittent reinforcement is ultimately desired and will effectively maintain established behaviors.

Prevention-conscious practitioners systematically use high-frequency behaviors to facilitate the development of low-frequency behaviors.

By using the principles of behavior management as a standard part of the teaching-learning process, practitioners need not anxiously wait for problems to arise in the classroom but can prevent them and use the time saved to teach children those things they must know to live productively in society.

EXERCISES

Quiz

1. Comment briefly on the following statement: "All behavior management interventions that are effective are ethical."

2. A continuum of behavior management interventions is:

3. List the three rights of children discussed in this chapter.

    a. _____   b. _____

    c. _____
4. Discuss in the space provided below, one of the rights of children listed in Question 3.

5. Discuss in the space provided below, the CEC standards for the ethical application of behavior management interventions.

Projects

1. Research the professional literature and write a 500-word essay on "The Ethics of Behavior Management."
2. Research the professional literature and write a 500-word essay "for" or "against" the use of physical punishment in the school.
3. Invite an attorney or a specialist in civil rights to discuss with your class the rights of children as enumerated in this text.
4. As a group conduct an inventory of behavior management interventions in a school.
5. As a group organize the results of the inventory conducted in Project 4 into a continuum of behavior management interventions. Make an effort to obtain consensus on the location of each intervention on the continuum.
6. As a group, discuss the ordering of the interventions as listed in this chapter.

REFERENCES

Allen, R. C. (1969). *Legal rights of the disabled and disadvantaged* (GPO 1969–0–360–797). Washington, DC: U.S. Department of Health, Education, and Welfare, National Citizens Conference on Rehabilitation of the Disabled and Disadvantaged.

Bandura, A. (1969). *Principles of behavior modification.* New York: Holt, Rinehart & Winston.

Bellack, A. S., & Hersen, M. (1977). *Behavior modification: An introductory textbook.* Baltimore: Williams & Wilkins Co.

Council for Exceptional Children Delegate Assembly (1983). Code of ethics and standards for professional practice. *Exceptional Children, 50*(3), 8–12.

Fargo, G. A., Behrns, C., & Nolen, P. (Eds.). (1970). *Behavior modification in the classroom.* Belmont, CA: Wadsworth Publishing Co.

Lewellen, A. (1980). *The use of quiet rooms and other time-out procedures in the public school.* Mattoon, IL: Eastern Illinois Area of Special Education.

Martin, R. (1975). *Legal challenges to behavior modification: Trends in schools, corrections, and mental health.* Champaign, IL: Research Press.

Nirje, B. (1967). The normalization principle and its human management implications. In R. Kugel & W. Wolfensberger (Eds.), *Changing patterns in residential services for the mentally retarded.* Washington, DC: President's Committee on Mental Retardation.

Skinner, B. F. (1953). *Science and human behavior.* New York: Macmillan Co.

Skinner, B. F. (1971). *Beyond freedom and dignity.* New York: Alfred A. Knopf.

Ulrich, R., Stachnik, T., & Mabry, J. (Eds.). (1966). *Control of human behavior.* Glenview, IL: Scott, Foresman & Co.

Author Index

Subject Index

Work Sheets and Forms

Work sheets and forms used in this text may be copied from the following pages as needed.

Target Behavior Selection Checklist

1. What is the target behavior to be modified? _____

_____

_____

_____

_____

2. Each characteristic of the behavior that should be considered in the target behavior selective process is listed below. An X should be marked by each characteristic as it is considered. The pertinency of these characteristics varies with the specific target behavior under consideration.

(X)	Characteristic	Comment
( )	1. Frequency	
( )	2. Duration	
( )	3. Intensity	
( )	4. Type	
( )	5. Direction	
( )	6. Observability	
( )	7. Measurability	

3. Restate the target behavior in precise and specific terminology. _____

_____

_____

_____

_____

Behavior Chart

Child _____

Observer _____ Date _____

Target behavior _____

DIRECTIONS: Indicate rate, frequency, etc., for vertical axis; hours, days, etc., for horizontal axis. Enter ordinate and abscissa points.

Ordinate points (rate, frequency, duration, percent, etc.)

0

Abscissa points (hours, days, sessions, treatment, etc.)

Date _____

Contract

This is an agreement between _____
Child's name

and _____. The contract begins on
Teacher's name

_____ and ends on _____. It will be re-
Date   Date

viewed on _____
Date

The terms of the agreement are:

Child will _____

_____

_____

_____

Teacher will _____

_____

_____

_____

If the child fulfills his or her part of the contract, the child will receive the agreed-on reward from the teacher. However, if the child fails to fulfill his or her part of the contract, the
rewards will be withheld.

Child's signature _____

Teacher's signature _____

Contract Work Sheet

Child _____

Teacher _____ Date _____

(X)	Tasks	Comments
( )	1. Establish and maintain rapport.	
( )	2. Explain the purpose of the meeting.	
( )	3. Explain a contract.	
( )	4. Give an example of a contract.	
( )	5. Ask the child to give an example of a contract; if there is no response, give another example.	
( )	6. Discuss possible tasks.	
( )	7. Child-suggested tasks: _____ _____ _____ _____	
( )	8. Teacher-suggested tasks: _____ _____ _____ _____	
( )	9. Agree on the task.	
( )	10. Ask the child what activities he or she enjoys and what items he or she wishes to possess.	
( )	11. Record child-suggested reinforcers.	
( )	12. Negotiate the ratio of the task to the reinforcer.	

Continued.

Contract Work Sheet—cont'd

(X)	Tasks	Comments
( )	13. Identify the time allotted for the task.	
( )	14. Identify the criterion or achievement level.	
( )	15. Discuss methods of evaluation.	
( )	16. Agree on the method of evaluation.	
( )	17. Restate and clarify the method of evaluation.	
( )	18. Negotiate the delivery of the reinforcer	
( )	19. Set the date for renegotiation.	
( )	20. Write two copies of the contract.	
( )	21. Read the contract to the child.	
( )	22. Elicit the child's verbal affirmation and give your own affirmation.	
( )	23. Sign the contract and have the child sign it.	
( )	24. Congratulate the child (and yourself).	

Point Card*

Child's name _____ Date _____

1	2	3	4	5	6	7	8	9	10
11	12	13	14	15	16	17	18	19	20
21	22	23	24	25	26	27	28	29	30
31	32	33	34	35	36	37	38	39	40
41	42	43	44	45	46	47	48	49	50
51	52	53	54	55	56	57	58	59	60
61	62	63	64	65	66	67	68	69	70
71	72	73	74	75	76	77	78	79	80
81	82	83	84	85	86	87	88	89	90
91	92	93	94	95	96	97	98	99	100

*Teacher circles the cumulative total.

Point Tally Form

Child _____ Date _____

Monday												
Tuesday												
Wednesday												
Thursday												
Friday												

TOTAL

Monday	
Tuesday	
Wednesday	
Thursday	
Friday	
Week	

Point Card for Multipurpose Token Economy

Child _____ Day _____ Date _____

Work period	Readiness	Social behavior	Work effort	Work success	Teacher comments
9:00-9:15			★	★	
9:15-10:00					
10:00-10:30					
10:30-10:45			★	★	
10:45-11:30					
11:30-12:00					
12:00-1:00			★	★	
1:00-1:30					
1:30-2:45					
2:45-3:00			★	★	

*Points for work effort and work success are not available during these periods due to the nature of the activity: opening exercises, recess, lunch, and closing exercises.

Time-out Log

Child _____

Supervisor _____

Date _____

Time		Behavior before time-out	Behavior during time-out	Behavior after time-out
Enters	Leaves			

Behavior Log Form

Target behavior _____

Child _____

Observer _____

Date	Time		Antecedents	Consequences	Applied interventions	Comments
	Begins	Ends				

WE VALUE YOUR OPINION—PLEASE SHARE IT WITH US

Merrill Publishing and our authors are most interested in your reactions to this textbook. Did it serve you well in the course? If it did, what aspects of the text were most helpful? If not, what didn't you like about it? Your comments will help us to write and develop better textbooks. We value your opinions and thank you for your help.

Text Title _____ Edition _____

Author(s) _____

Your Name (optional) _____

Address _____

City _____ State _____ Zip _____

School _____

Course Title _____

Instructor's Name _____

Your Major _____

Your Class Rank _____ Freshman _____ Sophomore _____Junior _____ Senior

_____ Graduate Student

Were you required to take this course? _____ Required _____Elective

Length of Course? _____ Quarter _____ Semester

1. Overall, how does this text compare to other texts you've used?

   _____ Superior _____Better Than Most _____ Average _____Poor

2. Please rate the text in the following areas:

	Superior	Better Than Most	Average	Poor
Author's Writing Style	_____	_____	_____	_____
Readability	_____	_____	_____	_____
Organization	_____	_____	_____	_____
Accuracy	_____	_____	_____	_____
Layout and Design	_____	_____	_____	_____
Illustrations/Photos/Tables	_____	_____	_____	_____
Examples	_____	_____	_____	_____
Problems/Exercises	_____	_____	_____	_____
Topic Selection	_____	_____	_____	_____
Currentness of Coverage	_____	_____	_____	_____
Explanation of Difficult Concepts	_____	_____	_____	_____
Match-up with Course Coverage	_____	_____	_____	_____
Applications to Real Life	_____	_____	_____	_____

3. Circle those chapters you especially liked:

1   2   3   4   5   6   7   8   9   10   11   12   13   14   15   16   17   18   19   20

What was your favorite chapter? _____

Comments:

4. Circle those chapters you liked least:

1   2   3   4   5   6   7   8   9   10   11   12   13   14   15   16   17   18   19   20

What was your least favorite chapter? _____

Comments:

5. List any chapters your instructor did not assign. _____

6. What topics did your instructor discuss that were not covered in the text?_____

_____

7. Were you required to buy this book? _____ Yes _____ No

Did you buy this book new or used? _____ New _____ Used

If used, how much did you pay? _____

Do you plan to keep or sell this book? _____ Keep _____ Sell

If you plan to sell the book, how much do you expect to receive? _____

Should the instructor continue to assign this book? _____ Yes _____ No

8. Please list any other learning materials you purchased to help you in this course (e.g., study guide, lab manual).

_____

9. What did you like most about this text? _____

_____

10. What did you like least about this text? _____

_____

11. General comments:

May we quote you in our advertising? _____ Yes _____ No

Please mail to: Boyd Lane
                  College Division, Research Department
                  Box 508
                  1300 Alum Creek Drive
                  Columbus, Ohio 43216

Thank you!